The book the professionals are talking about...

"Everything your mother forgot to tell you about whitewater rafting—and we all know that was a lot! Whether you run rivers with outfitters, rafting clubs, or friends, *Rafting!* can provide you with the knowledge, technique, and confidence to become more than a passenger on your next river adventure. If you're no longer content with just going along for the ride, *Rafting!* will show you how to get more than your feet wet."

— Phyllis Horowitz, Director, *American Whitewater Affiliation*

"A watershed event, and the double meaning is intended! *Rafting!* signals the emergence of rafting as a participant sport rather than a spectator sport.... Contains everything you need to know to be your own outfitter and guide."

— Dave Harrison, Editor-in-Chief, *Canoe Magazine*

"Bennett is a natural teacher with an infectious enthusiasm for whitewater rafting. His text is brimming with information and the joy of running wild rivers. *Rafting!* is required reading for all of our rafting students!"

— Bill Cross, Director, *Running Wild Whitewater School*

"Jeff's unique style of writing and whitewater insight provides everyone with that essential information necessary for a trip's success."

— Tom Wagner, General Manager, *North American River Runners*

"A comprehensive guide, of value to both beginning and experienced river runners. From equipment to *one-legged ducks* to the *SAFE* system of reading rapids, this book has everything you need to become adept at river running."

— Doug Tims, President, *Idaho Outfitters and Guides Association*

"The rafting community has been waiting a long time for a book like *Rafting!*. It lays out the basics in an informative and interesting style, and provides the first comprehensive written record of rafting's Renaissance Period—the 1980s. Jeff Bennett, an outstanding river guide and expert Class V rafter, has a full understanding of the sport, and it is evident in this book."

— Jack Nelson, Owner, *Cascade Outfitters*

"As a professional outfitter our goal is to provide our customers v   afe, enjoyable adventures. That means that our guides must understan'   's of rafting—from trip planning to running rapids, and from car to safety and rescue. ...The one book we recommend to all

— Mike Doyle and Dave Hammond, Owners, *Beyon*

"If you only have room in your library for one   ⟨,
Rafting! is the one to have!"

— David Bolling, Author, *How to Save a Riv.*   .ree

"Assembles, in detail, all the information rafters need to make river trips safer, more enjoyable, and better organized. This is the one book rafters will refer to as they plan their boating season, year after year."

— **Dennis Schell, President,** *High Country River Rafters*

"*Rafting!* provides the missing link between boaters and rivers. An extraordinary tool for rafters of any ability."

— **Dale Fuller, Director,** *North American Paddle Sports Association*

"It used to be difficult for the amateur to novice boater to teach himself the skills and lore of whitewater rafting. Learning even the basics required long apprenticeships or lots of trial and error.

But no longer! Jeff Bennett's extraordinary new guide puts together in one fun-to-read volume all the information you need to get started in rafting. Even experts will find a great deal of useful information from this leading authority on the sport.... A must for every river rafter's bookshelf!"

— **Richard Penny, Author,** *The Whitewater Sourcebook*

"*Rafting!* does an excellent job of covering the full spectrum of whitewater rafting and catarafting. From beginner to expert, this book is a must for any whitewater enthusiast's library."

— **Al Hamilton, Secretary/Treasurer,** *AIRE*

"The most definitive work on the subject to date. Jeff's thorough yet concise style helps bridge the gap between reading, understanding, and doing. A *must* read for anyone venturing out to play the wild waters."

— **Casey Garland, Founder,** *Rescue 3 Northwest*

"*Rafting!* hits you straight, hard, and fast. It gives you no-nonsense information in a realistic style and in a direct fashion. A must book for all boaters, from novices to experts."

— **Al Ainsworth, Director,** *North West Rafters Association*

"*Rafting!* educates with humor and style, and is the most thorough book on rafting I've ever read. Recommended reading for all of our guide training candidates!"

— **Matt Polstein, Owner,** *The New England Whitewater Center*

"This is the *only* book that takes you from the basic techniques needed to raft gentle rivers to the combat maneuvers required to run Class V rapids. Jeff's fondness for all types of rafting—gentle drifting or first descents—shines through in this book and provides a guiding light for all rafters who follow."

— **Dave Prange, International Whitewater Competitor,** *Team SOTAR*

RAFTING!

The Complete Guide to Whitewater Rafting Techniques and Equipment

JEFF BENNETT

Swiftwater Publishing Company
Portland, Oregon

*Few facets of my existence have brought me
so much joy as sharing my love of whitewater
with my river friends. This book is
for all of you.*

Edited by Tonya Shrives.
Additional editing by: Les Bechdel, Jim Cassady, Bill Cross,
    Casey Garland, Doc Loomis, Vera Loomis, Jack Nelson,
    Dave Prange, Julie Prange, and Gary Stott.

COVER PHOTO: Trinity River/Burnt Ranch Gorge.
    Copyright 1992 by Eric Burge/FlashBack Photographics
    PO Box 701, Lotus, CA 95651; (916) 626-7855

BACK PHOTO: Alan Hamilton on the North Fork of the Payette
    River. Photo by Mark Lisk/Mark Lisk Photography
    Boise, Idaho; Supplied courtesy of A.I.R.E., Inc.

Much of the gear shown in Chapter Three was supplied by Cascade Outfitters

Publisher's cataloging in publication data
Bennett, Jeff, 1961-
    Rafting! The Complete Guide to Whitewater Rafting
    Techniques and Equipment
    Includes index
    1. Whitewater rafting 2. Rafting (Sports) 3. Rivers
    ISBN 0-9629843-4-5
    Library of Congress Catalog Card Number 93-083649

Printed in the U.S.A

Printed on Recycled Paper

Your rafting adventure is just about to begin!

Whitewater rafting can sometimes get "too" exciting. Be careful, use sound judgment and quality equipment, and have fun!

A WORD OF CAUTION

Whitewater rafting, like any outdoor recreational activity, involves risk. Among the hazards of river running are damage to or loss of equipment, physical injury, or even death. The decision to accept or reject this risk is necessarily your own.

Rafting! is not intended to be a substitute for skill, knowledge, judgment, or quality equipment. It is merely an introduction to the sport of whitewater rafting, and is only a supplement to *hands-on* education by qualified professional instructors.

It is the author's hope that you will enter rafting carefully and thoughtfully, that you will seek professional instruction, and that all of your adventures will be safe, exciting, and memorable.

TABLE OF CONTENTS_____

FOREWORD

My skin crackled with electricity as our raft slipped onto the long, slick tongue leading into the heart of the rapid. All around me, cool canyon air reverberated with the thunderous applause of crashing waves. From my perch in the front of the raft I could hear our guide musing aloud, "Well, isn't it Jeff's turn to get doused?!" Suddenly, the immensity of the experience snatched away his final words. With my ears echoing the pounding of my heart, my remaining senses reeled in excitement. Our guide leaned on the oars one last time, turning our raft into the first standing wave.

Splash! Our raft surged skyward, twisting along the path of a huge, liquid rollercoaster. As we reached the crest of the first wave, a wall of water reared to meet us, then crashed down all about me. The river's icy fingers reached through the air and descended into the small openings in my paddle jacket. My body shivered, not so much from the chilling water, but from the surge of adrenaline that coursed through my limbs.

I imagined myself an explorer, a voyageur, a daredevil... flirting with death itself, but never feeling so alive!

Little did I realize the impact that first raft trip would have on my life. Today I reflect upon that first adventure with remarkable clarity and fondness. And no matter how many times I board a raft, I find myself captivated by the river, enraptured by whitewater, and consumed by the experience of running rapids.

I've now been fortunate enough to raft scores of rivers in many countries, and have shared countless river experiences with commercial passengers, friends, and fellow racing competitors. Amid my evolution as a whitewater rafter, I found myself riding from the peaceful rivers of my backyard to the cutting edge of the sport.

Using the finest equipment and techniques available, I pursued my penchant for Class V river explorations and first descents. Yet I never lost the simple fascination with the basic dynamics of running water. With each passing bend I let the river share its secrets, and have carried them with me from put-in to put-in.

It is my hope that this handbook captures and reveals those things rivers have taught me. It is not my intent to *teach* you how to raft, for only the river is the truest teacher, of which we are all forever a student. Instead, it is my intent to share with you my knowledge of whitewater in hope that it will enhance your own river running experience.

Whether you are about to embark on your first whitewater trip or your seasonal pilgrimage to a favorite river, I wish you the best with your whitewater endeavors!

ACKNOWLEDGEMENTS

This book is the culmination of years of river exploration. Along the way I met countless friendly faces and helpful compatriots who added significantly to my rafting endeavors. Without their support and contributions, this book would have been little more than a dream.

I would like to give special thanks to those who have spent endless hours with me, sharing river trips and tall tales, and those who have listened patiently while I babbled incoherently about river books and whitewater dreams. My helmet goes off to Al Ainsworth, Dan Baxter, Bill Bowey, Dan Buckley, Eric Burge, Fryar Calhoun, Bob Carlson, Bryan Cavaness, Jim Clements, John Connelly, Rick Croft, Jerry and Connie Davis, Dick DeChant, Mike and Bonnie Doyle, Dick Edgely, Jerry Eline, Rick Freimuth, Jim Foust, Dale Fuller, John Hall, Alan Hamilton, Dave and Carol Hammond, Lars Holbek, Ole Hougan, Megan Kalstad, Glenn Lewman, Steve Miesen, Dave Mullins, Rocky Perko, Scott Quinn, Ron Reynier, Beth Rundquist, Val Shaull, Dave "Harpo" Sher, Jim Stohlquist, Mike Strickland, Doug Zeal, and everybody else credited throughout this book.

I would also like to thank the following manufacturers, retailers, outfitters, publications, and organizations for their support: AAA Rafting, AIRE, The American Whitewater Affiliation, B&A Distributing, Beyond Limits Adventures, Canoe Magazine, Canyons Incorporated, Carlisle Paddles, Carlson Designs, Cascade Outfitters, Colorado Kayak, Columbia Sportswear, The Competitive Advantage, The Dig Dogs, Down River Equipment Company, Downstream Products, Eastern River Expeditions, Extrasport, FlashBack Photographics, Guy Cables Enterprises, High Country River Rafters, Hyside, Hy-Tek Helmets, Kokatat, Mountain and Surf Pro Shop, National Organization for River Sports, New England Whitewater Center, North American Paddlesports Association, North American River Runners, The North West Rafters Association, Northwest River Supply, OS Systems, Pacific River Supply, Paddle Sports Magazine, Paddler Magazine, Patagonia, Perception, Polzel Manufacturing, Power Bar, Predator, Preferred Modes, Project RAFT, Rapid Shooters, REI, Rescue 3 Northwest, Riken, Rios Tropicales, Rivers and Mountains, Sawyer Paddles and Oars, Sierra Designs, Whitewater Manufacturing, and Yakima.

Finally, I must thank my family—Paul, Bobbi, and Michelle Bennett—for having shared a singular vision of the world. One that knows no limitations, and bases quality of life on experience and adventure.

INTRODUCTION

Whitewater rafting bestows upon each of us endless opportunities for waterborne adventure. For some boaters, rafting adventures entail peaceful camping trips among majestic arid canyons or pine-covered slopes. For other boaters, first descents mark the apex of whitewater adventures. For still others, rafting ties friends and family together during lively river outings.

No matter which category you fall into, rafting is an endless process of learning, where experiences are piled atop of experiences, and where continuously evolving skills soon replace the misplaced strokes and ill-chosen routes of past trips.

Rafting! is a complete course in river running, with each chapter designed to build upon the ideas learned in the previous chapter. After a discussion on raft history and how to partake in your first raft trip, you will embark upon a journey through the jungle of available rafting equipment and accessories. Next, you will explore rivers themselves, probing underwater currents, surface hydraulics, and the many forces that make up whitewater rapids. Finally, actual river running will be covered, from basic maneuvers to the advanced techniques used on Class V rivers. As you move from chapter to chapter, you'll learn about safety and rescue, how to pack gear for overnight trips, how to plan rafting expeditions, and much, much more.

By the time you finish this book you should have a broad-based understanding of the concepts that underlie whitewater rafting. Hopefully, all of the information regarding safety will follow you from river to river, and you will glean enough information from these pages to plan a safe outing. Still, no book—especially one on whitewater sports—can replace the teachings of professional instructors and on-the-river application of these concepts. So, start easy. Take a trip with a commercial outfitter or some highly skilled friends. Sign up for a guide school in your area or join a club that emphasizes safety and enjoyment of whitewater rivers. Then, let your own desires dictate how far you will follow this sport.

With the sound judgment and finely tuned skills you'll develop, whitewater rafting will provide an endless source of recreational pleasure.

1

THE EVOLUTION OF RAFTING:
From Powell to Paddle Cats

"There warn't no home like a raft..." exclaimed Huck Finn in Mark Twain's timeless novel, *The Adventures of Huckleberry Finn.* Though first written in 1885, Twain's immortal words live on, emblazoned upon the pages of guidebooks, magazines, and outfitter's brochures. At a glance, it would seem as if rafting started when Huck shoved off onto the great Mississippi. But the evolution of rafting reaches much further into the past than Huck's childhood years.

Rivers and streams have been liquid highways for many millennia, transporting Indians in buffalo skin boats, French voyageurs in massive canoes, and early American explorers on log rafts. Though these craft bear little resemblance to today's high tech rafts, the techniques used to maneuver and propel river boats have changed little over the years. Rivers themselves—though subject to the forces of gravity, erosion, and geological change—have remained essentially the same.

For many North American rafters, modern raft history dates back to 1869, the year that John Wesley Powell led a team of explorers through the Grand Canyon of the Colorado River in decked wooden oarboats. Powell and his companions were brave souls, using the only techniques known at that time to test uncharted rivers and rapids. Approaching each new rapid, Powell's men heaved on their oars, backs facing downstream, hoping that a clean run through rapids would deliver their rigid craft to the safety of calmer pools below. Unable to maneuver their craft in this fashion, Powell's boats were crushed, capsized, and lost in rapids whose names live on in the genre of modern river tales. Yet in the midst of Powell's tribulations, the first glimpse of modern whitewater sport emerged:

> "With difficulty we manage our boats," wrote Powell. "They spin about from side to side, and we know not where we are going, and find it impossible to keep them headed down the stream. At first, this causes us great alarm, but we soon find there is but little danger; and it is the merry mood of the river to dance through this deep, dark gorge; and right gaily do we join the sport."

For almost three decades after Powell's historic Colorado River journey, boaters continued using the same equipment that had caused Powell so much consternation: heavy wooden craft that had to be sturdy enough to withstand being dragged around rapids as well as being pounded by rocks and hydraulics. The immense weight of these early boats meant that they were not only difficult to portage, they were quite unwieldy in whitewater. Early explorers also persisted in running rivers backward, much the same as Powell had done, sitting with their back to the rapid, and unable to easily view the dangers lurking downstream.

In 1896, Nathaniel Galloway, a hunter and trapper from Utah, revolutionized whitewater travel by turning his seat around and looking downstream. With this simple change came the ability to *face the danger*. When combined with Galloway's light, flat-bottomed craft, river travellers used their new found rowing techniques to slow down, position their craft, and maneuver around riverborne obstacles. By 1909 Julius Stone's Grand Canyon expedition—America's first paid commercial whitewater trip—uniformly used Galloway's techniques, tackling rapids with an effortless style that had eluded Powell many years earlier. A new era of whitewater travel had begun.

After World War II, surplus neoprene rafts—similar in shape, size, and design to modern rafts—found their way into the hands of private adventurers all around North America. Though impossibly heavy, shapeless, and quite unseemly by modern standards, these boats were durable and affordable, and they provided reliable flotation. It was probably with little surprise that the first real rafter discovered that early military assault rafts and ocean life rafts were well suited to Galloway's techniques. All a rafter had to do was fit the raft with a strong wooden rowing frame and the boat was all set to go.

As rafting spilled into the 1950s, a growing fraternity of river lovers took their equipment to new locations, accumulating many first descents, and attracting the interest of river admirers everywhere. It didn't take long before entrepreneurial rafters began taking paying customers along for the ride. In 1952, Bus Hatch, who had been running rivers like the Green and Yampa near Dinosaur National Monument, was granted the first commercial river running concession, and a new industry was begun. Meanwhile, river pioneers—like Georgie White, Smuss Allen, Shorty Burton, Mac Ellingson, Don Harris, and Amos Burg—were plying their favorite rivers, and gaining legendary reputations as news of their adventures spread. And out of these adventures arose the realization that these early neoprene craft were quite suitable for whitewater travel.

Georgie White, firmly devoted to building a safer and more responsive whitewater vehicle, approached Rubber Fabricators of West Virginia to build the *Green River*, an extraordinary whitewater raft that revolutionized raft design. The *Green River*, along with its smaller cousins, the *Yampa* and the *Selway*, actually looked like modern rafts. Their turned-up bows rose over cresting waves, while the remainder of the raft comfortably accepted rafters and their gear. Elsewhere, Bryce Whitmore worked together with R.C. Flemmings of RF Incorporated to manufacture some of the first rafts ever built for river running. Patterned after the Navy's 15-man *basket boats*—peculiar life rafts with arching overhead hoops designed to support sun-shielding tarps—the new raft deleted the basket raft's hoops and incorporated a new rip-stop nylon and neoprene material.

Not happy with the big water performance of the *Green River*, Georgie White designed the *G-rig:* an enormous three-part craft specially designed to safely float the Colorado River through the Grand Canyon. Applying the same concepts that culminated in Georgie White's G-Rig, Jack Smith constructed a new multiple pontoon raft known as the *J-Rig*. These massive craft were constructed of hot dog-shaped pontoons lashed side-by-side to form an immense barge that could withstand even the worst hydraulics of rivers like the Colorado, Fraser, and Ottawa. Interestingly, a miniaturized, yet similar, concept was applied in 1965 by Bryce Whitmore, who lashed rowing frames onto a handfull of small surplus pontoons to form incredible self-bailing rafts. One of Whitmore's creations was a two-tubed craft called a *Spiderboat*. However, it was Whitmore's four-tubed design which would have pleased Mark Twain, for this raft was respectfully dubbed a *Huck Finn*.

As rafting's popularity grew, the call for improved designs and materials rang throughout the canyons. Soon, people like B.A. Hanten, Lou Elliot, Eddie Sowden, and Vladimir Kovalik began working with manufacturers like Rubber Fabricators, Avon, and Rubber Manufacturers to design even better river rafts. By 1969, timeless craft like Avon's *Adventurer* and *Professional* appeared on rivers. Elsewhere, the practical designs of Gordon Holcombe and Vladimar Kovalik—the *Havasu, Miwok, Shoshoni,* and *Hopi*—sprung to life. Manufactured first through Campways, then later through Riken, these rafts joined the burgeoning showcase of legendary craft on new rivers throughout the world.

Following the onslaught of new raft designs in the late 1960s, rafting's evolutionary period all but disappeared by 1972.

After a long period of hibernation, raft designers clambered into rafting's renaissance age in the early 1980s. Gordon Holcombe—working first under the name of Holcombe Industries, then later with Maravia—had spent the 1970s working on military assault rafts. His rafts featured I-beam floors and self-bailing designs, but did not catch the popular attention of whitewater rafters. So, while Holcombe's military assault rafts quietly crept into the 1980s, other primitive self-bailing rafts began to evolve under the likes of Vladimar Kovalik, Rafael Gallo, and the Metzler Company of Germany. Still elsewhere, two visionary American rafters were busy collaborating on a self-bailing raft that would finally take the river running community by storm.

Building upon the floating mattress concept, Jim Cassady, Randy Shelman, and Glenn Lewman engineered a raft with a laced-in inflatable floor. Reclaiming and updating the appearance and aesthetics of the old surplus rafts, these new rafts had an inflated floor whose surface floated four to six inches above the river. That floor was then laced to the raft's side tubes through a series of matching grommets. When water fell over the raft's tubes and onto

A Russian ploht competing at the 1989 Chuya Rally. (Photo by Doc Loomis)

the floor, it slid sideways and back into the river through the lacing holes. These first generation self-bailing rafts were dubbed *SOTAR's*, an appropriate acronym for *State-Of-The-Art-Raft*.

By the mid-1980s, many other manufacturers were offering self-bailing rafts, and countless new rivers fell to the daring first descents of intrepid rafters. The long, heavily obstructed rapids that once marked the nemesis of standard-floor boats were now being run without the fear of swamping or losing control. For almost a decade self-bailing rafts were considered not only state-of-the-art equipment, but were the sole means of transportation on many Class V rivers.

In the late 1980s, rafting found itself entangled in a series of historical events of world-wide importance. Russia began dismantling its Iron Curtain, and as the barriers between East and West fell, human commonality and curiosity created links between the people of distant lands. In a moment of shared visions, a handful of rafters from the United States teamed up with Russian boaters to explore some of Asia's great rivers. Led by Jib Ellison, Project RAFT soon created a pipeline for American-Russian rafting exchanges.

In 1989, Russia opened the door to its most popular rafting competition—the Chuya Rally. Rafters from around the world came to compete on Siberia's Chuya River where they found two and four-person teams paddling curious-looking catarafts, and adept rafters maneuvering giant oar-powered plohts through seemingly impossible river mazes. Though oar-powered catarafts had already plied North American rivers in small numbers

15

for many years, these unique craft leapt to the forefront of river gear after the Chuya Rally, and swept the rafting community with their sensible designs. Soon, North American rafters began to see catarafts showing up on popular streams, with Russian-style paddle cats becoming a common sight. Today, catarafts are on the way to becoming nearly as popular as the more traditional rafts.

Now, thanks to the passion, creativity and imagination of rafting's pioneers, rafters have a myriad of raft designs from which to choose. From traditional standard floor rafts to high tech paddle cats, there are boats and accessories for any rafter and any river. And as we build upon the techniques drawn from more than one hundred years of experience, today's whitewater trips are among the safest ever undertaken.

Whether you are a first time rafter or a seasoned veteran of whitewater rivers, it is truly an exciting time to be a river runner, and to be a witness to the power and splendor of the river's mighty rapids.

2
GET WET:
Your First Rafting Adventure

With rafting showing up everywhere these days—on television, magazine covers, in colorful brochures—the tenderfoot may still scratch his or her head and wonder what it takes to get on the river. For the beginner, the first step into whitewater rafting can be intimidating and confusing. Unless you have some experienced friends, you're bound to ask yourself, "Where do I find whitewater? What do I need to know? Don't I need experience? Isn't rafting crazy?" Fortunately, rafting has grown into an enormous commercial industry. Hundreds of outfitters, outdoor clubs, and whitewater organizations cater to novices seeking to *get wet* for the first time.

OUTFITTERS: One of the easiest ways to get your first taste of whitewater is through a reputable commercial outfitter. In North America, rafting companies abound in just about any state and province that has hills and streams. You can find out about these outfitters in the yellow pages under *River Trips, Rafts and Rafting,* or *Guides.* Next, try contacting *America Outdoors* or one of the other outfitters organizations listed in the appendix of this book for a list of their members. Also check out your local outdoor store. They'll often have some brochures from local outfitters. Even government agencies such as the Bureau of Land Management, the National Forest Service, and local tourism departments maintain lists of qualified outfitters. If none of these prospects turn up a good outfitter, check out the advertisements in one of the popular outdoor magazines at your local bookstore.

One way to get your first taste of whitewater rafting is to go with a reputable outfitter.

Once you find an outfitter, inquire about the types of trips they offer. If you or members of your group don't care to paddle, ask the outfitter if they will carry you down the river in an oar boat, in which the guide has to do most of the work. More adventurous first-timers will probably enjoy the thrill of being part of a paddle crew on Class III rivers. Although many outfitters now offer rivers with Class IV and V rapids, ask the outfitter what you're getting into. Daring and physically fit novices can often run rivers with one or two *user friendly* Class V rapids, but only those with prior paddling experience should consider rivers with dozens of difficult rapids.

One easy way to figure out what types of rivers the outfitter offers is to read between the lines in their brochure. *Scenic float trips* are usually peaceful journeys along easy waterways with a few riffles to spice things up. *Fun for the whole family* often means the river has some whitewater, but that the rapids are forgiving for uncoordinated paddlers or misbegotten swimmers. Once the word *adventure* pops up—especially when combined with adjectives like *ultimate*—you're into more difficult whitewater. Unless you have paddled whitewater before, or have the utmost of confidence in your aquatic abilities, reorient your way of thinking and slide back to the *family class* trips for your first whitewater voyage. Remember, don't overestimate your abilities! It is better to leave the river hungry for more challenging adventures than to scare yourself out of the sport on your first trip.

CLUBS AND ORGANIZATIONS: Local outdoor clubs, whitewater organizations, and college outdoor programs offer appealing alternatives to the *pay to play* option offered by outfitters. Clubs and organizations can usually save you a lot of money by asking you to contribute your own food, transportation, and personal gear, yet they frequently offer the identical rivers that outfitters advertise in their brochures.

RAFT RENTALS: On some of North America's more popular rivers, it is possible to rent rafts, life jackets, and all of the necessary gear to undertake your own whitewater adventure. Since this alternative gives intrepid greenhorns direct access to whitewater, it is best to have an experienced river runner along for guidance and direction.

GUIDE SCHOOLS: If you are ever going to become serious about rafting—whether you ever intend to guide or not—one of the best things you can do is to enroll in a guide school. Guide schools will take you through all of the basics of river running, including river reading, rigging equipment, planning overnight trips, safety, and rescue. Even if you have several years of river experience, a guide school is well worth the money!

When selecting guide schools, don't be afraid to ask questions. Check out the school's reputation and safety record. Will it offer both classroom and hands on instruction? What is the student-to-teacher ratio? Will you get to do different rivers and use different equipment, or will you use just one raft on one river? If you really do want to become a guide, will they hire you or recommend you to other outfitters? What are the instructor's qualifications? The answers to these questions may vary widely. But, lucky for us rafters, guide schools abound. So, pick one that sounds the best, and *have fun!*

3

EQUIPMENT:
From Oars to Floors, Paddles to Pumps

The concept of floating on air-filled bladders isn't anything new. In fact, people were drifting on inflated animal skins thousands of years before the first surplus World War II rafts found their way onto whitewater streams. And, conceptually at least, today's rafts vary little from their ancient predecessors.

Rafts, in the most basic sense, are little more than misshapen balloons, high tech air bladders bent and distorted to conform to some waterlogged inventor's notion of the perfect river craft. Yet, despite the obvious simplicity involved in floating on air, today's high quality rafts are masterpieces of contemporary engineering. More than mere balloons, today's rafts are specifically designed for whitewater use. They are durable, handle well, and display a dazzling array of specialized accessories and options.

PART ONE: Basic Raft Anatomy

If you flip through the pages of your favorite whitewater catalog, or walk the aisles of your local rafting shop, it soon becomes obvious that rafts vary as widely as their manufacturers' imaginations. Then again, the closer you examine raft designs, the more similarities begin to appear. In the end, most rafts fit one of three categories: standard-floor rafts, self-bailing rafts, and catarafts. Other designs—such as J-rigs, G-rigs, triple rigs, and plohts—appear on North American rivers less frequently, so they'll only receive honorable mention.

Any fully assembled raft consists of many independent components, each of which is important to the raft's performance. The list of components includes tubes, baffles, seams, panels, thwarts, valves, floors, pressure release valves, D-rings, rubbing strakes, chafe pads, and carry handles. In the anatomy diagram, you'll see that most of these parts show up in a typical self-bailing raft. Standard floor rafts differ from self-bailing rafts only slightly, while catarafts, though unique in shape, display most of the features common to other rafts.

TUBES: All quality self-bailing whitewater rafts have one continuous outside tube that gives the raft its distinctive oval shape. The tubes, in turn, are divided by baffles or bulkheads into multiple air chambers. These independent air chambers keep the raft afloat even if one chamber is punctured, and add rigidity by keeping the internal air in place. In a typical twelve to eighteen-foot raft there may be as many as four separate tube cham-

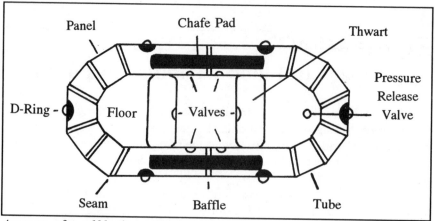

Anatomy of a self-bailing raft.

bers. One interesting twist on the multi-chamber design is the bladder system, which is similar to a car tire and inner tube. Rather than filling the outer tube with air, a bladder is inserted inside the outer tube, and the bladder is filled with air. If the inner bladder is damaged, it can be removed and patched faster and easier than a more conventional, single layer tube could be patched. The bladder system also lets manufacturers cut production costs significantly.

SEAMS AND PANELS: Tubes are manufactured from many separate pieces of material, and each *panel* is welded or glued together. These overlapping joints are then concealed and strengthened by welding or glueing narrow strips of material—known as *seams*—over the joints. When discussing the shape and configuration of panels at the bow and stern, rafters sometimes call the individual panels *miters*, which is just another word for panels.

Many PVC and urethane rafts are now being constructed with a *thermo-welding* process, which actually fuses the panels and seams together without the use of toxic glues or solvents. Welded rafts tend to be more bomb-proof than glued rafts since there is no possibility of a seam delaminating on a hot day. Nonetheless, glued joints and seams rarely separate and can be repaired.

VALVES: Each chamber has its own valve, with one of three types showing up on most rafts: military-style valves, Halkey-Roberts valves, and AD-1 valves. You open and close military-style valves by twisting the outer assembly, and air flows freely in either direction when the valves are open. The Halkey-Roberts and AD-1 valves have a spring-loaded center post that lets you pump air one-way into the rafts. To release the air, you just depress the post. Valves should be durable, maintenance free, and easily accessible. Some manufacturers place valves in the passenger compartment, which provides quick and easy access in an empty raft. However, frames and other equipment can cover the valves once the raft is fully loaded. Valves mounted on the outside of the main tubes provide easy access at any time, but run the risk of

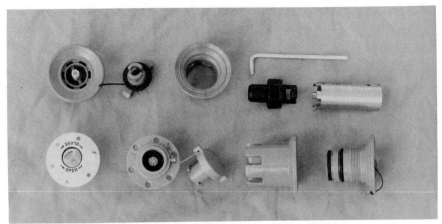

Raft valves (clockwise from top left): Low-profile Halkey-Roberts valve parts and tools; full-size Halkey-Roberts valve parts; HD-1 valve; plastic military-style valve.

damage in the event of a direct collision.

THWARTS: Thwarts are the inflated cross-tubes that run at right angles to the main tubes. Whether glued, welded, clipped, or strapped in place, thwarts help the raft maintain its shape by holding the main tubes an equal distance apart.

Besides adding torsional rigidity to a raft, thwarts give paddlers more surface area to brace themselves against. If you are going to be using a rowing frame, removable thwarts can be detached to add valuable storage space without compromising the raft's structural integrity. Keep in mind, however, that removable thwarts should have a bombproof binding system to keep them in place when they are needed (e.g., when paddlers need to brace their legs against the thwarts).

FLOORS: Rafting floors are generally described either as *standard* or *self-bailing*. In a standard floor raft, the floor is glued to the main tubes, in effect creating a giant bathtub. Some standard floor rafts are built with *wrapped floors*, which merely means that the floor continues upward around the outside of the main tubes. Wrapped floors generally extend up to a *rubbing strake*, which is an additional piece of thick, durable material bonded to the perimeter of the tubes to act as a protective bumper.

Self-bailing rafts have buoyant floors designed to float the floor's upper surface higher than the surrounding river level. When water enters the raft, it lands on the floor's top, then pours off the floor and out of the raft through a series of holes or slots.

Most self-bailing floors have either an *I-beam* or a *drop-stitch* construction. In I-beam construction, indented pleats run the length of the floor, giving the floor a common air mattress-like appearance. In drop-stitch

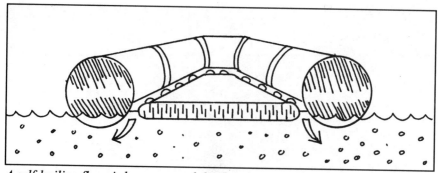

A self-bailing floor is buoyant, and the floor's upper surface floats higher than the surrounding river. When water spills into the passenger compartment it slides toward the sides of the floor, then exits back into the river through holes along the edge of the floor.

construction, thousands of tiny, equal-length threads hold the floor's surfaces equal distances apart. A drop-stitch floor has a smooth top and bottom, rather than the deeply channelled surfaces found on I-beam floors. Either type of floor can be attached to the raft by welding, glueing, or by lacing the floor to the main tubes with guy lines that run through matching slots or grommets.

The last floor component—the *pressure release valve*—saves self-bailing floors from being damaged from over inflation or hot, expanding air. The pressure release valve opens when internal air hits a preset pressure level, and lets the excess air out before it can do any damage.

ACCESSORIES: The most common raft accessories are *D-rings, rubbing strakes,* and *chafe pads.* D-rings are heavy-duty steel rings that are mounted on short, fixed straps, which are then sewn and glued beneath a patch made of the same material as the raft. D-rings provide a fixed point for strapping down frames and gear, tying your raft to a trailer, or for retaining a hand-line. Rubbing strakes and chafe pads are extra layers of heavy duty fabric that are bonded to the outer tubes to protect the raft from rock collisions and frame abrasion.

Another popular accessory found on many rafts is the carrying handle. Somewhat akin to the handles found on large suitcases, these handles make lifting and carrying a raft much easier.

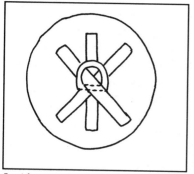

Inside anatomy of a D-ring

Plus, handles can even double as handholds when mounted inside the passenger compartment.

22

FOOTCUPS: Footcups look like sturdy, foot-sized cones constructed from raft material. If that doesn't conjure a mental image, visualize the back foot of a slalom waterski and you'll have the picture. When glued to the floor, they provide a secure place to put a paddler's feet. In fact, strong, properly mounted foot cups let paddlers wedge their feet deep in the cup and lean far out of the raft with total confidence, even in heavy whitewater. This is really important in Class V rapids, where a few extra strokes are more important than a passenger's ability to hold onto the thwarts! If things get *too* rough, the cup shape prevents the paddlers' feet from jamming, and allows paddlers to release their feet quickly.

Properly mounted foot cups should fit any paddler. Take your raft out for a test ride before mounting the cups and carefully observe where people's feet touch the floor. This will tell you the best location for the foot cups. Now, to keep your crew smiling—and inside of the raft—glue in at least one cup for the inside foot of each paddler. (To accommodate a broad range of preferences, mount the footcups at a 60 to 90 degree angle from the raft's long axis.)

FOOTCUPS

Footholds are to rafts what seat belts are to cars: they keep you in your seat when the going gets rough.

Before the days of footholds, rafters had to rely on extraordinary balance to keep paddling in rough whitewater, or they had to simply abandon paddling and hold on. Now, rafters can wedge their feet in footcups, brace against the tubes, and paddle confidently even in the throes of the roughest rapids.

PART TWO: Materials

Rafts are constructed from a variety of materials which vary in durability, life expectancy, stiffness, and overall *feel*. In order to give rafters some idea of how materials compare, I'll describe many of the fabrics and coatings used when this book was written. Keep in mind, however, that raft technology is ever-changing. By the time the ink dries on these pages, there will be something new on the market, and the only way to keep up with the new technology will be to read whitewater magazine reviews, obtain literature from raft manufacturers, and talk to local retailers. Still, the comparisons in this book will help you decipher manufacturers' claims and advertisements when new materials do show up.

Raft materials have two parts: the *base fabric* and the *coating*. It is the base fabric which provides tear and puncture protection. The coating provides abrasion resistance, air retention, and protection from ultraviolet rays.

BASE FABRICS: Base fabrics consist of cloth sheets made from woven or knitted polyester or nylon threads. Single polyester threads are less stretchy, but tend to be weaker if compared individually to nylon threads. Single nylon threads, in turn, are stretchier but stronger. I've said *single threads* since the cloth's *weave* can also affect how much each thread stretches. In fact, it is possible to weave a nylon thread into cloth that is less stretchy than polyester cloth!

One of the most common terms you'll hear regarding material is *denier*, which is but one of many factors used to figure out material strength. Denier measures the weight of one 9,000-meter-long thread, in grams—the heavier that thread is, the higher its denier will be. Quality whitewater rafts are usually constructed of materials with a minimum 420 denier, while more durable rafts usually display deniers of 1,000 or more. If you see two numbers describing the denier (i.e., 420/840), the fabric is woven from yarns of two different deniers. Since polyester tends to be a little weaker than nylon, polyester-based materials generally use a higher denier thread to achieve the same characteristics as a lower denier nylon cloth.

The quality of the base cloth can also be measured by *thread count* and *fabric weight*. Thread count simply measures the number of threads per inch while fabric weight measures the weight of one square yard of cloth. As with denier, higher numbers tend to indicate better materials.

COATINGS: Most fabric coatings fall into two general categories: synthetic *rubber coatings* and *plastomers*. Rubber coatings include hypalon (polyethelene chlorosulphone), neoprene (polychlorophene), and EPDM. Plastomer coatings include PVC (polyvinyl chloride) and urethane (ether based polyurethane). In turn, each coating may have different variations—for example, there are more than twenty neoprene compounds—but even the newest coatings will probably fall within these two groups. Common to all coatings are fillers such as stabilizers, UV inhibitors, anti-oxidants, and colored pigments.

HYPALON: Hypalon is a lightweight rubber coating developed by the DuPont Company. It stands up well to abrasion and UV rays, is fully cured when applied to the base fabric, and bonds securely to base fabrics. In top quality rafts, hypalon makes up almost 80% of the coating, while cheaper hypalon rafts might have as little as 25 to 50% hypalon. Many rafters like hypalon for its durability, long shelf life, ease of repair, and its ability to be deflated and stored in a tight bundle. On the other hand, hypalon rafts are usually more flexible than PVC or urethane rafts, and tend to *stick* to obstacles with greater frequency. Hypalon's sticky or rubbery feel is partly due to the nylon which usually comprises its base fabric. However, some manufacturers use stiffer base fabrics and higher quality hypalon coatings to give their rafts a more solid, slick, feel.

NEOPRENE AND EPDM: Two additional rubber coatings, neoprene and EPDM, are showing up on fewer and fewer whitewater rafts, but are still very effective for general whitewater use. EPDM is the least expensive coating available and is used on many economy rafts. If used on forgiving rivers, shielded from excessive UV exposure, and well maintained, an EPDM raft will last for many years. Neoprene has been around the longest. It is similar to hypalon, but it is heavier and less abrasion resistant. On the other hand, neoprene—especially top quality carbon black neoprene—holds air extraordinarily well and is remarkably resistant to UV degradation. Neoprene and EPDM, like hypalon, can be hand glued relatively easy.

PVC: While comparable in abrasion and UV resistance to hypalon, PVC (a plastomer) is a much lighter and stiffer coating than hypalon—especially when used with polyester base fabrics. PVC's light weight and increased rigidity lets rafts glance off rocks and hold their shape in powerful hydraulics a little better than the softer hypalon rafts. The trade-off for this increased rigidity shows up the moment you try to roll up your raft at the end of the day… PVC rafts don't wrap up as tightly, and may crack if rolled up in very cold temperatures. Also, as a plastomer, PVC isn't fully cured when applied to the base fabric. Instead, PVC's plasticizers leach out slowly, eventually leaving the PVC brittle and weak after many years of use.

One advantage of PVC rafts is their ability to be *welded* rather than *glued*. The welding process essentially fuses two pieces of fabric together (rather than holding them together with an adhesive), thereby creating an inseparable bond.

URETHANE: Urethane—another plastomer—is particularly durable and appears on many state of the art rafts. It is not only extremely rugged and long-lasting—perhaps more so than hypalon and PVC—it recaptures some of the *hand* of hypalon and can be welded like PVC. Urethane has been used alone (without any other coatings), or sprayed over other coatings like PVC as a protective outer layer. A few manufacturers have even developed multi-ply materials which layer three coatings of urethane with two layers of base cloth, taking full advantage of urethane's durability, flexibility, and resiliency.

ADHESION: The bonding of coating to the base fabric has a remarkable effect on raft materials. Since the coating adheres to the base fabric, the material works as a singular unit. If there is too much adhesion between the coating and the base fabric, the threads will be locked in place, and the material's tear resistance will be lowered. On the other hand, too little adhesion leads to delamination and lower abrasion resistance. The way coatings are layered can also be important. Some manufacturers use one coating on top of another to combine the best performance from each coating.

PART THREE: Design Characteristics

Many factors affect a raft's performance. For example, each of the materials discussed in Part Two react differently to rocks and rapids. But more importantly, a raft's shape and design affects how it will act in whitewater.

The most apparent differences between traditional rafts are their length, width, tube size, thwart size and attachment, number of thwarts, number of chambers, type of floor, and bow and stern shape. Each one of these factors can enhance or hinder a raft's performance depending on the type of river it is being used on.

LENGTH AND WIDTH: Most modern raft designers construct rafts with a width equal to about half of its overall length. Keeping that in mind, the more square feet of raft floor you have on the water, the more stable the raft will usually be. That's why rafters choose long, wide rafts for large volume rivers like the Thompson, Snake, Colorado, or Zambezi. Short, narrow rafts, on the other hand, work better on small streams that couldn't accommodate larger craft.

Moving beyond these simple ideas, you'll find that smaller rafts can be more exciting and lively than their bigger, more cumbersome cousins, but can also flip easier in powerful hydraulics. When it comes to turning a raft, a longer raft takes more time to pivot than a shorter raft, making it more difficult to maneuver through a technical, rock-strewn rapid.

TUBE SIZE: Tube sizes should be proportional to the raft size since they provide much of the raft's buoyancy, deflect water, and provide seats for paddlers. If the tubes are too small (less than 15 or 16 inches in diameter) waves will readily roll into the passenger compartment and paddlers will find that they are seated too low to paddle effectively.

SYMMETRY: Many traditional fourteen to eighteen-foot rafts have five to seven panels in the bow or stern sections (two to three panels on each side, plus one at the end). This creates a semi-rounded shape which deflects waves and holes that might knock the raft off course. Some manufacturers incorporate differently shaped bows and sterns into their rafts, creating *asymmetrical* boats. Rafts with smaller stern compartments have less gear space, but may make it easier for paddle captains to lock themselves into position. *Symmetrical* rafts have more storage space than asymmetrical rafts of equal size, and handle equally well when moved forward or backward.

RISE AND KICK: Rise—also known as *kick*—helps lift the bow over waves and holes, prevents diving in steep drops, and provides a drier ride through rapids. Stern rise also makes back ferrying (discussed later) easier by letting the stern slide over the water instead of trying to push it aside.

Building the right amount of kick into the raft is tricky. For example, too much bow rise creates a bulldozer effect and allows the raft to bend too much, both of which can cause the raft to run slower and stall in strong hydraulics.

Manufacturers incorporate these ideas into their designs, and offer rafts with a good compromise that works best in a variety of rapids.

In place of kick, some manufacturers use diminished tubes, which taper down to smaller diameters toward the bow and stern. Although less rigid than uniform diameter tubes, diminished tubes increase space in the passenger compartment and can, in theory, also help the bow pierce or ride over holes and steep waves. The piercing action of diminished tubes also makes for a wet ride.

WATERLINE: Waterline is the amount of the raft that is actually in the water. The waterline of an empty raft is governed by the raft's length, bow rise, and stern rise. But, once the raft is loaded, the added weight will cause it to sink deeper into the river's surface, extending the waterline toward the bow and stern. If the raft has a shorter waterline, it will spin faster but will be difficult to track straight in a chosen direction. The inverse is also true: a longer waterline helps the raft to track straight, but hampers its ability to turn.

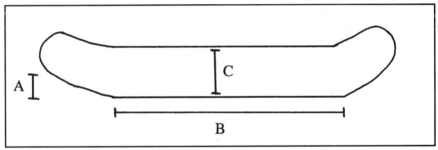

A raft's kick (A), waterline (B), and tube size (C) are among the design features that change the boat's feel and performance.

FLOORS: Floor design can have a profound effect on a raft's handling characteristics. *Standard floor rafts* capture water in the passenger compartment like a giant bathtub, rendering the raft heavy and unwieldy once it gets too waterlogged. To keep the standard floor raft light and maneuverable, the water must be bailed out manually. If there isn't a pool or eddy close by to pull into and bail, the extra water could be a real hazard. But on rivers with short, steep drops and long pools the standard floor raft works just fine. In fact, on forgiving pool-drop rivers, standard floor rafts can be more exciting for passengers. Also, the extra weight of tons of surplus water has been credited with helping more than a few rafts survive boat-flipping hydraulics.

Keep in mind that the best standard floors are very taught when the raft is inflated. That's because floppy, loose floors sag and hold more water, which makes bailing more difficult.

Self-bailing rafts, with their incredible water shedding capabilities, perform well in almost any type of whitewater. On small, technical streams the self-bailing raft remains light and nimble. On large volume rivers the self-bailer's

SELF-BAILING RAFTS

By the early 1980s I had become a fanatical river runner, leaping from canoeist to kayaker, and on to the leading edge of whitewater rafting. At the time, I was doing first descents on some pretty difficult rivers. The standard-floor rafts being used at that time were good, but could hardly stand up to the demands we placed upon them. As the rivers got harder, the old bathtub boats started to become a burden. I hadn't yet heard of the early self-bailing designs of Gordon Holcombe and others, and was in desperate need of a new, water-shedding craft.

In the Spring of 1982 Randy Shelman of Whitewater Manufacturing journeyed down to California to demo some prototype raft designs. As the operations manager for a local rafting company, I got to join a group of professional river runners on the North Fork of the American and to try out the new boats.

One boat was a modified Huck Finn, with smaller inside pontoons than the outside pontoons and with upturned ends. The design stirred a lot of interest, but I was intrigued by the second raft. This raft had the outer tubes of a conventional raft, but utilized a suspended plywood floor coated with indoor-outdoor carpeting. Strangely akin to a floating dance floor, it was the brunt of many jokes from my fellow rafters. Still, its self-bailing design had piqued my imagination.

After some more conversations with Randy Shelman and Glenn Lewman, we decided that a laced-in, I-beam inflatable floor should replace the heavy wooden boards. I felt so confident about this design that I sent Whitewater Manufacturing a deposit to make the boat, and even featured it in Pacific River Supply's new flyers before the first raft ever arrived!

When the first self-bailing rafts came off the assembly line in May of 1983, we were amazed. The new design worked like a charm. The raft stayed light and nimble, could be paddled or rowed, and displayed incredible buoyancy. By the time top California rafters like Jib Ellison, Bill McGinnis, Mark Helmus, Mike Doyle, Bill Carlson and Jack Morrison had tried it out, they all put in orders!

One customer said it was a state of the art raft, and we just reduced it to its acronym... SOTAR. Soon, self-bailing rafts started showing up on showroom floors everywhere, with manufacturers like AIRE, Maravia, Riken, Hyside, Northwest River Supply, and Avon incorporating self-bailing designs into hoards of top quality rafts.

The rest—as they say—is history.

— **Jim Cassady, Co-author**
Western Whitewater and *California Whitewater*

quick reactions lets rafters turn quickly into oncoming waves and deftly ferry around big holes or pourovers.

Self-bailing rafts, like standard-floor rafts, handle very differently from one another. For example, self-bailing rafts with smooth, flat bottomed drop-stitched floors are highly maneuverable and easy to turn, but may not track as well as deeply furrowed I-beam floors. (This can be a nuisance if the raft isn't built correctly. To keep the raft from continually sliding off course the floor must be correctly attached to the tubes at just the right height—an engineering feat accomplished by most reputable manufacturers.) I-beam floors, on the other hand, track quite well, but tend to take a little extra effort to turn.

Self-bailing floors are glued, welded, or laced to the main tubes through matching grommets or fabric hinges. One advantage of the removable laced-in floor is that it can be replaced if damaged, and can be separated from the raft for long portages. Only rarely do the ropes or straps holding the floor in place snap. Glued-in floors, on the other hand, don't have any ropes that could fail and are less complex. Glued-in floors can be built with a lower, faster profile, but they tend to bail slower since water has to exit through a limited amount of drain space.

Another lousy day in Paradise!

PART FOUR: Catarafts

With just a couple of pontoons and a frame making up the entire raft, the cataraft displays some distinct differences from other types of rafts—such as its lack of a floor. Since catarafts have no floor, there is no passenger compartment to bail. This cuts down on drag on shallow rivers, and lets the tubes pierce all but the most stubborn hydraulics. If the cataraft ever *does* find itself wrestling a sticky hole, the river will pour through the open tubes, making it harder to flip the boat. The decreased drag also makes *cats* faster to row and paddle than regular rafts.

The flip side of all this added mobility and stability is a big loss in buoyancy. Without a floor to provide added lift, all the weight of the frame, passengers and gear rests on two to six tubes. This makes it a tougher craft to outfit and use as a paddle boat, and means that rafters on multi-day trips must pick a cat big enough to haul all of their gear.

TYPES OF CATARAFTS: From short, sleek, highly rockered cats, to big multi-tubed cats, catarafts are as varied as their more traditional cousins. However, catarafts frequently incorporate many of the same features found on traditional rafts—D-rings, valves, multi-chambered tubes, baffles, and even rubbing strakes and wrapped floors. Accordingly, I don't think you'll be disappointed if I don't repeat everything I just said about raft components. (If you are severely disappointed, just flip back a couple of pages, start reading again, and substitute the word *cataraft* wherever you see *raft*!)

A cataraft.

OAR CATS AND PADDLE CATS

Almost any cataraft can be rowed or paddled with the right gear. Oar frames take great advantage of a cataraft's light weight by putting the weight of the rower and gear over the middle of the raft. This provides a low center of gravity and a central pivot point. Paddlers, on the other hand, must specially outfit their cats with saddles, quick release straps, or paddle frames instead of an oar frame. (See the section on frames for a more complete description.) These set-ups allow rafters to effectively straddle the tubes while bracing against straps or bars.

Some catarafts work better for paddling than others. Since the added weight of many paddlers spread across the tubes of large cats makes them difficult to turn, smaller cats seem to work a little better as paddle boats. Still, many outfitters have discovered how safe and maneuverable even the larger catarafts can be and have begun combining oars and paddles to create a great paddle-assist raft.

A paddle cat at the 1991 Costa Rica Rally. (Photo by Doc Loomis)

DESIGN CHARACTERISTICS: As with traditional rafts, tube length, width and shape all affect the cataraft's performance characteristics. Let's start by comparing a fairly standard set of cataraft tubes—those built like straight cylinders with pointed ends. Longer tubes, or multiple tubes, produce more

31

buoyant and stable rides—an important consideration on large volume rivers, or when additional gear or people are aboard. But the tradeoff for this increased stability is a slight decrease in the cataraft's ability to spin quickly. Shorter tubes, while not as buoyant, tend to turn faster without losing much of their ability to track well.

The addition of *rocker*, or tube curvature, drastically changes the way catarafts handle whitewater. Small cats with a lot of rocker have a very short waterline, offer little surface area for the river to grab and flip, and turn on a dime. Since they conform to the shape of some waves, highly rockered cats surf well, and make great playboats. Even larger catarafts gain a lot of turning ability when manufacturers build in a moderate amount of rocker to longer tubes. As always, there's a trade-off when rocker is increased. The decreased waterline brings with it less buoyancy—reducing the number of people or amount of gear that can be carried—and makes it more difficult to keep the boat on track when trying to ferry or maintain a straight line in currents.

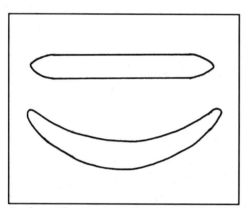

Rocker: The top tube has no rocker. The bottom tube shows a lot of rocker.

ROTOCATS: Rotocats are the newest addition to the rafting market, with their first significant acceptance coming in the early 1990's. Rotocats differ from ordinary catarafts in that they are molded out of solid plastic rather than welded together out of sheets of flexible fabrics. This lets rotocat manufacturers borrow both technology and designs from plastic kayak makers. In fact, the rotomolding process used to construct these catarafts lets manufacturers build in things like climbing and tracking edges, asymmetric hulls, and storage wells. This provides a unique ride—one that is stiffer and slicker than that of an ordinary cataraft—whether the cat is rowed or paddled. Of course this added stiffness doesn't ever go away. Rotocats aren't meant to fold up and store compactly, and the tubes retain their shape until someone runs over them with your cousin's giant pickup truck!

PART FIVE: Other Types of Rafts

On some rivers—especially giant rivers like the Colorado, Fraser, Thompson, and Katun—the raft of choice may be a *J-rig, G-rig, triple rig, Smith rig,* or *ploht.*

The *G-rig* was first designed by legendary Grand Canyon guide Georgie White and consists of three giant oval-shaped pontoons. The pontoons are lashed side-by-side with a motor mounted on the middle pontoon. These behemoths may measure more than 30 feet in length, and provide incredible stability even in the largest rapids.

The triple rig is remarkably similar to the G-rig, except that smaller, more conventional oar-powered rafts are used. When joined together as a singular unit, the individual rafts become a remarkably stable boat, capable of tackling treacherous stretches of whitewater even when heavily laden with passengers and gear. With frames mounted on the two outside rafts,

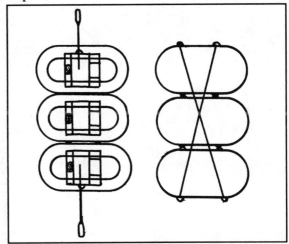

A triple-rig. The rope across the bottom prevents the end rafts from flipping up over the middle raft.

maneuvering a triple rig becomes a fantastic demonstration of teamwork: two guides are needed to operate the oars at either end of the rig. If all three rafts are fitted with rowing frames, triple rigs can be separated for smaller rapids, then reattached for the big rapids.

J-rigs, Jack Currey's innovative variation on the G-rig, consists of two to five sausage shaped tubes lashed side-by-side. The entire barge can also be fitted with a frame, and is usually powered by an outboard motor. The final type of giant motor-driven raft found on North American rivers is the *Smith rig.* The Smith rig combines a single donut-shaped pontoon—like the ones used on the G-rigs—but adds two of the sausage-shaped pontoons to the sides.

PLOHTS: Not to be upstaged by American ingenuity, Russian rafters have come up with a myriad of imaginative and inventive raft designs. Plohts, a generic name for many of Russia's favorite raft designs, are multi-tubed rafts which are joined together by steel or wooden frames.

Plohts, like big American catarafts, can be rowed or paddled by teams of rafters. But many plohts are rowed with oars over the bow and stern, more akin to North American sweep boats than catarafts. The sweep boat is nothing more than a traditional raft, but the sweep boat's rowing frame places the oars over the ends of the raft rather than over the sides. This lets one or two rowers maneuver the raft diagonally and horizontally with downstream ferries rather than using upstream ferries. Plohts, though frequently constructed from independent pontoons, are usually configured and rowed the same way.

A Canadian J-rig on the Thompson River.

A Russian ploht at the 1991 Chuya Rally. (Doc Loomis photo)

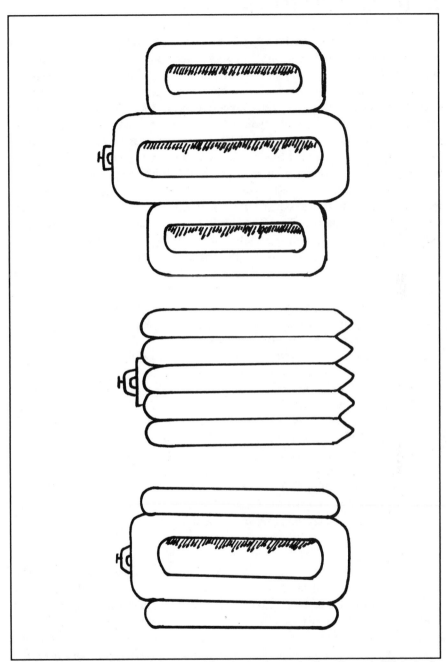

Types of rafts, from top to bottom: The G-rig (named after Georgie White), the J-rig (named for Jack Currey) and the S-rig (named for Ron Smith).

PART SIX: PURCHASING A RAFT

Buying a new raft can be a big investment, especially if you're going to purchase a top-of-the-line cataraft or self-bailer. But, fortunately for rafters, supply and demand economics have affected raft manufacturers the same as any other industry, and there are now rafts for almost any budget. However, budget shouldn't always be your biggest concern. You must also consider factors like the type of rivers you'll be running, the amount of abuse you expect to inflict upon your raft, and the amount of gear or passengers you'll be carrying. Since you may buy and use only one raft, your ideal raft will be a compromise that gives you as many desired features as you can get.

Don't be afraid to ask your local retailer—or the various raft manufacturers—questions. Most raft dealers are very proud of their products and are very informative. Since they want you to be happy, they'll frequently go out of their way to help you select the raft that is right for you. Before purchasing your next raft, consider each of these factors:

1. *Do you wish to row, paddle, or both?*
2. *Will you be running Class III rapids? Class V rapids?*
3. *Will you be running day trips? Overnight trips?*
4. *How many people and how much gear do you intend to carry?*
5. *How many days will you use the raft this year?*
6. *Will you be rafting small, steep rivers, or large, high volume rivers?*
7. *What is your budget?*
8. *What warranties will you get with the raft?*
9. *What is the dealer's/manufacturer's reputation?*
10. *Do you intend to use the raft commercially or on boat damaging rivers?*
11. *Where can you go for major repairs?*
12. *Will the raft be used for racing?*
13. *Will the raft ever be carried long distances?*

Next, take a look at the raft size selection table on the facing page. The last two columns indicate the approximate number of people that can comfortably fit in an oar boat or paddle raft without much added gear. To find a raft that might fit your needs for day trips, figure out how many people you intend to carry, then select the raft that matches that number from the left column. If you plan to do many overnight trips, your extra gear will have the same affect on the table as extra people. Get a larger raft so that you can fit all your equipment comfortably inside.

RAFT LENGTH	RAFT WIDTH	TUBE SIZE	ROWING/ PEOPLE	PADDLE/ PEOPLE
10 Feet	5 Feet	16 Inches	1-2	2-3
12 Feet	6 Feet	18 Inches	2-3	3-4
13 Feet	6 Feet	18 Inches	3-4	3-6
14 Feet	6.5-7 Feet	20 Inches	3-5	4-8
15 Feet	7 Feet	21 Inches	4-5	6-8
16 Feet	7.5 Feet	22 Inches	4-6	6-10
18 Feet	8 Feet	24 Inches	5-6	8-10

Raft size selection table for standard floor and self-bailing rafts: The chart above provides a useful starting point for selecting the proper raft by its capacity rating. Keep in mind that rafts aren't all the same shape and size as described above. Also, factors such as the amount of gear you plan to carry and the type of rivers you will be rafting will affect your choice of raft.

PURCHASING CATARAFTS: Buying a cataraft is much the same as buying traditional rafts. First, ask yourself the questions listed on the previous page, then discuss your answers with manufacturers and retailers. If you think that most of your outings will be one-day trips, or that you'll be rowing without passengers, the giant multi-tubed cats may be overkill. Pick a smaller cat that is still buoyant and stable enough to survive the rapids of your favorite rivers. (If you're real adventurous, highly rockered sport cats work phenomenally well on very small, steep streams or with paddle saddles, and are a great toy for almost any rafter.) If you plan to carry extra gear and passengers, start looking at catarafts with larger or additional tubes.

USED RAFTS: Used rafts can be a great way to break into the private whitewater game. Since properly maintained equipment lasts for many years, you're likely to find quality rafting gear available at reasonable prices.

When looking for a used raft, spend enough time to adequately *kick the tires.* Ask a lot of questions like "How old is this raft?" "What rivers have you used it on?" and "Does it hold air?" Next, inflate the raft and listen for air leaks. Inspect the material for any fading or discoloration that might indicate too much exposure to damaging ultraviolet rays. Check the seams to see if they're intact, and see how carefully any patches have been applied. You should also check to see that the valves open and close smoothly. To check the integrity of the baffles, inflate one chamber at a time. Finally, the true measure of the raft's prior use and care is its floor. Examine the floor in good lighting to see if the material's outer coating is worn away from the base cloth. Expect to find some wear, but if large patches of cloth are showing through, chances are the raft has seen some heavy use.

Keep in mind that used equipment is bound to have some damage—patched tubes, broken D-rings, marred floors. But, with some time and effort, many rafts can be inexpensively reconditioned and used for many more years.

PART SEVEN: Frames

Rowing frames—constructed from aluminum alloys, steel, or other metals—secure gear, stiffen the raft, support a rower's weight, and provide a fulcrum for the oars. Wooden frames, which work just as well, are slowly disappearing into rafting's nostalgic history. Looking into the future, new materials will inevitably fall into the hands of innovative frame builders, giving rafters broader choices in frame construction, durability, and design.

TRADITIONAL RAFT FRAMES: Basic rowing frames consist of side rails that rest atop the tubes; cross bars to keep the frame square; oarlock stands to hold pins or oarlocks; and a seat for the rower. As builders add new pieces and bars to the basic frame, raft frames become more varied and personalized. For example, some rafters prefer slanted seats—long boards which slant downward toward the rower's feet—over more conventional seats,

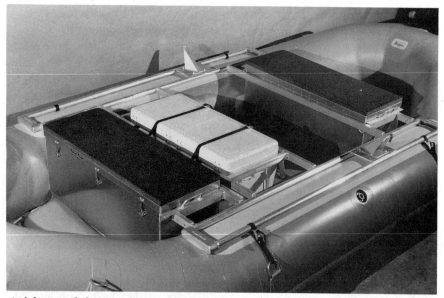

A deluxe raft frame, with two kitchen boxes and a cooler. (Photo courtesy of Cascade Outfitters)

while other rowers prefer the comfort of a large padded seat. A dropped foot brace, mounted across from the rower's seat, is often added to frames in order to give the rower a solid platform from which to start pulling the oars. Other additions—such as ammo can wells, cooler retainers, movable oarstands, and breakdown frames—add some luxurious amenities for the rafter willing to invest a little more in his own indulgences.

Frames can be built to fit in the center of the passenger compartment, or can be built to fit in the stern. If there is only one guide, and no one else around to assist with paddling, the center frame works best since it puts the pivot point near the middle of the raft. Stern frames, on the other hand, are often used in conjunction with paddle teams to provide some extra power when the guide really needs it.

SELECTING A FRAME: What type of rafting do you plan to do when rowing? One-day trips or overnighters? Steep, technical streams or broad, lazy rivers? Will you be in a traditional raft or a cataraft? There are so many frames available today that it is easy to select and tailor one to your needs.

If you plan to spend most of your time doing short trips on very difficult rivers, all you'll probably need is a sturdy bare-bones frame. A simple add-on for cataraft frames is a set of sturdy footplates, which provide a solid platform when you're standing up, shifting weight, or pushing through huge waves and holes. Frames that have a built-in cooler retainer are nice for almost any river, and expand your raft's versatility by turning it into a food carrier. If you plan on doing long trips with a lot of gear, larger, more complicated frames may make river life easier by supplying multiple tie-down points and wells for kitchen boxes or ammo cans.

Frames also come with a variety of seat options, including tractor-style seats, flat boards, cooler seats, and slant boards. Cooler seats or flat boards provide the least seating stability for a rower, but make it easy for an oarsman to move about the passenger compartment. Tractor seats and slant boards, on the other hand, hold the rower more firmly in place, allowing the oarsman to concentrate on rowing rather than staying in his seat.

Before you buy any frame, your first step will be to determine your raft's dimensions. Take these measurements, and tell them to your retailer. They will then be able to recommend the right frame for your raft.

1. *Center compartment width: the distance between the main tubes in the center compartment.*
2. *Center compartment length: the distance betweent the thwarts in the center compartment.*
3. *Tube size: the tube diameters (the raft manufacturer will be able to tell you this if you don't know).*
4. *The size (in quarts) and make of the cooler you plan to use.*
5. *If you own a self-bailing raft, also measure the distance from the top of the main tubes to the top of the floor.*

OTHER CONSIDERATIONS: Any frame should be free of burrs or sharp corners that could snag and puncture tubes or injure paddlers. If the frame breaks down into separate sections, make sure that the pop buttons or cotter pins don't rub against the raft's material. Finally, it's always a good idea to cover the bottom of the frame and the frame corners with padding to help save the skin of both your raft and crew.

CATARAFT FRAMES: Frames—an essential component of any cataraft system—are much more critical to the performance of a cataraft than they are to traditional rafts. Cataraft frames tend to be stronger and better supported than traditional raft frames since they must hold the pontoons firmly in place while the river's hydraulics try to tie the whole rig into a pretzel.

Since cataraft frames don't have floors, some rafters install durable safety nets across the bottom opening. The reasons for this are obvious: on my first cataraft ride, I stared at the Class III rapids gurgling beneath the open bottom of the cataraft and felt like I was on a trapeze without a net. Many rafters prefer leaving the interior open, rather than using a net, so that they can put their feet down and walk the boat across shallows. The open floor design also lets the rower climb through the center when the cataraft is upside down.

A recent addition to the cataraft frame market is the *paddle saddle*. Paddle

Some catarafters install safety nets across the floor. This helps the rower stay aboard if bounced from his seat, but makes it impossible to climb back through the center if the raft flips.

saddles allow paddlers to ride the tubes like a horse while maintaining a firm grip on the raft. Whether constructed from the same curved metal tubing used to build raft frames, or merely built out of quick release strap harnesses, paddle saddles cradle rafters' legs while they kneel on top of the tubes. At the same time, the saddles provide support and protect the lower legs by keeping them up off the river's surface. (See the photo of the paddle saddle in action on page 31.)

COOLER FRAMES: A cooler frame is a narrow rectangular frame designed to hold a cooler firmly inside the raft's passenger compartment. They're great for single day trips or for light overnighters, and can even be used to keep dry bags and other gear off the floor.

PART EIGHT: OARS

From the timeless aesthetics of wooden oars, to the simple reliability of aluminum and composite oars, whitewater oars are built to be durable enough to withstand powerful hydraulics and menacing boulders, yet light enough to respond all day long to a rower's efforts.

OAR CONSTRUCTION: Most contemporary oars fall into three categories: *wooden, aluminum,* and *composite oars.* The first category—wooden oars—have been used since rafting first began. Whether crafted from solid ash, or laminated from strips of douglas fir, wooden oars flex and straighten during the course of a single stroke. To many rafters, the feel of a wooden oar is incomparable.

Aluminum oars now equal wooden oars in popularity due to their sturdy construction, ease of maintenance, and ability to accept different blades or oar extenders. Starting with a hollow aluminum shaft, aluminum oars are coated with a colorful protective plastic or vinyl sleeve, fitted with a solid handle at one end of the shaft, and a cavity specially designed to accept removable blades at the other end. Usually sold separately, the blades have a pole-like end which slips into the shaft's cavity and locks into place. This allows easy replacement of damaged blades, more compact storage with the blade removed, and even lets rafters change from one blade size to another.

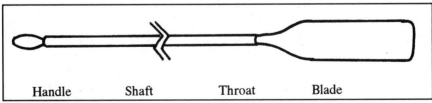

Handle   Shaft   Throat   Blade

Parts of an oar.

Composite oars are constructed from a multitude of exotic materials, including fiberglass, carbon, and graphite shafts, and polypropylene or compressed foam handles. When properly laminated, these materials can mimic the feel of a wooden oar while providing much of the durability of aluminum oars.

SELECTING OARS: Oars come in so many different materials—all of which have good and bad characteristics—that your choice of material is a personal one. Ask your retailer and friends many questions. Do you want a complete oar, or do you want interchangable parts? Are you willing to maintain a wooden oar in exchange for its great feel? Do you prefer the lightness of a graphite shaft over the heavier wooden and aluminum oars? Or do you simply want the no-nonsense durability of an aluminum oar?

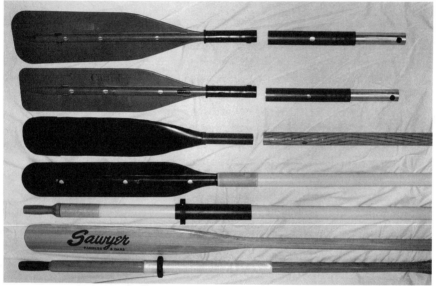

Oars come in a wide variety of materials and lengths.

When purchasing *wooden oars*, it is important to buy the best wood you can afford—one that combines great bending strength and medium flexibility with high impact resistance. For medium to heavy-duty river use, fir, ash, oak and spruce make fantastic oars. Laminated softwoods—such as fir and spruce—also hold up well to the rigors of river running if properly constructed. Ash oars are frequently cut from a solid piece of wood and are considered by some to be the toughest oars available. However, ash's quality does not come without a price. Ash oars tend to be heavier and more expensive than other woods. Other types of wood, such as basswood and cottonwood, don't last as long in tough river conditions, but work well for light-duty use.

Before buying a wooden oar, examine it closely. The strongest oars will have grains running parallel with the shaft, and will be free from strength-sapping knots. If the oar comes painted, the manufacturer may be trying to conceal flaws. The throat of the oar—the point where the shaft and blade meet—should be thick and strong. Test the oar's flexibility by holding the oar out to your side at a 45 degree angle with the blade touching the floor. Then, while holding up the handle with one hand, exert pressure half way down the oar with the opposite foot. A good oar will have some flex, but not too much.

OAR LENGTH: It is important to pick out the right oar length for your raft. Generally, a properly sized oar leaves one-third of the oar's overall length between the oarlock and your hand. First-time buyers can generally select a proper oar length by measuring the distance between oarlocks or pins, then adding 50% to that distance to get the proper oar length. Another way to estimate proper oar length is to simply take 2/3 of the length of the raft.

Keep in mind that many factors govern oar length: longer oars may be needed on wider rafts, rafts with large tubes, and on frames with high or widely spaced oarlock stands; shorter oars might be better on technical streams and in stern rowing frames; larger bladed oars may perform best on a large volume river or when the raft is heavily laden. Even a rower's strength and arm length will affect oar length selection: strong, long-armed rowers often like a slightly longer oar.

RAFT LENGTH	RAFT WIDTH	OAR LENGTH
11-12 Feet	5-6 Feet	7-8 Feet
12-13 Feet	5.5-6 Feet	7.5-9 Feet
13-14 Feet	6-7 Feet	8-10 Feet
14-16 Feet	6.5-8 Feet	9-11 Feet
16-18 Feet	7-8 Feet	10-12 Feet

Oar length selection table: this provides a rough estimate for proper oar length based on the size of your raft.

SETTING UP OARS: No matter which oar you buy, you may need to do some finishing work before it is river-ready. If you have purchased a set of unfinished wooden oars, they will require special treatment before you can take them out on the river. Here's what you'll need to do:

1. *First, paint the entire oar with a light coat of quality wood sealer. (I'd recommend using linseed oil.) To get the best results, try to do this when the air is at least 70 degrees fahrenheit. Let the sealer dry completely.*
2. *Next, paint the entire oar with a high oil content marine spar varnish that has been thinned slightly with a quality varnish thinner. This should be done by brushing the varnish on in the same direction as the wood's grain. Again, let this coat dry completely. (In place of varnish, many rafters use marine grade paint.)*
3. *Finally, apply another coat of varnish or paint in the same manner as the first coat. Let it dry completely, and your oars will be finished.*

If you are using oarlocks, the next thing any oar will need is an *oarstop*. These tight fitting rubber or plastic donuts slide or bolt onto the shaft where it rests against the oarlock, and prevent the oar from sliding out of the oarlock and into the river. Oarstops should be positioned about 1/3 of the way down the oar from the handle. To install your oarstops, start by marking the point on the shaft where the oarstop will go. Next, slide or bolt them into place on the oar shaft. Finally, put the oars in the oarlocks to make sure that the handles are positioned comfortably for you.

Oarstops are usually used with *stopper sleeves* that slide over the shaft and protect it at the point that the oarlocks rub the shaft. (Without the sleeve, the oarlocks can quickly cut deep grooves in any oar material.) As an alternative to sleeves, many rafters form a protective shield by wrapping 60 to 70 feet of solid-braided 1/4 to 3/16 inch multifilament polypropylene rope or parachute cord tightly around the shaft and glueing it into place. (This can also be done with about six feet of seat belt strapping or 1-1/2 inch webbing.)

PINS AND CLIPS AND OARLOCKS: *Pins and clips* and *oarlocks* are the two most common tools for supporting an oar midway on a rowing frame.

In a pin and clip system, a vertical steel rod, called a *thole pin*, is placed into the oarlock stand and bolted into place. A plastic or nylon *stirrup* is mounted in a U-shape on the pin to hold the oar in place if the oar pops loose from the pin. Finally, the oars are fitted with beefy steel clips, which are bolted securely to the shaft with two or more radiator hose clamps. Once everything is in place, the oar can be jammed perpendicularly onto the pin where it is free to pivot around the pin's axis.

Note that when using pins and clips, the oar should be kept in front of the pin (toward the bow) so that it doesn't create too much stress. The added benefit of this oar position is that it lets a rower execute a few extra strokes after an oar pops loose if a stirrup was used to hold the loose oar in place. Also, to prevent accidental injury, the pin is kept as short as practicable, and is capped with a large plastic or rubber ball which is threaded onto the top of the pin.

Pins and clips have long been a favorite of beginner rafters with little or no rowing experience since they keep the oar length and blade angle perfectly set at all times. Experts also like this feature because it cuts down on the number of missed strokes in difficult rapids. The drawbacks of pins and clips are that the oar can only be *shipped* parallel to the raft, not drawn into the raft. Also, since the blades can't be feathered, or twisted, they occasionally catch strong submarine currents in heavy hydraulics.

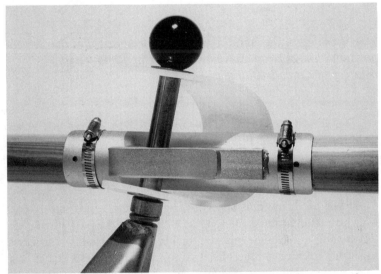

*A complete **pin and clip** set up, showing a properly mounted oar and a stirrup. (Photo courtesy of Cascade Outfitters)*

OARLOCKS: Oarlocks—steel U-shaped oar retainers—allow more oar movement than pins and clips, but take some getting used to. With oarlocks, the rower can twist or *feather* the oars (which makes rowing against the wind or through big hydraulics easier), draw the oars into the raft, or pull the oars out of hydraulics. The tradeoff for this added flexibility is that the blade may twist in the wrong direction just when you need to make a critical stroke. One cure for this problem is the use of an *Oar Right*—oar stoppers with a guide that keeps the oar aligned vertically in the oarlock. Oar Rights recapture the blade angle benefits of pins and clips, while letting the rower ship and feather the oar freely.

45

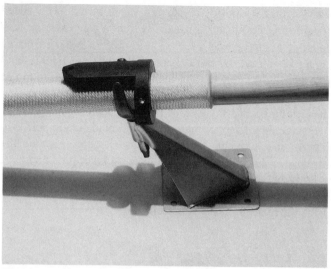

*This oar is in an **oarlock** which is mounted on the oarstand. The oarstop shown here is an **Oar Right**. (Photo courtesy of Cascade Outfitters.)*

SETTING UP OARS AND OARLOCKS: Unless you've already got a good feel for how you like to position your oars, mount the oarstops and clips on the shaft such that the oar handles are never less than a fist's width apart. This will prevent your hands from getting caught between the handles, and will maximize your leverage on the blades.

If you are using pins and clips, bolt the thole pins into the oarlock stand with just enough pin showing to accommodate the oar, stirrup, and cap ball. (Most thole pins come pre-set, making customization unnecessary.) Next, adjust the opening on the clip with a rubber mallet so that it snaps securely onto the pin, but pops free if it hits a rock or gets caught in a powerful hydraulic. (If you make the clip opening too small, the oar will violently pop free of the pin when it finally releases.) Finally, mount the oars inside the stirrup on the bow side of the pin. That way the oars can still be used if they pop free.

If you are using oarlocks, adjust the oarlock opening with a rubber mallet so that it is slightly narrower than the oar shaft. This will hold the oar in place while rowing, but will let it pop free under intense pressure. Once properly adjusted, the only way to insert an oar is to slide it in blade first. Also, to avoid losing the oarlock, thread a sturdy cotter pin through the oarlock's base.

When you mount oars on either pins or oarlocks, you may also wish to add a short *safety line* to retain the oar should it pop free. The safety line should be just long enough to reach from the clip or oarstop to the oarlock stand, and it shouldn't be so short that it prevents you from shipping the oars inward. Keep in mind that the safety line is a matter of personal choice. Some rafters prefer not to use these safety lines because they could entangled passengers in the event of a flip or wrap.

PART NINE: Paddles

Paddle rafting may be exhilerating for your crew members, but it tests the limits of your paddles. Rafting paddles must be able to withstand the same rigors as oars: rock collisions, powerful hydraulics, and the torque that results when paddlers pit their strength against the river's current.

The main considerations in choosing rafting paddles are length and materials. Most rafters use paddles ranging from 54 to 60 inches in length, with the 60-inch paddle being the most popular length for commercial customers. Paddle captains, on the other hand, frequently prefer slightly longer paddles—66 to 72 inches long. The extra length gives the captain added leverage when executing his ruddering strokes. (I like the extra length because I can reach forward and poke inattentive passengers when they're not paddling correctly!)

Paddles, like oars, come in a variety of materials. Outfitters usually use paddles constructed with aluminum shafts and some type of plastic handle and blade since they are durable and reasonably priced. However, many experi-

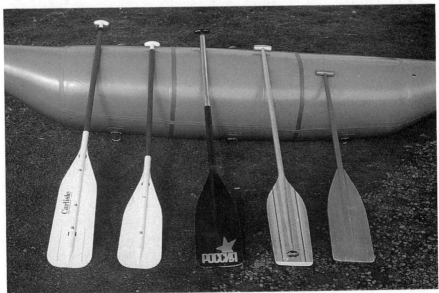

Raft paddles come in a variety of shapes and materials.

enced paddlers are discovering that wooden paddles—constructed from ash, fir, and other woods—and composite paddles sacrifice a minimal amount of durability, while their light weight makes paddling easier. In fact, many top rafting competitors choose wood and fiberglass paddles for their light weight, incredible feel, and stellar performance characteristics.

The last criteria to consider when selecting paddles is blade size. Paddle blades are generally seven or eight inches wide by twenty inches high. Guides often like beefier blades—up to eight inches wide by 26 inches high—which gives them some extra leverage to crank the stern around. However, the rest of the crew will find that the larger blades slow down their stroke rate and require some extra muscle to move.

PART TEN: Essential Riverwear

The first layer of protection between you and the river environment is your personal gear: clothing, life jackets and helmets. Carefully designed and selected riverwear not only improves the quality of your river experience, it makes whitewater rafting much safer. Wet suits, dry suits, life jackets and helmets protect rafters from the debilitating effects of hypothermia, provide supportive flotation in powerful currents, and protect swimmers from injury amid rock-strewn channels.

CLOTHING: Novice rafters are frequently astonished when they first discover how cold most rivers are. Whether fueled by snowmelt, rainfall, or dam releases, the water temperature in many popular rivers is cold enough to require some form of outerwear, even on the warmest days.

When choosing riverwear, select garments that meet three criteria: (1) comfort; (2) flexibility; and (3) sufficient insulation to ward off the onset of hypothermia. This may mean that shorts or bathing suits are sufficient when the river is forgiving and the air is warm, but this is often the exception to the rule. Experienced rafters should consider river and air temperatures, the type of river they'll be rafting, and their expected level of activity to determine their clothing requirements. Novices, on the other hand, can follow the *120 degree rule*: if air and water temperatures combined equal less that 120 degrees fahrenheit, don wetsuits, drysuits, paddle jackets, and booties to stay warm. You can always peel off layers during the trip if you get *too* warm!

WETSUITS: Wetsuits made of body-hugging neoprene have been a favored form of insulation for many years. A *farmer john* style wetsuit—which leaves the arms and shoulders uncovered—provides the first layer of insulation, with pile sweaters and paddle jackets or dry tops comprising the outer layers.

The wetsuit works by shielding unprotected skin from direct splashes, and traps a thin film of water between the suit and your skin during swims. Once water fills the suit it is warmed by your skin and insulated from the river by the suit itself. Wetsuits also provide some extra flotation and padding—nice things to have if your swimming a boulder-strewn river.

When selecting a wetsuit, try not to get the same type of suit worn by scuba divers. A rafter's higher activity level and increased range of motion demands a thinner wetsuit than their diving brethren. A thickness of 1/8th inch (2-3 millimeters) provides both warmth and flexibility. Also check for proper fit. A properly fitted farmer john wetsuit will follow the contours of your body without being too tight.

PADDLE JACKETS AND DRY TOPS: Paddling jackets and dry tops are high-tech rainjackets similar in design to the upper half of a drysuit (described below). The main difference between paddling jackets and dry tops is in their ability to shed water. The more affordable paddling jackets combine loose layers of waterproof cloth with water resistant neoprene or lycra closures at the neck and wrist. The dry top, on the other hand, incorporates waterproof latex closures at the neck and wrist.

Both paddle jackets and dry tops are effective when you're sitting up in the raft, but allow water to enter through the waist opening when you're swimming. They're usually used as an outer waterproofing layer with wet suits, and help prevent chilling blasts of cold water from finding their way down the front of your wet suit, especially when worn over a synthetic sweater. However, on warmer days, paddle jackets and dry tops can be enough to keep hearty rafters warm with nothing more than a synthetic sweater underneath.

A wetsuit (left) and drysuit (right).

DRYSUITS: Drysuits differ dramatically from wetsuits in both appearance and function. Instead of trapping water near the skin, the drysuit keeps water off your body by enclosing it in a loose fitting layer of waterproof fabric. The suit has a large waterproof zipper or flap closure that allows easy entry and exit, and is made totally waterproof with tight fitting latex gaskets at the neck, wrist, and ankle openings.

Though drysuits lack the insulating qualities of wet suits, they are baggy enough to fit over inner layers of clothing. As in other outdoor sports, the best way to choose clothing that will keep you warm is to follow the *layering* concept. The innermost clothing layer should wick sweat away from your skin, while the next layers should be warm and absorbent. Since the dry suit will seal in body moisture, it is important to choose synthetic materials like nylon or polypropylene fleece.

OTHER CLOTHING ACCESSORIES: Booties, gloves, and insulating caps vastly improve the quality of your rafting experience on cold rivers. Thick neoprene booties with semi-rigid soles keep feet warm and provide decent traction during slippery portages. In warmer climates, specially designed river sandals (with extra straps to hold them securely on your feet) work great. Waterproof caps help the body retain an enormous amount of body heat by providing another layer of insulation over your head. Even hands can be kept comfortably warm with neoprene gloves.

LIFE JACKETS: Life jackets—also called *personal flotation devices* or *PFD's*—must be worn by rafters on any river. They not only increase your buoyancy in the event of a swim, their foam-filled shells provide some extra insulation on cold days, and even provide some welcome body armor in the event of a swim.

When choosing or purchasing life jackets, you must consider two important factors: *fit* and *flotation*. A properly fitted life jacket is comfortable enough to wear all day, and doesn't interfere with rowing, paddling, or swimming motions. It will cinch snugly around your torso and won't ride up over your face or head in rapids. Many life jackets achieve a customized fit through the use of different sizes (from extra-small child sizes to extra large sizes), flexible contoured foam panels, and buckled cinch straps.

To make sure you're getting the best fit possible, try a few on. First select a life jacket that has ties or straps that tighten at the waist. Then, after you put on the life jacket and cinch the ties, have a friend yank on the shoulders. If the life jacket fits properly, it will only budge slightly while remaining comfortable. Keep in mind that you'll be adding bulky layers of riverwear under the jacket when you're out rafting, so make sure there's enough space left to accommodate your clothing.

The second factor in selecting a proper life jacket is *flotation* or *buoyancy*. Life jackets work on some fairly basic principles. An average person is surprisingly buoyant, weighing only ten to twelve pounds when immersed in water (less if you're thin, more if you're heavy). So, anything that attaches to

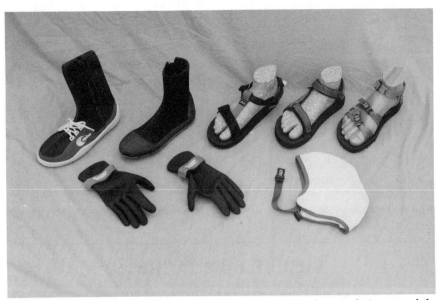

Accessories: a selection of neoprene booties, specially designed river sandals, gloves, and a helmet liner.

your body and provides more upward lift than your body's sinking weight will increase your buoyancy.

The main goal of a life jacket is to keep your mouth and chin above water long enough to let you breathe. But before you can decide how much flotation *you'll* need on your next river trip, you'll need to evaluate your own abilities and the river's difficulty. Ask yourself what type of water you will be paddling; how much you weigh and your body type; the clothing you intend to wear underneath the life jacket (a wet suit can add 6 to 8 pounds of buoyancy, and an air-filled dry suit can add more); whether you are likely to swim this river; and whether you're a strong swimmer.

If you're a weak swimmer or about to embark on a very difficult run, a life jacket with maximum flotation may increase your safety during a swim. However, the more foam that's added to the life jacket (to increase its buoyancy) the more it will interfere with your ability to swim, row, or paddle. Also, high flotation life jackets might make it tougher to escape holes or reversals. Strong swimmers on gentle rivers may be able to get away with slim, low flotation life jackets.

Since there are so many factors in choosing a life jacket, ask your dealer to help you in selecting one, or get a couple of life jackets so that you'll be ready for anything.

Life jackets range from beefy, high flotational jackets (left) down to slim low float jackets (right).

RESCUE LIFE JACKETS

US coast guard regulations discouraged innovation in US life jackets design, but European equipment designers rapidly filled in the creative gaps, coming up with practical and safety-minded personal flotation devices. These designs finally caught on in North America in the early 1990's, and now provide a great alternative for safety-conscious rafters and rafters who spend a lot of time on Class V rivers.

A rescue life jacket differs from ordinary life jackets by the type of accessories attached to the jacket. Items like an integral quick-release harness or belt—which provides a belay point for swimming rescues or vertical rescues—and lash points for carabiners and short throwlines are common to most rescue life jackets.

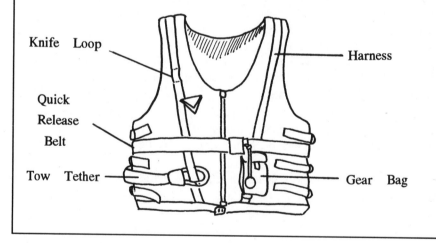

HELMETS: Helmets have become de rigeur for rafters on many whitewater rivers, and are mandatory on any Class IV and V outing. Helmets consist of a sturdy outer shell, a shock absorbing liner, and a chin harness designed to keep the helmet on your head. Outer shells can be made of plastic, fiberglass, kevlar, or other rigid and strong materials. However, since reputable whitewater stores are unlikely to carry helmets with shells made of inferior materials, the shape and fit of the outer shell becomes more important than its durability.

A properly shaped and fitted helmet covers the entire head—including the top of the head, temples, and ears—but remains unobtrusive to the wearer. Some helmets even have face-guards to protect against facial injuries caused by rocks, flailing paddles or collisions with other paddlers.

When selecting a helmet, check out its liner. You may prefer foam padding over a suspension type of shock absorbing system, but either system works well. Finally, make sure that the helmet fits your head comfortably: the chin strap should hold the helmet securely in place such that the helmet won't ride up and expose your forehead, or slide down and block your vision.

Well-designed helmets cover all of the important parts of the head, including the forehead, temples, and ears.

4

SADDLE UP:
Assembling Your Gear and Crew

A fully outfitted raft is like a fine car: it looks great just sitting there, but it doesn't work worth a darn until there's somebody sitting behind the wheel.

In this chapter you'll do much more than inflate and climb aboard your raft. You'll learn different ways to rig rowing frames; different ways to seat crew members; and how to select the best seating configuration for the river you're running.

PART ONE: Inflating Your Raft

Well, now that you've identified the jumble of equipment piled at your feet along the riverbank, it's time to assemble your gear and come up with a clean, serviceable system.

PUMPS: Since rafts float better and hold more weight when they have a lot of air in them, let's start out by inflating the raft. Pumps specially suited to rafting range from powerful 110 volt, AC electric blowers to affordable hand and foot pumps. The big AC blowers are wonderful timesavers. But, un-

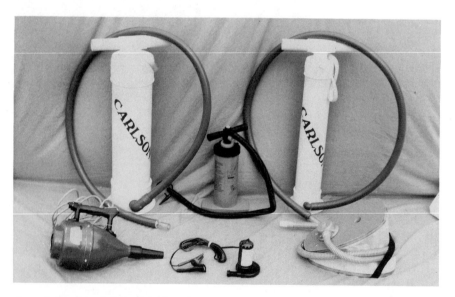

A variety of manual and electric pumps. Top row: handpumps. Bottom row from left: big blower, LVM, footpump.

less you're inflating your raft near an electrical outlet or generator, you'll probably use one of the more common battery powered DC air pumps. Twelve volt pumps attach to a car's battery and put out about 1.5 to 2.5 pounds per square inch in air pressure. These pumps are used to give the raft its full shape, then a manual hand or foot pump is used to *top off* the raft with the final bit of extra air pressure. Topping off the raft with manual pumps increases the life span of your electric pump, and will make your raft much stiffer on the river.

Manual pumps can be hand or foot powered and come in a variety of sizes. Hand pumps with large, wide diameter barrels enable you to pump up rafts fast and more efficiently, while smaller hand pumps are easy to carry on your raft. (Don't be deceived by size—some small pumps blow out air on both the up and down stroke of the handle, making inflation fast and easy.) Any raft pump should have a durable hose and a nozzle sized to fit your raft's valves perfectly. Also, some pumps work in reverse and can actually suck air out of a raft. This handy deflation feature helps get the last bit of air out of your raft before putting it in storage.

INFLATING THE RAFT: Before you blow up your raft, think of two things: (1) don't exceed your raft's recommended air pressure rating (usually 2-3 pounds per square inch), and (2) blow up the chambers slowly and evenly. By adding air evenly around the raft you'll avoid over-pressurizing—and possibly damaging—the delicate baffles that separate each chamber. The addition of the *proper* amount of air makes the raft perform at its best. (Underinflated rafts can be sluggish and more prone to wrapping, while overinflated rafts are more susceptible to tearing or flipping.)

To properly inflate your raft, first put just enough air in each chamber to give the raft its normal shape. Next, go back around again and top off the raft by adding air to each chamber until the raft is fully inflated. (Don't exceed its recommended P.S.I!) When you're done, look at the tubes. Smooth surfaced, identically-sized tubes will tell you that you've blown your raft up correctly, while a crease in any tube above a baffle means that the chambers aren't equally inflated. Figuring out if your raft is properly inflated takes a little bit of experience, and can be done with an air gauge or by feel. A raft is usually fully inflated when a struck fist bounces firmly off the tubes.

WHEN INFLATING YOUR RAFT: *(1) first use an electric or manual pump to merely bring the raft up to shape, inflating all chambers evenly; (2) top off the chambers evenly to prevent undue stress on the baffles; (3) check pressure periodically by hand or with a gauge, especially on hot, sunny days; (4) to prevent floor damage, never place hand or foot pumps on the floor when the raft is on the ground.*

PART TWO: *Rigging the Frame*_____

THE FRAME: If you're going to be rowing, the next item on your pre-river agenda will be to strap the frame to the raft. If the frame needs to be assembled, do that outside of the raft to avoid pinching the raft's fabric. Also, put the raft in the river before you add the frame. That way you won't find yourself fifty feet from the shoreline trying to muscle an overweight pile of raft material and steel across rocks, grass, or dirt.

Most raft frames are designed to sit right in the center of the passenger compartment, and for good reason. Saddled with little more than a central rowing frame and an oarsperson, a raft floats like a giant bowl or saucer, its pivot point directly over its midline. So, by placing the oars over the middle of the raft, the rower can easily spin either end of the raft with single and double-oar turning strokes.

I like to strap down the frame after I've already inflated the raft, especially if the frame will hinder easy access to the valves. However, some rafters prefer to top off the raft after the frame has been strapped down so that the straps will be extra taught. If you fit in the latter category, take care not to overstress lash points such as D-rings and thwarts.

LASHING DOWN FRAMES

When selecting straps to hold down the frame: (1) use straps that are just slightly longer than the minimum length needed to secure the frame; (2) use enough straps to hold the frame firmly in place; (3) adjust the straps so that the free ends face the rower... that way the rower can quickly tighten loose straps without climbing all over the raft or missing too many strokes.

PART THREE: *Loading Accessories*_____

SPARE OARS: On anything except short roadside raft trips, rafters should carry at least one or two spare oars. Firmly lash the spare oars to the frame's siderails with short straps or quick release buckle systems high above the water line so that they won't snag on rocks or hydraulics. While some rafters prefer to lash the spare oars to the frame with the blade facing the bow, this could actually cause the oar to swing wildly if the front strap loosens or fails. Try mounting the spare oar with the blade facing the stern.

SPARE PADDLES: Spare paddles should be strapped crosswise onto thwarts and held firmly in place by looping a strap once around the shafts, then once around the thwarts. Do your best to keep the blades and handles out of the way of shins and knees to prevent injuries when the going gets rough. Although paddles can also be stored at an angle in the stern, or even lashed to the outer tubes, never lay paddles on a standard floor. Rocks can snag the paddles, damage the floor, and injure paddlers' feet.

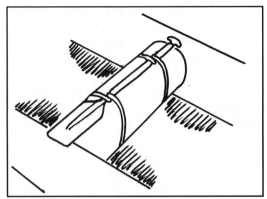

Carry spare paddles strapped across the back thwart. Loop straps around handles to prevent loss or excess movement.

BOWLINES: Bowlines—about 50 to 75 feet of rope tied to the raft's front D-ring—come in handy in many situations. You'll use it to tie the raft to shore, for lining difficult rapids, and for tying the raft up when it is being stored. When not in use, keep the bowline neatly coiled and safely stowed to avoid entangling passengers.

There are three basic ways to store a bowline. Perhaps the easiest way is to clip a *bowline bag* (which looks like an oversized throwbag) to the bow D-ring. This bag retains the rope in loose coils when not in use, and seals shut with a pull closure so that the rope won't snake free. (A loose bowline is a hazard to crew members, and can jam between rocks.) Two more innovative ways of storing the rope in a safe coil are found in the appendix.

HANDLINES: If your raft is equipped with a full set of exterior D-rings, a handline can be threaded through each D-ring around the perimeter of the raft. Once in place, the handline provides a grab point for swimmers, and

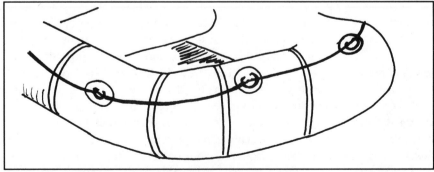

Handlines should be taught to prevent entanglements. To prevent excess movement, loop the line through each D-ring twice.

makes pulling the raft ashore easier. As with any loose ropes, the handline is considered a safety hazard—especially if it hangs loosely—by some rafters since it can entangle limbs or snag on life jacket clips. Other rafters like the security it affords.

When rigging an exterior handline, use nylon or polypropylene line at least half an inch in diameter, or use one inch wide nylon tubular webbing. Tie one end of the line to the stern D-ring with a half hitch, leaving about two feet of extra line hanging from the knot. Then, starting with the next D-ring, pull the rope as tight as possible and wrap it once around the D-ring before moving to the next D-ring. Continue this process until the rope can be knotted back to the loose rope at the stern with a square knot.

BAIL BUCKETS: I have yet to figure out where to put a bail bucket to keep it from getting broken or endangering passengers! However, most rafters prefer to hang the bucket away from passengers in the stern of paddle rafts (near the guide), or in the center compartment of oar boats (near the rower). Alway keep the bail bucket securely stowed on a short leash, yet readily available for those all too frequent moments when your raft begins to resemble your bathtub.

STOWING OTHER GEAR SAFELY: In later chapters, we'll learn to properly pack and load a raft for overnight expeditions. But in this chapter we're concerned with keeping the raft trimmed and performing at its best. Gear, like passengers, adds a lot of weight to the raft and makes it more difficult to maneuver. Accordingly, it is just as important to load gear such that it won't hinder your raft's performance. To accomplish this, keep three things in mind: (1) don't overload the ends of the raft; (2) keep the heaviest gear low in the raft; and (3) leave enough open floor space for passengers' feet or for bailing standard-floor rafts.

If you're rowing just yourself and one or two day's worth of gear, loading your oar raft is pretty easy. You can lash all of your gear down in the stern without worrying much about doing wheelies all the way down the river. But as you add more gear—like when you are on extended river trips—you'll want to give more consideration to gear placement. Don't just randomly toss all of your gear in the stern. Keep in mind the three points just mentioned.

In paddle rafts, gear placement becomes a bit more challenging. Since lots of space must be left for paddlers' feet and legs, less room is left for gear. There are a number of ways to overcome the disadvantages of paddle rafting. First, consider leaving some of your gear at home. Not only will that make life on the river less complicated, it will make your raft lighter and more maneuverable. Next, consider leaving some of your paddlers at home. If you pick the right raft, and have enough paddle power to handle the river, the extra paddlers will just take up valuable gear space. Finally, think of the most compact and efficient way to store your gear. This means taking a few extra minutes to compress your gear tightly into dry bags, and tying them into the center of the raft where they'll rest over the raft's pivot point.

PART FOUR: Passengers in Oar Rafts

PASSENGERS: In an empty oarboat, one or two passengers can sit in the bow compartment without upsetting the raft's balance. (In fact, the only thing you'll probably upset if you put either passenger in the stern compartment is *that passenger*, especially if they have a fancy for front row seats!) But by the time the third passenger climbs aboard, it's time to either move the frame back a bit, or to start drawing straws to decide who gets the back seat. The more body weight the raft has to carry, the more important it is to spread that weight around evenly.

Most guides will find that a few intrepid volunteers will leap into the bow compartment before the river trip, while the more apprehensive members of the crew will crawl towards the stern. The end result of this type of natural selection is that you'll obtain a happy medium in both seat selection and weight distribution without having to ruffle anybody's feathers.

Keep in mind that you'll need to leave plenty of room to operate the oars. Forewarn the passengers that you'll be leaning forward and backward frequently while maneuvering the raft, and that they should be prepared to give you some extra space if necessary.

An oarsman and crew tackling some fun rapids.

PADDLE ASSISTS: Stern-mounted rowing frames are frequently used on commercial trips when a paddle captain needs extra leverage to guide a paddle crew through difficult rapids. Also known as *hybrid* rigs and *paddle assists*, the stern-rowed raft lets the guide shout commands forward at the paddle crew while reaping the powerful benefits of a long set of sturdy oars. In a clutch, the guide can override an uncooperative crew and make an important move. The stern frame's drawback is that when the crew isn't paddling, the raft's pivot point is so far back that the raft becomes more difficult to turn than a center-rowed raft. Also, the oarsman sits on a proverbial catapult seat which can toss him forward when the raft hits big holes or jars to a halt at the base of steep drops.

The same paddle assist concepts that work with stern frames can be applied to center frames. By seating a couple of paddlers in the front compartment, the rower gains some extra power, ballast, and flexibility. This helps on all types of rivers: in steep, technical rivers, where narrow chutes or big boulders frequently interfere with the oars, the paddlers can take over and help execute critical maneuvers. On large volume rivers, where big haystacks or breaking waves are the norm, the bow paddlers add paddle power and can throw their weight forward in big hydraulics. This takes some of the workload away from the rower, and makes the raft stronger overall.

A stern-mounted oar frame gives the guide a lot of power and control over the paddle crew on challenging rivers.

PART FIVE: Paddle Crews

Now it's time to shed the frame, ditch the oars, and grab some paddles. Paddle rafting is the ultimate in team-oriented adventures. But before each paddle trip, spend a few moments teaching each passenger how to brace in the raft and where to sit.

A SOLID FOUNDATION: Since paddle strokes use every muscle in your body, each paddler has to lock in to the raft by pressing their legs against thwarts, slipping their feet into footcups, or using friction and balance to stay aboard. Paddlers should seat their buttocks far enough out on a tube so they can reach the water, but not so far out that they'll fall overboard when the first wave or rock hits. Sitting on the thwarts or floor—though it seems safe and comfortable—simply won't do. It puts the main tube between the paddler and the river, and makes paddling impossible.

Legs and feet should stay inside the raft. This not only puts most of the paddler's body weight inside the raft, it places a tube between their limbs and bone-crushing rocks or logs. On large, obstacle-free rivers, some paddlers prefer riding *cowboy style* with their outer leg dangling in the river. Though acceptable when there are no rocks present, this style of paddling places more of the paddler's body weight outside of the tube, making it easier to fall out.

Once you're comfortably seated, lean the lower part of your legs against a tube or thwart. If the raft lacks foot cups, push your feet half way under a thwart. (*Never* put your whole foot or leg under the thwart since that increases the risk of entrapment or compression injuries.) If a foot cup *is* available, slip your foot far enough into the cup to get a solid grip, but not so far that your foot won't easily slide out in an emergency. With feet, legs, and butts properly planted on the raft, you'll be ready to tackle the rapids.

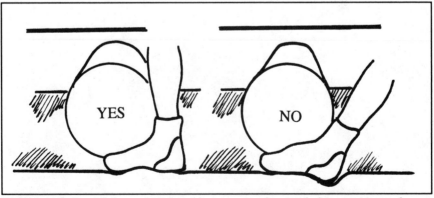

If your raft doesn't have footcups, brace your feet and shins against tubes or thwarts. However, never wedge your feet all the way under thwarts.

SEATING PADDLERS: On gentle rivers, guides can be hard pressed to give their passengers a really exciting ride. On some easy rivers I've gone so far as stacking all of the passengers in the stern compartment, then paddling into small, deep rapids with the bow riding high in the air. With each passing wave, the bow would bounce higher and higher, until it finally flipped backward, sending us all into the drink. It made for a great laugh on warm, gentle rivers, but gave us a quick lesson in how improper weight distribution affects your rafting success.

Three considerations go into positioning members of your paddle team: (1) *even strength distribution;* (2) *even weight distribution;* and (3) *adequate room to paddle.*

Even strength distribution begins with the most important member of the crew: the paddle captain. In North America, the paddle captain sits in the stern compartment. From there, the captain can watch oncoming rapids and crew members, call out paddle commands, and execute the powerful rudder strokes necessary to guide the raft.

Using a five or six-man team as an example, the next most important passengers are the bow paddlers; they set the pace for the rest of the crew (under the commands and watchful eye of the paddle captain), control the front of the raft, and take charge of the bow line. In a well-balanced paddle raft, the bow paddlers should be the strongest and most capable paddlers in the team—able to react quickly to commands and willing to paddle fearlessly in the midst of difficult rapids. (If the strongest bow paddler is seated *diagonally*

A six-man crew properly seated in a fourteen-foot raft.

from the guide, the guide and that paddler can sometimes maneuver the raft when everybody else is too nervous to move!)

The last two or three paddlers should be seated as follows: two paddlers should sit near the middle of the raft, while the last passenger can sit in the stern next to the guide. (Keep in mind that each paddler needs enough room to move around or their paddle strokes may get tangled up with other members of the crew.)

VARYING THE SIZE OF THE PADDLE TEAM: The same concepts that apply to five-man teams work with any odd-numbered team: if you have three paddlers, seat the guide in the stern and the other paddlers in the bow or center compartment. If you have seven paddlers, seat the guide in the stern and spread the other paddlers evenly throughout the raft. In large, even-numbered paddle teams, the last paddler can sit next to the paddle captain since proper guiding technique keeps the guide's paddle on *one side* at all times. However, if the raft is only half full (half empty?), make the stern the captain's private domain so that she has plenty of room to move around.

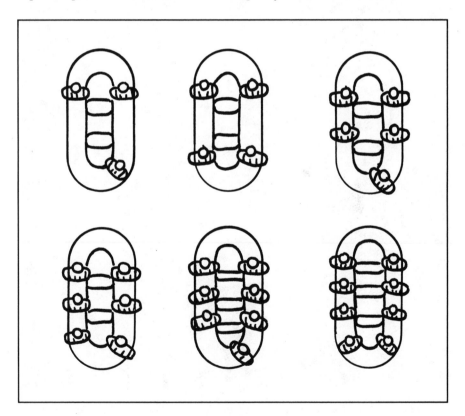

Different ways to seat paddlers: in each configuration paddlers are seated to achieve even strength distribution, even weight distribution, and are given adequate room to paddle.

"A river is never silent. Even its deepest pools thrive with dark and dreamy utterance. They shelter more than we can say we know...." **Brian Turner, Listening to the River**

5

RIVER MORPHOLOGY:
The Dynamics of Running Water

From my boyhood days in Eastern Massachusetts, to my most recent adventures on the steep rivers of the Sierra, Cascade, and Rocky Mountain ranges, I've been enthralled with moving water. As a child, I'd dash outside during Spring freshets to watch water collect and flow through small roadside gulleys. Tossing tiny sticks into these meager currents, I'd stare transfixed as these make-believe rafts descended the miniature pebble-strewn rapids. Even today, standing high atop a rocky precipice while scouting a new rapid, I feel the same inspiration that roused my imagination many years ago.

To the ordinary landlubber, whitewater rapids are a primal source of fascination. Flowing like unbridled liquid avalanches, rapids are breathtaking in their beauty, yet awe inspiring in their power. But to an experienced river runner, rapids are predictable and orderly. Obstacles, constrictions, and even changes in volume or gradient have definite and reliable effects on the river's surface. The seasoned veteran knows these effects intimately and can anticipate how currents and rapids will affect a raft.

In this chapter we will disassemble and examine rivers. Rather than looking at the big river picture, we'll dissect rapids into tangible components, like pieces of a puzzle. Then, once we've gained an understanding of how the pieces work and fit together, we'll reassemble the puzzle and form real live rapids much like the ones you'll really see on your next river trip.

PART ONE: A Look Beneath the Surface

WATER MECHANICS: Ask the average river runner how water moves and in what state, and they're likely to respond, "It moves downhill in West Virginia." Well, yeah, that's a correct response. But ask a hydrologist about water movements, and they'll mention three very different states: *laminar, turbulent*, and *chaotic*. Each state describes a different pattern of currents, and appears at different places with the river system.

For many rafters *laminar flow* is the most comfortable type of current to experience, for it is laminar flows that are the most safe and predictable. Laminar flows show up on smooth, straight riverbeds where, if we were to slice the river from bank to bank, we would find some distinct patterns. As the diagrams on the following page show, rivers have multiple sheets of water, each moving at different speeds. The small circles and long arrows represent the fastest moving sheets and are located near the center of the river below the surface. Large circles and short arrows represent slower sheets, their downstream progress hampered by friction from the riverbed, banks, or air. Between each sheet there's a zone of mild shearing, better described as an interface between two laminar sheets moving quite independently and at different speeds.

To *feel* the differences between laminar sheets, let your raft glide freely across the river surface. If you plant your paddle deep in the river, you will feel a forward tug. That tug is caused by subsurface laminar sheets moving forward faster than the sheets on the surface. If you've ever fallen out of your raft in a big, powerful river, you may have experienced a *tunnel effect*, as if you were trapped inside a giant horizontal tube that wouldn't let you go. That is because the core of the river (just below the surface) is an independent laminar sheet totally separated from its surrounding sheets. Once in the tunnel, the shear zones hold you inside until your life jacket finally propels you back toward the surface.

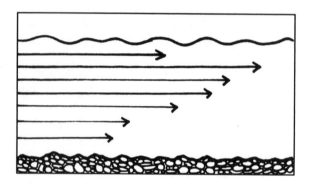

In this example of laminar currents, the longer arrows represent faster currents and appear just below the surface. The currents near the riverbed are slowed by friction.

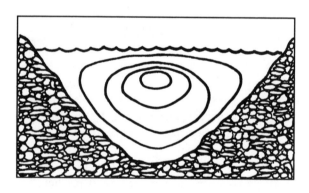

In another example of laminar currents, the smaller circles represent the faster flows.

Turbulent flows arise wherever obstacles obstruct the current. An obstruction forces too much water into too little space, which in turn forces one laminar sheet into another. When this happens, the laminar sheets begin to break up, leaving smaller ribbons of current which seek their way independently through the neighboring currents.

Rafters should look for turbulence at places like chutes, where the independent ribbons slip free and create ripples or waves on the river surface. In another example, turbulence appears in eddies. Here, an obstacle compresses the laminar sheets together as they slip around the obstacle. Then, the turbulent zone appears behind the rock where the laminar sheets break up. The zone of turbulence (the eddy) is separated from the passing laminar sheets (the main current) by an abrupt boundary rafters call an *eddy line*.

As the main current slip past an obstacle, the straight lines (laminar currents) begin to shear off and rotate behind the obstacle (turbulent currents). In this case, the result is an eddy.

At the extreme end of water behavior patterns—just as with many rafters' behavior patterns—there is *chaos*. Simply put, chaos is an utter state of confusion. The river's normal flow lines disintegrate and bounce around randomly. Interestingly, all of this commotion cancels itself out, leaving little real movement at all. Probably the best example of chaos is the ordinary hole (discussed in detail later in this chapter): at the base of a steep slide (like at the back of a rock or ledge) too little water tries to fill too large a space, and settles on trying to be everywhere at once... chaos. Though the water explodes randomly throughout the hole, the hole itself ends up being stationary.

Within any river, other universal patterns emerge. *Helical currents* flow outward from the bank along the surface until they collide with the main current. There they spiral downstream, dive and work their way back toward the bank under the surface.

If you have ever swum a river before, you may have noticed that the last few feet to the shore seemed harder to swim than anything else. That's because the helical currents were pushing you away from the bank, out toward the center of the river.

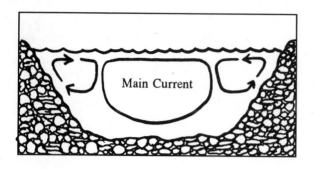

Helical currents flow away from the bank on the surface, meet the main current, then dive. Next, the water works its way back to the bank, then rises along the shore to repeat the cycle.

In the main current you'll find *horizontal and vertical meanders*. In horizontal meanders, the main current weaves back and forth across the river trying to make one complete trip from one bank to the other and back again in a distance equal to eleven times the channel width. In vertical meanders, the main current climbs from deep pools to shallow riffles and back again at a rate equal to three to seven times the channel width.

Since meanders can be kind of confusing, a couple of examples are in order. Let's start off with horizontal meanders. First, pick a bend in the river. Next, measure the river's width. Finally, multiply the river's width by eleven. Now, if you proceed downstream that distance, you would theoretically find another bend in the river where the current completes a horizontal meander. For vertical meanders, measure the distance across the river at a pool, multiply by three to seven, float that distance downstream, and—voila—another pool. (Now, before you go try out these experiments, I've got to add a disclaimer: currents don't always get their way. Banks are constantly eroding and rerouting the main channel. So, it's a constant battle between the hydrodynamics of water and the impediments of new boulders.)

So, what does all of this scientific mumbo-jumbo mean for river runners? Well, each of these well-defined properties influences the shape and feel of rivers in ways that rafters can see and understand. For example, the river's desire to follow its meander route causes it to lean against any bank that gets in its way. As the river continues to lean on that bank, the water's erosive power gradually carves out a new bend. Next, something different happens. Since water only travels in a linear course, the current piles up on the outside of the bend where it has to travel faster than the water on the inside of the bend to reach the same point downstream. At the same time, the outer flow hits the bank, dives toward the bottom, and creeps along the bottom toward the slower currents at the inside of the bend.

The net effect of all this activity is that the fast moving water on the outside of the bend keeps acquiring erosive power, continues to gnaw at the outerbank, and slowly pulls part of the bank into the current itself. At the same time, the slow water along the inside of the bend loses its ability to support the eroded particulates and deposits them on shallow bars. If the pro-

Horizontal meanders work back and forth across the river, continually pressing against the outside bank. Left to its own accord, the meander will erode the outside bank until the riverbed takes on the same shape as the meander.

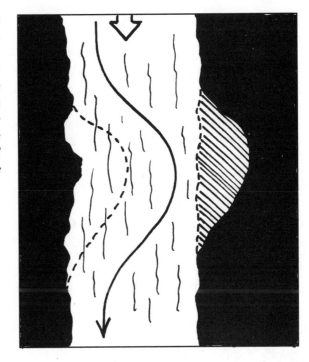

Vertical meanders rise and descend as the current flows downstream. Eventually, this action creates alternating shallow sandbars and deep pools.

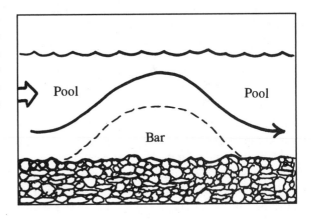

cess continues, deeply undercut cliffs, exposed roots, and overhanging trees begin to appear along the outside of the bend, while the inside bend becomes increasingly shallow and waterless.

PART TWO: River Characteristics

Rivers outwardly display a broad range of emotions—at times calm and soothing, at other times angry and riotous. But inwardly, rivers are lazy by nature. Water can be compared to a train running lazily along a track. It just keeps rolling in the same direction unless something comes along and knocks it off course. Water, just like trains, follows a path of least resistance as it is pulled downhill by its natural engine—gravity. So, then, why do rivers and rapids look so different from one another?

There is much more to whitewater rivers than water's natural tendency to follow a course of least resistance. Obstacles clutter the main channel in places, riverbeds descend more steeply in places, and water levels fluctuate with seasonal rains, snowmelt, or droughts. In the end, three factors have a profound effect on the intensity and character of whitewater rivers: *volume, gradient,* and *changes in river structure.*

VOLUME: River volume is measured in cubic units per second. In the United States, the foot is used for the cubic unit, and the correct term is *cubic feet per second,* or *cfs.* In metric countries, the meter is used in place of the foot, so river volumes are measured in *cubic meters per second,* or *cms.*

Simply stated, cfs and cms measure the amount of water that passes a specific point each second. However, the proper formula is the river's width, times its depth, times the current's velocity. For example, a river twenty feet wide by ten feet deep, with a current flowing five feet per second has a flow of 1,000 cubic feet per second. *(10' x 20' x 5 feet per second = 1,000 cfs).*

Using this basic formula, you can see that the addition of more water—say from a recent rain or a tributary—to the same 10' x 20' river changes the speed of the current. For example, double the flow of the river, making it 2,000 cfs instead of 1,000 cfs. Since the river's depth and width haven't changed, the additional water must move *twice as fast* to make the formula work: instead of moving five feet per second, the velocity jumps to ten feet per second. *(20' x 10' x 10 feet per second = 2,000 cfs).*

Changes in volume or river velocity have some important effects that rafters need to understand. Since water is *heavy*—weighing 8.33 pounds per gallon, or 62.4 pounds per cubic foot—the addition of a few cfs or an increase in river velocity causes a big change in the amount of force that water exerts on a raft or swimmer.

Let's look at this by going back to the cubic foot of water. Instead of using just one cubic foot of water, slice a long rod of water out of the river one foot wide by one foot high. Now, make that rod the same length as the river's flow in cfs. For example, if the river is flowing at 1,000 cfs, make the rod one square foot wide by 1,000 feet long. Now, the weight of that long pillar of water flowing past a designated point in the river doesn't have a force of just 62.4 pounds, it is backed by the force of 1,000 cubes of water, or *62,400 pounds!* Fortunately, the fluid properties of water lets much of that force slide around a raft, rock, or body unnoticed. However, a raft held in place against the main current—say, during a wrap—can prove just how powerful and heavy the river really is. The wrapped raft is held tight by thousands of pounds of pressure, making it very difficult to remove.

Up until now, we've assumed that rivers move downstream at a constant rate of speed. However, as you will soon discover, rivers flow upstream in places and at differing speeds within the same section of river. In an eddy, reverse currents can flow upstream toward an obstacle just as fast as the main current's downstream velocity. This makes the velocity differential between the two currents as much as double that of the main current, and creates powerful *rotational* or *twisting* forces. Rafters caught on the interface between the currents have to fight the current's desire to spin their raft wildly.

Rotational forces are also found where fast and slow currents meet. As the faster currents pass the slower currents, friction pulls pieces of both currents free and causes them to rotate. The interface between the two currents is not as dramatic as those found in eddies, but is still enough to spin your raft around unless you fight to keep it straight.

MORE ON VELOCITY: A change in velocity—whether from an increase in gradient, a narrowing of the river, or an increase in flow—changes the river's force dramatically. It works like this: for every doubling of the current's velocity, the force exerted by the water quadruples. This added force can exert itself on anything in the water's path, or it can be used to support debris suspended in the river's current. (That is why flooded rivers can lift and displace giant boulders, or transport giant logs like overgrown corks.)

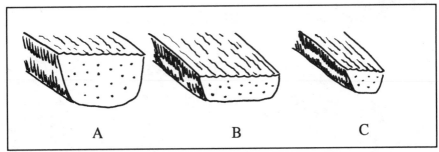

This diagram shows three cross sections of one river at different places. In diagram A, the river is broad, deep, and flowing slowly. In diagram B, the river is the same width, but shallower, forcing the river to flow faster. Finally, in diagram C, the river is both shallow and narrow. Here, the river must flow the fastest.

RIVER SIZE: Without even looking at a river up close, rafters can get some idea how *big* a river is by looking at its average flow. In a very general sense, rivers can be categorized as small, medium, or large. Small rivers can range from a few hundred cfs up to about 1,000 cfs, medium-sized rivers can range from 1,000 to 6,000 cfs, and some large rivers can exceed 100,000 cfs! Still, this type of description is pretty subjective. One rafter's *small* may be another rafter's *big* depending on their point of view. Also, rivers grow and shrink in size and power with seasonal water fluctuations or dam releases.

GAUGES: Many governmental agencies monitor river flows. In turn, rafters can obtain water level information by finding out which agency monitors the rivers they plan to run and asking that agency for the information. If you're not quite sure which agency to contact, check out the guidebooks in the appendix—many list the phone numbers to call for each river they describe.

One problem I've run into with gauges is that many agencies monitor water levels on a *gauge height* basis. Rather than simply announcing the flow in cfs or cms, you'll obtain a gauge height in feet or meters. All this information tells you is how high a river has climbed up an oversized ruler placed in the river at a set location. To use this information you'll have to know the river intimately, or ask someone to correlate the gauge height with river flow. Again, many of the guidebooks explain how to do this. If that doesn't work, the agencies themselves usually maintain a correlation table.

The Colorado River through the Grand Canyon is an example of a large volume river. (Photo by Doc Loomis)

GO WHEN IT FLOWS

Let's start off with a basic premise: "river running is a lot of fun when there's enough water to float your raft." Having said that, you're probably thinking, "Great. I just spent $15.95 on this dumb book so that Jeff can tell me that I need water to go rafting." Well, yeah. Sort of. Just try showing up at a river at the wrong time of year and you'll see what I'm saying.

Rivers obtain water from three sources: snowmelt, rainfall, and springs. Plus, if a hoard of engineers arrived with blueprints and bulldozers long before you did, your river might also get water released from dams and big conduits. Planning river trips involves a little bit of understanding as to how each of these water sources affect rivers.

Snowmelt rivers typically inhabit the foothills of grand mountain ranges like the Rockies, Cascades, or Sierras. After a few days of hot Spring weather, the snow liquifies and releases its watery contents to the tug of gravity. As the water trickles downhill, it collects in ever growing rivulets until it is finally large enough to be called a creek or river.

Rain-fed rivers work in the same way, except that falling rain replaces melting snow as the system's driving force. In rain-fed watersheds it frequently takes a few days of rain before the ground stops absorbing all of the available moisture. (This is why Summer rains rarely fill rivers quickly.) Then, once the ground is saturated, the surplus water spills downward, and the millions of tiny raindrops collect to form giant streams.

By looking at a river's flow history, you can tell whether it is a rain or snow-fed river. If the river's flow peaks during the warmest days of Spring, it relies primarily on snow for its water, while a river that peaks in the middle of the region's rainy season is a rain-fed river.

For rafters, this information is important for selecting the best time of year to go rafting. Since rivers are dangerous at peak and flood stages, the optimal time to run a river is usually before or after the peak has been reached. On small streams with limited watersheds, peak flows might only last a day or two after a heavy storm, while some larger rivers might subside slowly after hitting their peak water levels.

To learn about any river's optimal season, first consult some local guidebooks or call one of the government agencies listed in the appendix. Next, check with guidebooks and other boaters to obtain recommended levels for river running. Finally, plan your trip so that it coincides with the time that the river reaches the levels rafters consider the safest and most fun for river running.

FLOW VERSUS DIFFICULTY: Trying to correlate changes in water volume with the river's difficulty rating is nearly impossible. On most rivers, rapids become more difficult as water levels rise, while rapids disappear beneath gentle blankets of swift water on other rivers. Nonetheless, rafters should remember that larger volumes and faster currents bolster the river's power and can turn gentle rivers into powerful hazards.

GRADIENT: In North America, gradient is described in *feet per mile* (fpm) or *meters per kilometer* (mpk). Both ratings measure a river's average descent over a given distance.

To figure out a river's gradient you will first need to know three things: the elevation at the put-in, the elevation at the take-out, and the distance between the two points. Here's an example of how these numbers work: if the put-in is at an elevation of 3,000 feet and the take-out is at 1,200 feet, the river drops 1,800 feet in that section. Now, if the section to be rafted is 36 miles long, the river drops 50 feet per mile. (1,800/36 = 50). Here's the formula: *(Put-in elevation - Take-out elevation) ÷ Miles = Gradient.*

Rapids appear where the gradient of one section of river exceeds the river's average gradient, and pools form where the gradient dips below the overall average. So, if a river descends evenly over its entire length, the rapids might be long and constant. But if the river alternates between pools and drops the rapids might be short but intense. The most severe example of a *pool-drop* river would be one that descends very little in its placid stretches, then plunges violently over giant waterfalls.

As with the other descriptive factors, gradient gives you some clues about the character of a river. Most whitewater rivers have an average gradient of ten to one-hundred feet per mile. However, it is becoming quite common to see rafters boating rivers with gradients upward of 200 feet per mile. Still, one rule of thumb should be kept in mind, especially when exploring new rivers: *the steeper the river, the more difficult the whitewater.*

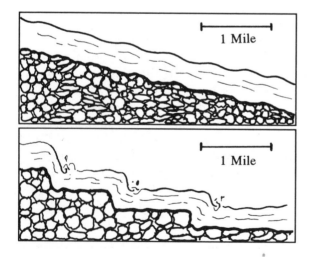

*In a **continuous** river, the water falls gradually over the steadily descending riverbed.*

*In a **pool-drop** river, the river alternates between calm pools and steep rapids.*

PART THREE: Surface Features

River structures are seldom uniform. Riverbeds descend more steeply in some places than others, cliffs narrow and confine channels, and obstacles clutter and obstruct the main current. Each of these structural changes have profound effects on the river, some of which we have already discussed: if the same amount of water is forced into a smaller space (i.e., between two cliffs), its velocity will increase dramatically; if the main current descends down a steep slide, the gentle laminar currents will gradually give way to turbulence or chaos; and if the river travels around a bend, the currents along the outer banks will move faster than those found along the inside of the bend.

Since rafters like to spend most of their time above the river's surface (after all, a majority of rafters rate their whitewater success in terms of avoiding submarine adventures and close encounters with aquatic creatures), it is the *surface* effects of changes in river structure that we are most interested in. So, let's step away from the river, scramble to a point high upon the bank, and start looking at the river's surface features.

Let's begin with a calm, straight river—one that flows freely over an unobstructed channel. Then, let's make some changes. As obstacles enter the current, rapids begin to appear. Here you'll find chutes, waves, holes, and eddies... the things river runners call *fun*—at least if they're not too large or dangerous.

TONGUES: At the top of many rapids, the main current enters a slick, smooth-surfaced ramp called a *tongue*. Tongues are typically "V" shaped, with the tip of the V pointing downstream. These *downstream tongues* form between rocks, cliffs, or shallows, and point out the deepest, least obstructed channel. There may be just one large tongue, or there may be many tongues of different sizes. When there's more than one tongue—like when there are large boulders or islands dividing the river into many channels—the safest and deepest tongue will usually be either the largest tongue or the one that begins dropping the soonest. (The reason for this is that channels that wait longer before they begin to drop lose water to deeper channels. So, by the time the smaller channel reaches the base of a rapid, it may consist of boulder fans barely wet enough to float a raft.)

The second type of V is the *upstream V*, which has the tip of the V pointing upstream. Upstream V's are shockwaves created by obstacles that pierce or lurk just beneath the surface. Unlike tongues, the upstream V is a warning sign—a signal to rafters to steer clear or else risk damaging their boats on the partially submerged obstacle.

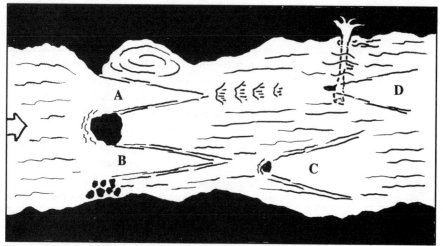

Tongues (A and B) show deep, clear channels, while upstream V's (C and D) show subsurface hazards. Rafters should stay on the tongues and avoid the upstream V's.

STANDING WAVES: Standing waves are one of the most fascinating and entertaining of all river features. From the small erratic riffles of your local creek, to the giant haystacks of large volume rivers, standing waves provide rafters with the ultimate aquatic rollercoaster ride.

No discussion of river waves would be complete without some comparison to *ocean waves*. Although ocean and river waves may look remarkably similar, there are some distinct differences. First, river waves are stationary and remain at the same location as the forces or obstacles that form them. Ocean waves, on the other hand, travel toward shore where they dissipate or crash as they roll up the beach. Second, water travels through river waves, releasing its energy as it goes, while the water inside ocean waves hardly moves at all. Instead, the water inside the ocean wave transfers its energy as the wave rolls toward the beach.

WHAT FORMS A WAVE: Many things form waves: subsurface boulders, changes in gradient, converging currents. But ultimately, most waves are created from a change in water speed. Since water can't be compressed like air, it moves faster when it is confined by narrow streambeds or obstacles. In fact, water gains speed whenever it: (1) is squeezed *horizontally* between banks or boulders; (2) is compressed *vertically* over rocks or river bottom; or (3) when it falls down a steeper section of riverbed. Waves are associated with all three changes in water velocity.

The most common standing waves are those which form at the bottom of downward sloping riverbeds. Here, the potential energy stored in fast, downward moving water dissipates gradually when it hits the bottom of the slope. In the most basic example of a sloping river bed, there are no obstacles to interfere with the formation of standing waves. As the river reaches the end of the slope, a series of waves—or *wave train*—forms, with each wave lining up perpendicular to the main current. The first wave in the train is usually the largest, with each successive wave diminishing in size. (*Tailwaves*—another name used to describe standing waves—are wave trains that begin at the base of a rapid.)

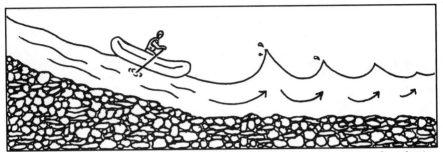

Standing waves form when the current slows down at the base of a sloping riverbed.

Standing waves also appear after cliffs, shallow gravel bars, boulder piles, or other obstacles force a broad river into a narrow channel. Since the river has less space to occupy, it is forced to travel faster. The moment the channel reopens, the energy stored in the fast moving water dissipates in the form of standing waves.

Submarine boulders or ledges can also form waves. Here, the current picks up energy as it travels faster over the top of the obstacle, then releases it downstream in a series of waves. A hump or cushion—not a standing wave—forms above the obstacle, followed by standing waves downstream. Since waves formed by rocks and boulders frequently stand alone, their solitary presence foretells of the obstacle beneath the surface.

Still another cause of standing waves is converging currents. *Convergence waves* often form where two channels meet, or where a tributary spills its current into the mainstream. Water piles up and gathers energy at the convergence, then releases the excess energy gradually in the form of standing waves. If the cause of the convergence is a deflection of the main current back upon itself by cliffs or steep banks, the waves that bounce off the cliffs are sometimes called *reflection waves*.

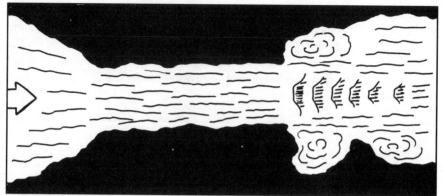

Standing waves form where the fast current of a chute meets the slower moving water below.

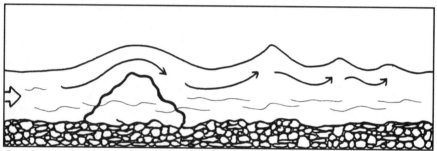

Standing wave forming after a boulder.

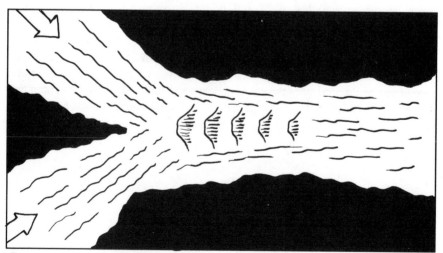

Convergence waves forming where two currents meet.

78

DIAGONAL WAVES: When a submerged ledge or boulder cuts diagonally across the main channel, surface waves won't line up perpendicular to the main current. Instead, the first wave or two below the ledge will lunge upward at an angle to the main current, forming *diagonal* or *lateral* waves. Diagonal waves also appear wherever submerged boulders, converging currents, and constricted channels deflect waves at an angle to the main current. No matter what forms the diagonal waves, the waves following the first few diagonal waves realign themselves with the main current just like any other standing wave.

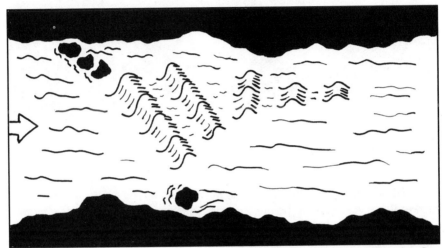

Diagonal waves forming after a submerged diagonal ledge. After the first couple of waves, the tail waves realign themselves perpendicular with the current.

HAYSTACKS: Haystacks are the mountain peaks of the riverscape. Although they look like towering, peaked standing waves, they're actually formed from converging standing waves, each contributing its energy to force the haystack higher than its surroundings. With all of this energy packed into one wall of water, haystacks are rarely stable—they tend to dance around on the river's surface and surge randomly.

BREAKING WAVES AND STOPPERS: When a wave becomes too large to support its own weight and shape, it starts spilling the highest water down the wave's upstream face. Whether they're called *curlers, curling waves, breaking waves*, or *reversals*, these waves can be very powerful. If enough water is falling down the upstream face, it can carry sufficient force to stop and flip your raft—hence the name *stopper*.

When a standing wave becomes too large to support its own weight, the crest falls down the wave's upstream face. This rafter is wisely avoiding the powerful breaking wave across the river.

PILLOWS: When the current collides with an obstacle, some of the current flows vertically up on the obstacle's upstream side and forms a mound of water called a *cushion* or *pillow*. These mounds stand higher than the surrounding river and disclose the presence of boulders and other obstacles. As pillows grow, they eventually become too large to support their own weight. When that happens, the highest water spills down the upstream face, creating a hydraulic much like a breaking wave.

Pillows form where the current collides with the upstream side of an obstacle. The current rises upward on the obstacle, forming a cushion, then settles back down as it slips around the side of the obstacle.

80

A pillow—or, rather, the lack of a pillow—also reveals a major river hazard: *undercuts*. To spot an undercut from your raft, watch the river. Whenever the current collides with an obstacle without forming a pillow, beware! It is a certain indication that the obstacle is undercut, and that the current is diving under the obstacle—just where you don't want to be! Since powerful currents can carry rafts and swimmers beneath undercut ledges, banks and boulders, they are to be treated as some of the biggest hazards to be found on whitewater rivers.

This paddle captain is giving the "thumb's up" because his team avoided the dangerously undercut rock in the upper left hand portion of the photo.

ROOSTERTAILS: Roostertails are pillows gone berserk. Like pillows, roostertails form when a fast current piles into the upstream side of a rock or boulder. However, rather than building smoothly upon the shoulder of the rock, the rock slices through the current and deflects water into the air, creating an aerial fountain in the shape of a rooster's tail.

There are two types of roostertails: *upstream* and *downstream roostertails*. Upstream-angled roostertails form when the rock is tilted upstream, and are identified by the fan of water deflecting through the air in an upstream direction. Downstream roostertails are caused by downstream tilted rocks and fan water through the air in a downstream direction.

Rafters should avoid any kind of roostertail since the exposed rock and fast moving currents can combine to tear or wrap the raft in an instant.

The upstream roostertail (left) and the downstream roostertail (right) pose serious hazards to rafters and should be avoided.

BOILS: Boils are upwellings in the river current caused by things like underwater boulders, undercut ledges, and converging currents. Here, the river surface looks like a giant boiling pot of water.

HOLES: When water pours over a rock or ledge, the water plunges down a *falls* toward the riverbed then flows downstream along the bottom of the river. A deep cavity appears in the river surface just downstream of the falls. In an effort to fill this cavity, the river grabs surface water from downstream and pours it in a reverse direction back into the cavity. (This zone of upstream currents is called the *backwash*.) Viewed from the side, the hole's currents rotate like a wheel, with the surface rolling upstream, and the bottom rolling downstream. This rotating liquid vortex goes by many names, including *hole, reversal, souse hole,* and *stopper.*

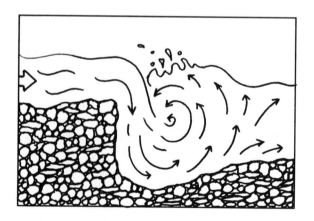

A hole: the water falling over the ledge escapes downstream along the riverbed, while the water at the surface flows upstream to fill in the cavity. If the hole is large enough, rafts and swimmers can actually get caught in this vortex.

Holes, like waves, come in all shapes and sizes. Large holes—sometimes called *keepers*—can hold and flip a raft with ease, while small holes can be crashed or avoided. Getting to know the difference between friendly and unfriendly holes is one of the most important skills any rafter can have. Fortunately, there are four factors which reveal the intensity of a hole: (1) the *height, angle,* and *volume* of the falls; (2) the *shape* and *width* of the hole; (3) the hole's *depth*; and (4) the *length of the backwash*. These factors mix and match in countless ways, but understanding how they work together will reveal a lot about a particular hole. Let's start by looking at *the falls.*

Water plunges downward at the upstream side of a hole. Generally, the steeper and taller this *falls* the more severe the hole. In vertical falls—often called *pourovers*—water plummets toward the bottom of the river and can create a deep hole with a small pocket of violently opposing currents, especially if the pourover is more than a few feet high. Sloping falls, on the other hand, can create long zones of backwash—a perilous hazard for rafters.

Falls with a lot of water usually create stronger holes than low volume falls. In a tight, constricted channel, the whole river might plunge over a sharp ledge. This can create a nearly impenetrable hole that can easily trap and hold rafters. On the other hand, a small boulder in the middle of a broad stream might only create a small hole—one barely big enough to be noticeable, or one that is just big enough to splash your crew. In any case, the addition of more water to the falls generally makes for a more powerful hole.

There are four different shapes which could describe almost any hole: *smiling, frowning, horizontal,* and *diagonal.* Each shape describes the hole's appearance from an imaginary perspective upstream. In a *smiling* hole, the middle of the hole is the furthest upstream, while the hole's outer edges curl downstream and away from you. This lets some of the current—and anything floating on it—escape laterally out of the hole. Because of this, smiling holes are the safest holes to run. If the outer edges curl back at you, the hole is frowning. *Frowning* holes focus much of the current's energy toward the middle of the hole, creating a powerful magnet for anything stuck in its grasp. For rafters, this can spell disaster. Large frowning holes can make lateral escapes nearly impossible, and can hold rafts and swimmers indefinitely.

Horizontal holes show up in two places: at the base of artificial dams, and at the base of river-wide ledges. If the volume of water flowing over the ledge is even all the way across the river, the resulting hole forms a forboding bank-to-bank obstacle for rafters. Like frowning holes, these types of holes can be powerful and dangerous, making escape very difficult.

The final type of hole—a *diagonal hole*—appears wherever an obstacle or ledge cuts across the channel at an angle to the current. Diagonal holes have one side further upstream than the other, and contain a current which slides downstream across the face of the hole. By moving the raft to the downstream end of the hole, it will eventually slip free of the hole and back into the main current—hopefully upright.

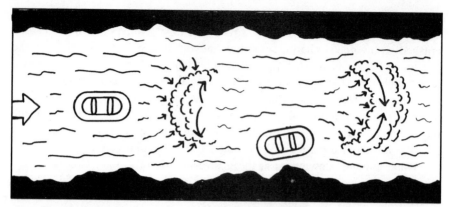

A smiling hole (left) and a frowning hole (right). The surface current in the smiling hole kicks outward and provides an escape route for rafts, while the frowning hole's surface current kicks inward, creating a powerful trap.

A river-wide horizontal hole (left) and a diagonal hole (right). The horizontal hole has no escape route and can trap a raft. The diagonal hole, on the other hand, has a surface current that kicks from the top of the diagram to the bottom. A raft caught in the diagonal hole will eventually wash up on the right (lower) bank.

Hole width and *hole depth* are the next factors that indicate the strength and danger of any hole. Hole width is measured perpendicularly across the current. Wide holes are much more difficult to exit than are narrow holes and should usually be avoided. Hole depth describes how far beneath the surface the recirculating current extends, and is determined by the speed and volume of the falls. In deep holes, the falls forces water all the way down to the riverbed. From there, the current climbs back toward the surface and repeats the cycle without letting much water escape. On large volume rivers, a rafter trapped in its grasp could be in real trouble. Not only can the downward current behind the rock slam swimmers against the river bottom, there is only a narrow zone of escape directly on the bottom of the river.

Shallower holes don't extend all the way to the bottom of the river and are usually much safer for rafters, all other factors being equal. Since the hole's rotating currents only reach part of the way to the riverbed, swimmers can easily swim out from under the upstream currents utilizing the free flowing downstream current.

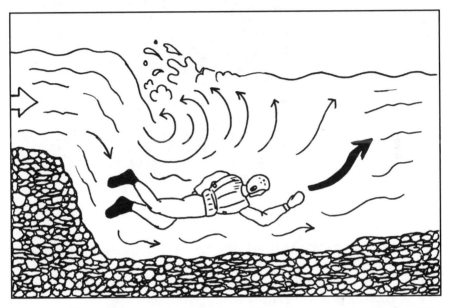

In this shallow hole, the downward current only extends part way to the riverbottom and allows easy escape under the backwash. In deep holes—especially those in which the falls plunges all the way to the riverbed—escape is much more difficult.

BACKWASH: The term *backwash* describes the zone of upstream current which forms downstream of a hole. In some holes, an object floating on the surface twenty or more feet downstream of the falls can travel back upstream on the backwash, only to find itself caught in the swirling maelstrom yet another time. Rafters can follow an easy rule of thumb: "the longer the backwash, the more difficult and dangerous the hole."

SPOTTING HOLES: Holes can appear anywhere a ledge or boulder lurks beneath the surface. But since the river plunges over the obstacles, the hole itself might be hard to see from upstream. Still, there are signposts that reveal the hole's presence to observant rafters. In a rapid, look for the calm, smooth hump which forms as the water stays level when passing over a submerged rock. If you can see beyond the hump, look slightly downstream for the foamy backwash. Gradually you will get better at spotting holes, and eventually you'll be able to discern fun, runnable holes from hazardous holes just by looking at them from upstream.

To spot holes from upstream, look for a smooth hump in the river's surface, or for the backwash that forms at the base of the hole. Both can be seen in this photograph.

LOWHEAD DAMS AND WEIRS: Lowhead dams and weirs include a variety of artificial structures. Many lowhead dams were originally designed to divert water into grain mills or irrigation networks. Now they are built for such purposes as flood control and power generation.

Fabricated from cement, asphault, rebar, and rip-rap, most lowhead dams are installed straight across the river channel, with walls rising out of either end of the dam. As the water drops over the top of the dam, it slides down a smooth face, spilling onto a flat or angled apron. Then, as the water plummets into the pool below the dam, the currents form *incredibly dangerous* holes.

Holes below lowhead dams can extend all the way across the river, are very straight, display a lot of power, and have a long zone of backwash. Any one of these factors could create a very dangerous hole in their own right. But when combined, they form one of the most hazardous obstacles known to whitewater enthusiasts. In fact, a great number of river-related fatalities are due to lowhead dams. For rafters, I've got only two words of advice: *steer clear!* Even runnable looking lowhead dams contain dangerous currents, and many contain nasty piles of submerged rebar, trapped logs, and construction debris.

When on the river, watch for artificial structures and smooth, riverwide horizon lines. These signs can tell you that a dam is coming up and that it is time to pull to the bank!

WATERFALLS: When holes get too big for their britches, we call them waterfalls. To me, waterfalls include pourovers, slides, or any type of drop that's high and steep enough to make me think twice before I raft it. In many ways, waterfalls are no different than holes. Each waterfall has a downward plunging current, a zone of backwash, and can be any of a number of shapes or sizes. Accordingly, everything we just learned about holes applies to waterfalls.

Waterfalls can be detected from upstream by their distinctive horizon lines. When you first start rafting, keep a keen eye downstream. If the river seems to suddenly disappear without going around a bend, pull over and walk downstream. It may be that the gradient has simply increased, or it could be that the river is about to plunge over a waterfall. As you start to discern the differences between rapids and falls, things like nearby trees and large boulders, or even the sound of the water, will give you clues as to whether the river is about to pour over a dangerous waterfall.

Don't try this at home, kids!

EDDIES: I've waited until the end of this chapter to discuss eddies for two reasons: first, eddies combine almost everything mentioned so far about currents and river features. They have oppositional currents, appear opposite of pillows behind obstacles, and contain both laminar and turbulent currents. Second, eddies are the most important hydraulic formations for rafters to know and understand. They provide gentle parking zones for loading and unloading rafts, safe havens for scouting or resting before the next drop, and can even make cross-river maneuvers easier.

Eddies are found behind any obstacle that deflects the main current—boulders, bank protrusions, even bridge abutments and logs. No matter what the obstacle is, it has the same effect: when the main current collides with the upstream face of the obstacle, it works its way around the obstacle and accelerates. This leaves a depressed zone of low pressure behind the obstacle. Water from downstream actually flows *upstream* toward the obstacle to fill in the gap, creating a pocket of current moving in the opposite direction of the main current. (For an example, see the diagram on page 67.)

A feature called an *eddy line* marks the narrow divide between the oppositional currents of the eddy and the main current. Here, the currents of the eddy and main channel mix and swirl. On powerful, large volume rivers, the eddy and main current might rise to two different levels, causing the currents of the eddy and main channel to wrestle violently along the transition zone. When there is a visible wall of water blocking the entrance or exit from the eddy, rafters call the eddy line an *eddy fence*.

Two factors affect the intensity of an eddy: (1) the size and shape of the

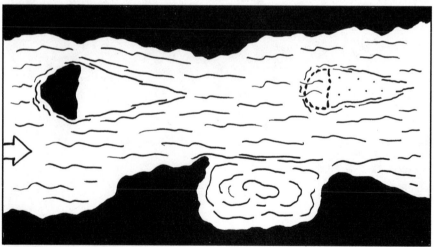

A solid green eddy forms behind an exposed midstream boulder (left) and the peninsula (center). An aerated white eddy forms behind the partially submerged boulder (right).

obstacle, and (2) the velocity of the current. If the obstacle has chiselled, well-defined edges, it will sever swift currents sharply from the eddy, creating a crisp eddy line and stable eddies. On the other hand, rounded obstacles and slow currents allow the currents to mix, weakening the eddy and melting the eddy lines. Shallow obstacles can create eddies even if they don't pierce the river's surface. As the river slides over the top of the obstacle, it loses its momentum and swirls in an aerated pocket. The foamy eddy that is formed behind the obstacle is called a *white eddy*, while the more solid eddies are called *green eddies*. The last type of eddy contains powerful, vertical boiling currents. For lack of a better term, call these *boiling eddies*.

PART FOUR: The Big Picture

The thing that makes rafting so exciting is that no two rapids are alike. The river features we've discussed in this chapter vary not only in size and intensity from river to river, they mix and match in a myriad of combinations. Some rivers might contain long series of gentle waves interspersed with calm pools, others might display steep boulder gardens punctuated by steep holes, and still others might have giant haystacks bordered by vicious eddy fences.

As you move from one river to another, the same distinctive hydraulics will be found again and again, and their distinguishing characteristics will become comfortable and familiar. You'll soon associate solitary waves or pillows with submarine boulders, strange water fountains with surface piercing rocks, and smooth humps of water or foaming backwash with holes. Eventually, each feature will direct you to safer channels, or forewarn you that any attempt at running some rapids is at your own risk.

PART FIVE: Rating the Rapids

There are two universal systems used by rafters to classify the difficulty and intensity of rapids. The most common system is the *International Scale of River Difficulty*, which grades rapids on a scale of I to VI. In the Southwestern United States, another system, known as the *Deseret Scale* or *Grand Canyon System*, is sometimes used. This system rates rapids on a scale of 1 to 10. Unfortunately, neither system is perfect. Rapids change constantly, and are affected by water level fluctuations and shifts in the riverbed. Rafters might rate rapids differently depending on their attitude or skill level. Also, the pursuit of more difficult whitewater has resulted in a downgrading of many rapids. Rapids that used to be considered Class VI (extreme) have been downscaled to Class V after many successful descents. So, river classifications are little more than a starting point for finding out about any river. You should gather as much additional information about rapids as you can find.

THE AWA RIVER RATING SCALE: The American Whitewater Affiliation has published the leading version of the *International Scale of River Difficulty.* Here it is:

"This is the American version of a rating system used to compare river difficulty throughout the world. This system is not exact; rivers do not always fit easily into one category, and regional or individual interpretations may cause misunderstandings. It is no substitute for a guidebook or accurate first-hand descriptions of a run.

"Paddlers attempting difficult runs in an unfamiliar area should act cautiously until they get a feel for the way the scale is interpreted locally. River difficulty may change each year due to fluctuations in water level, downed trees, geological disturbances, or bad weather. Stay alert for unexpected problems!

"As river difficulty increases, the danger to swimming paddlers becomes more severe. As rapids become longer and more continuous, the challenge increases. There is a difference between running an occasional Class IV rapid and dealing with an entire river of this category. Allow an extra margin of safety between skills and river ratings when the water is cold or if the river itself is remote and inaccessible. "

Class I: Easy. Fast moving water with riffles and small waves. Few obstructions, all obvious and easily missed with little training. Risk to swimmers is slight; self-rescue is easy.

Class II: Novice. Straightforward rapids with wide, clear channels which are evident without scouting. Occasional maneuvering may be required, but rocks and medium-sized waves are easily missed by trained paddlers. Swimmers are seldom injured and group assistance, while helpful, is seldom needed.

Class III: Intermediate. Rapids with moderate, irregular waves which may be difficult to avoid and which can swamp an open canoe. Complex maneuvers in fast current and good boat control in tight passages or around ledges are often required; large waves or strainers may be present but are easily avoided. Strong eddies and powerful current effects can be found, particularly on large-volume river. Scouting is advisable for inexperienced parties. Injuries while swimming are rare; self-rescue is usually easy, but group assistance may be required to avoid long swims.

Class IV: Advanced. Intense, powerful but predictable rapids requiring precise boat handling in turbulent water. Depending on the character of the river, it may feature large, unavoidable waves and holes or constricted passages demanding fast maneuvers under pressure. A fast, reliable eddy turn may be needed to initiate maneuvers, scout rapids, or rest. Rapids may require "must" moves above dangerous hazards. Scouting is necessary the first time down. Risk of injury to swimmers is moderate to high, and water conditions may make self-rescue difficult. Group assistance for rescue is often essential but requires practiced skills.

Class V: Expert. Extremely long, obstructed, or very violent rapids which expose a paddler to above average endangerment. Drops may contain large, unavoidable waves and holes, or steep, congested chutes with complex, demanding routes. Rapids may continue for long distances between pools, demanding a high level of fitness. What eddies exist may be small, turbulent, or difficult to reach. At the high end of the scale, several of these factors may be combined. Scouting is mandatory but often difficult. Swims are dangerous, and rescue is difficult even for experts. Proper equipment, extensive experience, and practiced rescue skills are essential for survival.

Class VI: Extreme. One grade more difficult than Class V. These runs often exemplify the extremes of difficulty, unpredictability and danger. The consequences of errors are very severe and rescue may be impossible. For teams of experts only, at favorable water levels, after close personal inspection and taking all precautions. This class does **not** represent drops thought to be unrunnable, but may include rapids which are only occasionally run.

Class III whitewater.

PART SIX: The Rating Game

The International Scale of River Difficulty—the most popular whitewater rating system in the world—lumps all rapids together in one of six classifications. Though these generic categories work well when making basic comparisons between rivers or rapids, rafters have had to fine tune the descriptions to keep up with the vast spectrum of rapids being run today.

By adding mathematical signs and decimals, the International Scale explodes into a long list of highly descriptive ratings, with smaller increments between classifications. Using plus and minus signs, a rapid which spans a gray area between the International Scale's Class III and IV ratings can be rated *Class III+* (slightly harder than Class III) or *Class IV-* (slightly easier than Class IV). By the time all of the potential ratings are tallied, the International Scale's six classifications multiply into 15 classifications (Class I-, VI- and VI+ are rarely used).

At the upper end of the whitewater scale, a decimal system has emerged which helps distinguish one Class V rapid from another. Similar to the numerical system used by climbers, the Class V rating system classifies rapids Class V.1 (easy Class V) to V.10 (extremely difficult). This system keeps the occasional Class V rafters from getting into something above their skill level.

Remember that any rating system is subjective, and that as time goes by, rafters will keep getting better. What was rated Class V ten years ago may be rated Class IV today, and today's Class IV's may be the Class III's of the next decade. Rely on your own skills and judgment, and don't let anyone—or any system—tell you what you can or can't do!

Class V.1 or Class V.10? You be the judge! (Photo by Julie Prange)

6

PROPULSION BASICS:
Different Strokes for Different Boats

Steering a raft through whitewater embraces two very distinct activities acting together in harmony: reading rapids and executing the proper set of maneuvers. Watching a skilled oarsperson or finely-tuned paddle team running a difficult rapid reveals both the simplicity of individual oar and paddle strokes, and the complexity of combined whitewater maneuvers.

This chapter provides the most critical tools for learning how to maneuver rafts through whitewater: basic oar and paddle strokes. From the basics of backrowing to the intricacies of forward paddling, this chapter gives you your first glimpse of the techniques you'll need to successfully run rivers. It is your opportunity to put your hands on the wheel and feel what it is like to propel a raft on the river.

PART ONE: Oar Strokes

BACKROWING: Backrowing—or *pulling* on the oars—is the foundation of many raft maneuvers for two reasons: it slows the raft down in relation to the current and provides the foundation for the ferrying techniques discussed later in this chapter.

Before you take your first backstroke, let's talk about the four phases that make up any stroke: the *reach, catch, power*, and *recovery phases*. In the backstroke, the *reach phase* pushes the oarblades backward and the handles forward. Make your reach by leaning comfortably forward, arms outstretched, and pressing the handles downward. This will lift the blades clear out of the river behind you. In the *catch phase*, lift your hands, dipping the blades back through the river's surface until they barely disappear. Now it's time to pull the oars through the water in the *power phase*. Pull straight back on the handles, dragging the blades through the water until your hands come close to your chest. The stroke ends with the *recovery phase*, which begins with pushing the handles down again, popping the blades free of the surface. The oar is recovered by pushing your hands forward, which sets up the oars for another cycle.

So, there it is... the basic backstroke. Now, let's make the backstroke more powerful and effective by adding a little leverage. First, make sure one or both feet are planted squarely on the footbar. This will give you a solid platform to brace against as you begin pulling back on the oars. Next, concentrate on using the powerful muscles of the legs and back, and think of your arms and hands as little more than giant gaff hooks connecting your torso to the oars. Finally, focus on moving the oars in level planes both beneath and above the river surface. Don't let the oars dive in huge submarine arcs, and avoid lifting the oars too far out of the water. This will save a lot of energy, and will add to the effectiveness of your strokes.

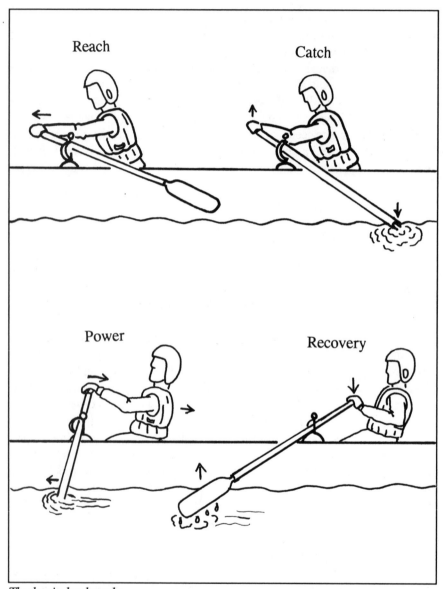

The basic backstroke.

PORTEGEE: The portegee—or *pushing* the oars—is just the opposite of backrowing. In fact, a more descriptive word for the portegee would be *frontrowing*.

In the portegee, the rower leans back, pulls the oar handles close to the torso, and lifts the handles. This plants the blades into the river toward the bow. The rafter then begins the stroke's power phase by leaning forward, pushing the handles outward, and straightening both arms.

The portegee is less effective than backrowing because it relies on the weaker muscles of the front torso. However, it is very useful in gentle rapids, and is frequently used to give a raft the last bit of push up a steep wave or through a strong hole. To make the stroke a little stronger, put one foot on the floor close to your body and push with your legs.

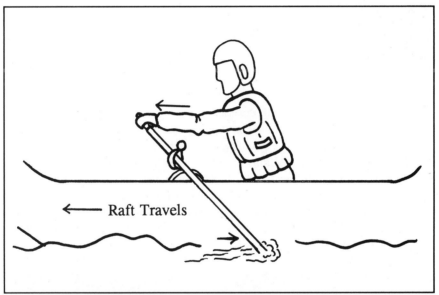

The portagee or push stroke.

TURNING: Basic oar turns are based on a simple theory: *one-legged ducks swim in circles*. Applying this theory to rafts, the basic oar turn requires only one oar. No matter whether you pull or push this oar, the raft is going to turn. If you backstroke on one side, the bow will pivot toward the oar being pulled and the raft's downstream movement will slow just a bit. If you need to execute a more powerful and speedy turn, push on one oar while simultaneously pulling on the opposite oar. This technique, called the *double oar turn*, causes the bow to quickly spin toward the oar being pulled without any loss of forward motion.

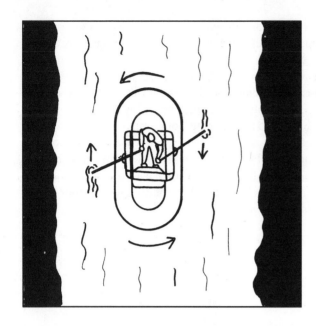

The double oar turn uses both oars to spin the raft. Pull on one oar and push on the other at the same time. The raft will spin toward the oar being pulled.

REFINEMENTS: Beyond the basics of backrowing, portegeeing, and turning, there are a few more rowing skills considered essential on any river.

First, in narrow or rocky channels there may not be enough room to hold the oars in their outward position. Instead, it may be necessary to get the oars out of the way of nearby obstacles. The technique for getting the oars out of harm's way is called *shipping*. Oars can be *shipped forward* by tucking the blades against the side of the bow, or *shipped backward* by tucking the blades against the side of the stern. The final shipping technique—which only works with oarlocks—is to pull the oars straight into the passenger compartment.

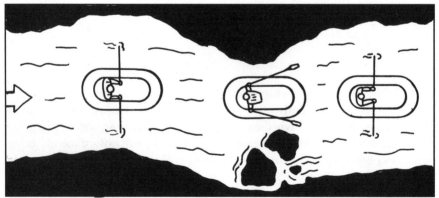

When running narrow slots, oars can be shipped forward (as shown here) or backward to that they don't snag rocks or cliffs.

MORE ROWING TIPS

There will be times when shipping an oar gives the river carte blanche to push your raft wherever it desires. However, if you shipped your oars with the blades facing forward, you can still control your raft with subtle sculling movements.

Even when the blades are tucked close to the raft near the bow, one blade can be lifted out of the water, planted a foot or so from the tube, and pulled back to the tube. The result of this mini-stroke is a quick sideways motion of the raft toward the oar. To move the raft away from the oar, just plant the blade right next to the tube, then push it outward a foot or two. If you are using oarlocks, try doing the same thing while sculling the blades in a figure eight pattern just beneath the surface. You may be surprised at the amount of control you gain over your raft in tight chutes.

*Rafters using oarlocks will find that they can also **feather**, or rotate their oars in the oarlocks by turning their wrists to and fro. By twisting the handles, the blades can be turned horizontal to the river. This can be real nice on windy days, when the blades can be feathered flat as they are drawn through the air. Also, feathering can give experienced rowers a more intimate feel of the currents beneath the surface of the river.*

In shallow or technical rapids, oars have a way of snagging obstacles and popping free. To avoid this, always keep an eye on your downstream oar so that it doesn't catch rocks or boulders, and use your upstream oar to maneuver. If you find yourself having to maneuver around big boulders, try sticking your oars in passing eddies to add extra power to each stroke. Finally, anticipate each stroke and strive for smooth power.

— Gary Stott, Cascade Outfitters

SWEEP BOATS AND PLOHTS: Sweep boats and plohts use long, sturdy oars (often called *sweeps*) mounted parallel with the raft's long axis (over the bow and stern). This is quite different than regular oar rafts, which mount the oars sideways over the left and right gunnel. The raft is then run with its long axis parallel with the current, with the guide standing in the center of the raft. To move the raft back and forth across the river, the guide pulls or pushes the oars and relies on ferry angles. Since these craft are steered more than they are rowed, they are designed for use on rivers with consistent currents. On pool-drop rivers, or rivers with very slow stretches, it is difficult to propel these rafts downstream unless they're turned sideways.

For these craft, good rowing technique begins with a solid stance, and the whole body is leaned into or away from the oar to create long, smooth, powerful pushing and pulling strokes. In larger plohts and sweep boats, it is common to have two or more guides controlling the oars. The extra body weight and strength of the additional oarsmen can generate a tremendous amount of power. Finally, since it is nearly impossible to slow the descent of these type of craft without first turning them sideways, anticipating maneuvers and following less drastic routes can become important.

The long oars (sweeps) of sweep boats and plohts make lateral maneuvers easier than they would be with conventional oar rafts.

PART TWO: Basic Paddle Strokes_____

For team-spirited whitewater adventure, few experiences compare to paddling rapids with a finely synchronized crew. Working in unison, paddlers can achieve the same degree of success in rapids as their oar-wielding brethren while giving every crew member a chance to get involved.

The paddle strokes used in rafting have evolved significantly over the last decade. Traditionally, rafters paid little attention to the subtle yet effective techniques used by other whitewater paddlers, such as open canoers. But following the advent of competitive raft racing, rafters began to take a closer look at those paddling techniques. Now, many of the same strokes that power canoes and C-1's are used in paddle rafting with little or no modification. Only the raft's large tubes and difficult seating positions alter the paddling techniques.

In this section we will look at a myriad of paddle strokes, ranging from the forward and backstroke, to advanced strokes like *cross-bow draws* and *farback strokes*. It builds on the configurations learned in Chapter Four for seating paddlers, and takes you through every basic stroke used in running easy to intermediate rapids.

THE GRIP: Good paddling techniques start with proper hand grip and hand position. First, look at the diagram of the paddle. Note that the paddle consists of a handle, shaft, throat, and blade. On a typical rafting paddle, the handle is shaped like a hot dog or a "T."

The *T-grip* is designed to let paddlers wrap their fingers over the top of the handle with their thumbs underneath. (As easy as that sounds, you'd be amazed how many people wrap both hands around the shaft—just take a look in some outfitters' brochures or in your favorite river magazine!) Keeping the upper hand on the T-grip is very important. It stabilizes the paddle, controls the blade angle, and lessens the chance of dropping your paddle. However, a white-knuckled grip isn't necessary. A gentle grip works perfectly with the anatomically shaped T-grips, and saves your hand from fatigue.

The lower hand is called the *shaft hand*. The shaft hand wraps around the shaft with the palm facing forward (toward the bow). If possible, the shaft hand should also be placed 2-1/2 to 3 hands' widths up the shaft from the throat to provide maximum effectiveness.

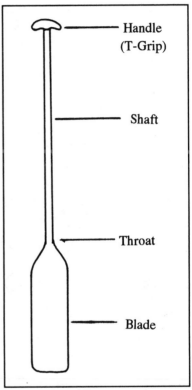

A typical paddle.

THREE CATEGORIES: Conceptually, all paddle strokes fall within one of three categories: *power strokes, turning strokes,* and *braces. Power strokes* move the raft forward and backward. Hence the main power strokes are the forward and backward strokes. *Turning strokes* are more complicated since there are many ways to turn a raft. Forward and backward strokes, when used in combination on opposite sides of the raft, turn the raft. Still, true turning strokes include *pry, sweep,* and *drawstrokes,* each of which can be used near the bow and stern to control the speed and direction of the raft's spin. When the same strokes are used to drive the raft laterally, without turning, they aren't technically turning strokes, but they'll be included in the same section to keep matters simple.

The final category is *braces*. Rafters are only beginning to discover how useful canoe-style braces are in rafting. Whether you're on a technical creek that wants to flip your boat as it passes through a steep, narrow slot, or you're on a giant river that threatens to dislodge you from your raft with each passing wave, braces provide a way to keep yourself in the raft and the raft upright.

THE BASIC FORWARD STROKE: The forward stroke is the most important stroke in the paddler's arsenal since it uses the powerful muscles of the torso. To execute the basic forward stroke, lean forward while thrusting the paddle forward. The lower arm becomes straight as the paddle reaches its maximum comfortable extension, and the upper arm remains slightly bent at eye level. Now, keep the blade at right angles to the tube, pull it toward you with your lower hand, and push forward with your upper hand. End the stroke just forward of your hips (if you let the blade pass your hips, you might get thrown off balance).

The basic forward stroke: pull with the shaft hand while pushing with your upper hand.

THE ADVANCED FORWARD STROKE: Few paddlers will find it necessary to perfect their forward stroke beyond the simple technique just described. However, racers and advanced rafters can add power and efficiency to their forward strokes by using the techniques developed by world class canoeists.

The advanced forward stroke is both beautiful and fluid when properly executed, but actually consists of four phases: the *reach, catch, power* and *recovery* phases.

Start the *reach phase*—which follows the last stroke's recovery

100

phase—with your blade held perpendicular to the raft. Raise the paddle and extend it toward the bow, keeping your lower arm straight and your upper arm slightly bent at eye level. At the same time, rotate your outside shoulder (the side nearest the river) forward. At full extension, your upper body leans forward 15 to 20 degrees for a little extra reach, but your hips stay stationary and your lower back straight. Now, your torso is *wound up* in preparation for the catch and power phases of the forward stroke.

In the *catch phase*, the paddle is planted in the river close to the side of the raft. To get a good catch, keep your paddle nearly vertical, about 70 degrees to the river surface.

Now comes the heart of the stroke—the *power phase*. Pull the paddle back by rotating your shoulders and waist back without bending your lower arm (keep it comfortably straight, not stiff). At the same time, keep your hands close to the outside of the tube with the paddle as vertical as possible. This paddle posture captures energy that would be lost if the paddle were pushed down on, rather than pulled through, the river.

The *unwinding* of the torso during the power phase provides an enormous amount of power during the first five to seven inches of the stroke, but the power quickly diminishes before the paddle reaches the hips. Accordingly, short, fast strokes work much better than longer, less efficient forward strokes.

Start the final phase of the forward stroke—the *recovery phase*—just forward of your hips. (Continuing the power phase past your hips causes the paddle to shovel or lift water, and pulls the raft imperceptibly downward rather than driving it forward.) The blade is sliced out of the water by twisting the wrists slightly, then the paddle is lifted and returned to the catch position. By rotating the paddle such that the blade is parallel to the water, it can be moved forward with very little wind or water resistance.

The forward stroke: "wind up" your torso by rotating your waist and thrusting your outside shoulder forward, and hold the paddle vertically out over the tube. During the stroke's power phase, rotate your torso back to its starting position.

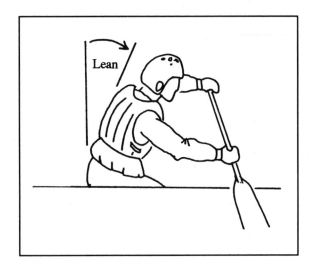

Lean

THE BACKSTROKE: The backstroke is, in many ways, just the opposite of the forward stroke. The paddle is held in the same manner as in forward strokes, but the paddler begins the stroke by rotating the outside shoulder backward and reaching the paddle toward the stern. In the backstroke's catch phase, the paddle is planted in the water slightly behind the hips. Run through the power phase by rotating your outside shoulder and waist forward until the paddle ends just in front of your hips. (At this point, the tendency of many paddlers is to simply leave the paddle where it was planted and lean against the current rather than to finish the stroke. Though a full stroke works much better, it can be hard to move the paddle in heavy whitewater.)

One way to increase the power of your backstroke is to use your hip as a fulcrum. Lean the shaft against your outside hip and rotate your outside shoulder forward while pulling the inside shoulder and arm backward. This creates more power than arm strength alone, and works great in situations where the raft must be slowed suddenly. However, when using this technique, rocks, eddies, and strong hydraulics can pole vault you out of the raft or injure tender joints. So, *be careful!*

The basic backstroke: Plant the paddle behind you and rotate forward while pulling with your upper hand. You can use your hip as a fulcrum to add power to the stroke, but beware of submerged rocks and powerful hydraulics.

THE BASIC PADDLE TURN: Turning a raft with paddles works the same way as with oars: the bow always turns toward the side applying the backstroke. To turn the bow to the right, the right side back paddles while the left side forward paddles. To turn the bow to the left, the right side forward paddles and the left side back paddles.

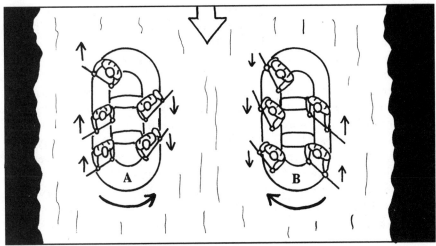

The basic paddle turn: raft A is executing a left turn, while raft B is executing a right turn.

Since forward strokes and backstrokes are all it generally takes to turn a raft, the term *turning stroke* is almost a misnomer. However, when rafters started borrowing strokes from canoers they didn't stop with just these two strokes. Rafters picked up a whole slew of strokes specially developed to control the speed and trajectory of the canoe's spin. As it turns out, many canoe strokes work equally well in rafting, especially when they're used by bow or stern paddlers.

Keep in mind that this book describes how strokes *ought to look*, not how they're going to look when you try them on the river. So, even though it's a good idea to know how each stroke works in theory, don't expect to pull them off exactly as they're described here. On the river you are more likely to use variations of both basic and advanced strokes, and you are equally likely to use each of them in an infinite number of combinations to get you where you want to go.

THE SWEEP STROKE: The sweep stroke carves a broad arcing path along the side of the raft. Properly executed, the sweep stroke turns the raft *and* moves it forward or backward (i.e., a forward sweep also moves the raft forward, while the back sweep moves the raft backward).

When doing either forward or back sweep strokes, hold your upper hand lower than usual so that the paddle shaft angles downward, across the tube, and into the water at a 45 degree angle. (This position allows maximum extension in the reach phase of the stroke, while keeping the paddler safely within the raft.) In the catch phase, plant the paddle as far forward as possible and keep the blade parallel to the tube with its power face turned out. Now, keep your shaft arm comfortably straight and start the power phase by pulling the paddle through an arc away from the boat. In other words, if the paddle begins in front of you, at 12:00, right side paddlers should trace the paddle through a path from 12:00 to 3:00-4:00 before beginning the recovery phase. Remember to rotate at your waist and to use the powerful muscles of the torso, not your arms!

When a forward sweep stroke is properly executed by one bow paddler, the bow turns away from the paddler. However, stern and center paddlers will discover that their forward sweeps have little effect on the raft. For stern paddlers, the *reverse sweep* stroke is a powerful tool. As you may have guessed, the reverse sweep is the same as a forward sweep, except in reverse. The critical difference between the two strokes is in paddle position. During the reverse sweep, the catch phase begins at 6:00 (directly behind the paddler) and ends at 3:00 or 2:00. Also, the reverse sweep spins the bow toward the *paddling* side.

Sweep strokes: the bow paddler turns the raft to the left with a forward sweep. To turn the raft to the left from the stern, the stern paddler executes a backward sweep.

THE DRAW STROKE: Draw strokes excel in difficult rapids when you have to move your raft laterally without turning it. In a fix, they can be used when there isn't enough time to turn a paddle raft around an obstacle, or when the raft's path has to be diverted sideways on steep, sliding rapids. Draw strokes also help in big, heavy water when rafts get knocked off track. Bow paddlers can quickly turn rafts into oncoming waves and holes with draw strokes while remaining set up to forward stroke.

To start the draw stroke, rotate your body outward (toward the river) until you're facing 90 degrees away from the raft. Next, reach both hands out at a right angle to the raft and plant the paddle nearly vertical in the water. Now, pull the blade directly toward you and the side of the raft while keeping the shaft as vertical as possible. If done correctly, the raft will actually move toward the paddle. Finish the stroke before the paddle hits the tube by twisting your wrists to release the blade and lift the paddle from the water.

The draw stroke: reach directly out to the side of the raft and pull the blade back toward you. Keep the paddle vertical throughout the stroke and finish the stroke before the paddle hits the tube.

THE CROSS BOW DRAW: While only one bow paddler actually performs a cross bow draw at a time, the *cross bow draw* describes a team-based maneuver. With a cross bow draw, a well-tuned team can dramatically slow a raft's descent while quickly moving it laterally.

In the following example, a cross bow draw is used to move a five-man paddle team quickly to the right: the right paddlers reach out to the right and perform a draw stroke; the paddle captain either draws to the right or reaches behind the raft to draw the raft *upstream*; the back left paddler does a back stroke; and the front left paddler reaches out across the bow and performs a draw stroke on the *right* side. If everyone balances the timing and strength of their strokes, the raft will slow down and move to the right. To get it to move to the left, just reverse each paddler's role in the cross bow draw.

PRY STROKE: A pry stroke is just the opposite of a draw stroke: the blade is planted close to the tube and is pushed outward by pulling the upper hand inward while pushing out with the shaft hand. When properly done, the pry stroke moves the raft sideways away from the paddle. Since raft tubes interfere with the pry stroke, it is not as effective for rafters as it is for canoeists, but it provides an excellent turning stroke for paddle captains. Also, if you need to *supercharge* a draw stroke, just add some pry strokes on the opposite side of the raft.

Paddle captains, sitting on or near the stern, can execute the pry by twisting their waist and shoulders around, planting the paddle in the river behind the raft, then uncoiling the torso while pushing the blade away from the raft. If the pry is executed off the captain's right hip, the bow will turn to the right, while a left-sided pry will cause the bow to turn to the left. For more power, the paddle captain can use her hip as a fulcrum. (When using the pry stroke, beware of submerged rocks that could catch your paddle and throw you off balance.)

The pry stroke: The pry stroke works best in the stern, and is often used by paddle captains to turn the raft. Using your hip as a fulcrum, pull your upper hand inward and push your shaft hand outward. If you're doing a pry on the right side of the raft, the bow will turn to the right.

BRACING: It is the definitive image of *yahoo* rafting: a crew of slack-jawed, wide-eyed rafters holding their paddles at various levels over their heads while screaming *we-e-e-e-e!* I call this *gaping* or *air bracing*. Most of the time, these paddlers are paying an outfitter good money to let them do that. But some of the time, paddle captains are nursing ulcers as they try to guide uncontrolled rafts through whitewater rapids.

It takes a while to convince paddlers that paddling actually increases your likelihood of staying aboard in medium-sized rapids. First of all, you are more attentive when you're paddling, so you are usually better attuned to changes in the raft's direction. Also, the upward pressure the river exerts on your paddle blade during strokes can actually push you into the raft. This upward thrust, in a very basic way, is the foundation of bracing.

If the raft bucks or tips violently, you may find your side of the raft dipping precariously downward, exposing you to the grasp of an overly amorous river surface. The lower your tube sinks, the less likely you are to maintain your grip on your seat. One way to keep yourself aboard is to execute a *low brace*.

Think of the *low brace* as an outrigger made out of your paddle. To execute the low brace, cock both your wrists and knuckles downward so that you can slap the river surface with the back side of your paddle blade. At the same time, hold the shaft almost horizontal to the river's surface. Now, as your paddle hits the water, push down with your shaft hand while lifting up at the T-grip. Keep your body weight low and shift it horizontally into the passenger compartment, bringing the paddle in with you as you go. If your raft doesn't flip, the low brace might provide just enough leverage to keep you high and dry.

Another bracing technique is called the *high brace*. Think of the high brace as a draw stroke that you use to pull one side of a raft downward when the river has already shot it skyward. Since your side of the raft will be higher above the river than usual, start off by leaning out over the tube to reach the water. Next, hold your paddle with your knuckles pointed upward, elbows bent slightly, and the shaft more horizontal than in a draw stroke. Now, reach out and do a draw stroke, but try to shovel some water back toward you. If all goes well, the extra weight and downward pull will settle the raft back down on the river.

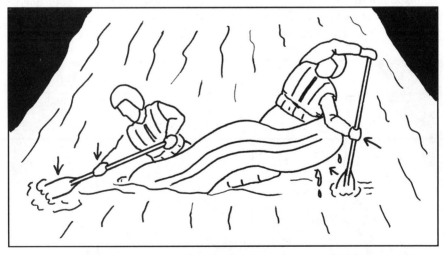

The low brace (left) is used as a last resort to stay aboard a bucking raft. To low brace, slap the surface with the back side of the paddle blade, push down with your shaft hand, and lift up with your upper hand. At the same time, shift your weight inboard. The high brace (right), is like a draw stroke, but is used to keep a raft from flipping.

PART THREE: *Advanced Paddle Strokes*

There are many more strokes which rafters have borrowed from canoeists and kayakers. Since the more exotic strokes are difficult to execute from the passenger compartment of a large raft, few of these strokes have made it into the common river runner's handbag of tricks. However, the paddle cat restores the flexibility of a canoe or C-1, making these strokes possible. In paddle cats, paddlers can—and often do—paddle both outside and *in between* the tubes. It may take some practice to perfect these strokes, which are used predominantly for catching tight eddies or executing quick turns around obstacles. Still, they're nice to try out on easy rivers, and may be just the key to a great racing time or clean Class V descent.

FARBACK STROKE: The farback stroke is a forward stroke in reverse—the paddler rotates her torso outward and backward toward the stern, plants the paddle behind her, and pulls it toward her.

CROSS AND HYBRID STROKES: When paddling between the tubes of a cataraft, paddlers can perform strokes that mimic the outside strokes. In the *cross forward* stroke, the paddle is thrust forward to the catch position inside the tubes. The blade enters the water such that the shaft tilts about 20 degrees from vertical, with the shaft hand about six to ten inches forward of the upper hand. Now, the power phase of a cross stroke uses more of a pelvic thrust, with the hips moving forward and the upper torso straightening upward until the blade reaches a point between the knees and torso. (Don't let your hands leave the front of your body.) To end the stroke, twist your wrists to unlock the paddle and make a recovery by slicing it forward underwater.

Paddle cats open up a whole new set of paddling options. With Paddler A executing a farback stroke, and Paddler B executing a cross forward stroke, the raft will turn to the right.

7

PADDLE CAPTAINING:
The Art of Whitewater Choreography

Paddle rafting straddles a gray area between shared elation and communal frustration. When a paddle crew perfectly executes difficult maneuvers in intense whitewater, the feeling is incomparable. But when a paddle team falls out of synch and lets the raft ricochet off of rocks and hydraulics, paddle rafting can be a nerve-wracking endeavor.

Paddle captains provide the critical link between the raft and its engine... the paddlers. Part coach, choreographer, cheerleader and drill sergeant, paddle captains strive to balance paddlers' strokes, translate maneuvers into understandable paddle commands, and provide the necessary inspiration to complete a successful descent. All the while, the paddle captain picks the course through rapids and executes turning and rudder strokes to keep the raft moving along a safe course.

PART ONE: The Pre-Trip Lecture

Effective guiding begins long before paddlers ever board your raft. Good paddle captains immediately break the ice, and open up cordial lines of communication with their crew. They also explain all of the rafting techniques that will be used, and discuss all of the emergency procedures that will be followed. What the guide says in this speech—and how funny or foreboding the lecture sounds—depends on the river, the types of rafts being used, the caliber of the day's crew, and so on. Still, some basic points should always be stressed during this introductory lecture:

1. *Introduce the guides, the equipment, and the river.*
2. *Give the passengers some idea of what to expect during the trip (i.e., rapids, scenery, photographic opportunities).*
3. *Assign passengers to oar or paddle rafts depending on the available equipment, their personal preferences, and their capabilities.*
4. *Outline safety precautions such as keeping lines tightly stored, rafts bailed out, and lifejackets securely fastened. Also note the importance of proper river wear to make the trip more safe, comfortable and enjoyable.*
5. *Go over the paddle commands, being sure to include unique commands like highside, dig in, or get low.*
6. *Discuss emergency procedures, highlighting what to do in the event*

of a flip or swim.

7. *Include anything else that will make the river trip safer and more enjoyable for your crew.*

PART TWO: *Seating the Captain and Crew*_____

In North America, *paddle captains* usually sit as close to the stern as they can get so that they can maximize the reach and power of each stroke. (In some countries, paddle captains sit in the bow, and on some rivers, there are paddle captains in the bow and stern.) The stern seat provides extra clearance for guiding strokes, and adds a few inches of reach to the guide's strokes. This extra reach translates into better leverage on the water, and more power with which to turn the raft.

In some instances, paddle captains won't be able to sit in the back of the stern: short paddle captains, or captains confronted with high stern rises, may have to sit on the side tube just like the other paddlers to be able to reach the river; small-tubed rafts may not provide enough flotation to support the paddle guide; and heavy captains might push the stern down far enough to bulldoze water during back ferries.

SEATING THE CREW: Take a moment to refer back to the seating configurations suggested in Chapter Four. Since paddle rafting relies heavily on the forward stroke, it is best to place the strongest, most experienced paddlers in the bow. Good bow paddlers respond quickly to the guide's commands, set a good example for the rest of the crew, and provide some muscle where it is needed the most. The weakest paddlers should be seated in the middle of the raft, with additional strong paddlers seated toward the stern. Also strive to balance the strength of the paddlers on both sides of the raft.

PART THREE: *Guiding Strokes*_____

Paddle captains can use all of the strokes discussed in Chapter Six, but the turning strokes—such as the sweep, pry and draw—are the most useful. These strokes change the raft's angle quickly, setting the raft up so that the crew can assist in making maneuvers. The only new stroke to add to the paddle captain's repertoire is the *rudder stroke*. In this stroke, the paddle captain places the paddle behind the stern, at 6:00, with the blade parallel with the raft's axis. Now, as the raft moves forward, the paddle can be turned slightly in either direction to change the angle of the bow.

New guides may feel a little confused the first time they sit in the captain's seat since many strokes have a reverse effect on the raft. For example, if the

Guides can use the paddle as a rudder to steer the raft through whitewater.

guide is paddling on the right side, a draw stroke will turn the bow to the left, while a pry stroke will turn the bow to the right. A forward sweep carried past 3:00 will turn the bow to the left, while a reverse sweep initiated at 6:00 will turn the bow to the right. Practice guiding in easy rapids, and soon the raft's movements will feel natural.

One common urge among novice paddle captains is to switch sides with their paddles—ruddering with the paddle on the right hip one moment, and on the left hip the next. Since the raft is unguided when your paddle is out of the water, it is better to learn to guide and stroke from just one side. Right handed paddle captains usually keep the paddle on their right side, and only paddle on their left in extraordinary circumstances.

PART FOUR: Paddle Commands

Paddle commands are nothing more than one or two-word descriptions of strokes, maneuvers, or techniques like highsiding. The paddle captain bellows these commands like a crazed aerobics instructor, while the paddle crew responds with the appropriate strokes.

BASIC COMMANDS: The basic paddle commands are *forward paddle, back paddle, left turn, right turn, and stop* (or *drift*). Each one describes a stroke by the same name, although *stop* or *drift* merely means *stop paddling*. To get the crew to respond appropriately to these commands, the guide should

111

explain each command and the corresponding set of strokes ahead of time. Then, in the pools above the first rapids, the crew can practice responding to the commands, starting with the easiest ones first (forward paddle, back paddle, and stop). As paddlers get better at executing the correct strokes, the guide can start giving turn commands, eventually building into complex commands like *draw right* (paddlers on the right side execute draw strokes), *dig* (bow paddlers execute big forward strokes through large waves or reversals), or *get down* (crew sits low in the raft to avoid falling out).

MORE COMMANDS: As paddle teams enter rapids, the likelihood of hitting obstacles, getting stuck in holes, or drifting sideways toward giant haystacks becomes more serious. In anticipation of these mishaps, guides should explain how hydraulics are going to affect the raft, what an unexpected collision with a rock could mean, and how to handle all of the situations they expect to encounter. At the same time, the guide can tailor different commands to evoke an appropriate response from the crew.

Pre-trip discussions should include some comments about holding on and getting low in the raft. This move is important in steep drops, big holes, or violent eddies where a low center of gravity helps keep paddlers aboard. To make the "hold on and get low" commands easy, give the command a short name like *get down* and have the crew practice leaning into the raft so that they respond naturally when you give the command.

The paddle captain can call out a *dig* command in big hydraulics to get the bow paddlers to dig their paddles deep into the solid water while the rest of the crew forward paddles strong and fast to prevent a stall.

Be flexible in your choice of commands, and match them to the requirements of the river. Keep in mind that commands should be easy to understand, should sound different from one another, and should roll off your tongue quickly. The shorter and faster your commands, the more impressive your crew's response will be.

FINE TUNING: Since there is always some time lag between commands and strokes, paddle captains have to anticipate moves and talk fast. Any hesitation on the part of the captain is intensified by the delay in paddlers' reactions. By anticipating the next move, paddle captains have a chance to form their thoughts before translating them into verbal instructions. Still, in fast moving whitewater, some commands must be given and changed within a split second. If a guide thinks about the command too long (*hmm, does a draw stroke turn the bow right or left?*) the raft might get eaten in a hole before the answer emerges. Sometimes it is better to say something and be wrong than to say nothing at all. If you choose a wrong command, at least you'll see the negative effect right away and can fix it, versus trying to figure it out in your mind.

Lag time also affects how the paddle team paddles together. Many times, one bow paddler starts paddling a moment before the other bow paddler. Since the middle and stern paddlers follow the strokes of the person in front of them, the whole raft falls into a syncopated rhythm that makes the raft wiggle back and forth. Tell paddlers to keep their heads up to see what *everyone* is doing, not just the person in front of them. That way, the whole raft will work together as one synchronized unit.

Another delay phenomenon seems to happen after paddlers start stroking. Rather than stopping on command, excited paddlers keep on paddling... usually until your screams get their attention or someone taps them on the shoulder and tells them to cut it out. One of the easiest ways to cure this problem is to limit the number of strokes in your command. Rather than just yelling, "forward paddle," say *"forward two strokes."* If your crew listens to you carefully, you'll have gained an upper hand over the chronic over-strokers. Then, if you need more strokes, you can just add a few more in a new command.

YOUR VOICE: Many things influence paddle teams, like the intensity and decibel level of your voice. If you really want to see your crew paddling, raise your voice and shout something like, "Paddle faster! C'mon!!" If power strokes aren't necessary, save your voice for the big rapids downstream. Also, offer helpful criticism to weak paddlers in order to balance the team's strength. Remember that *you* are the captain. Don't let paddlers do what *they* want, teach them to do what *you* say!

THE SEASONED TEAM: The longer a paddle team works together, the more harmonious their actions become. Rather than constantly responding to guiding commands, team members develop a feel that tells them when they are paddling in synch, or when their strokes are unproductive. Teams that have paddled many rivers together require few, if any commands, other than comments about route selection. With these types of teams, it is easier to explain which path you want the raft to follow ("let's go to the left of the first rock, then back to the right to get around the hole") and let everybody feel what it is they're supposed to do. Occasional commands like "straighten the raft up," or one or two of the standard commands will keep things moving smoothly.

8
WHITEWATER:
Running the Rapids

Although quality whitewater rafts are delightfully buoyant and stable in gentle water, they are little more than mindless, inflatable vessels, subject to the whims of currents and oarstrokes. In severe whitewater an unguided raft follows the same course as other flotsam, sometimes into the heart of danger, sometimes avoiding obvious obstacles. By now you've learned the oar and paddle strokes that boaters use to harness a raft's capabilities. Now it's time to combine those strokes into definite maneuvers, to expand your knowledge of river features, and to learn the fundamental techniques necessary to run rapids. This is your next big step toward becoming a whitewater rafter!

FIVE TYPES OF MANEUVERS: Amazingly, every type of maneuver known to whitewater rafters falls within one of five categories: (1) maneuvers that keep you *parallel* with the current; (2) *ferries*; (3) *turns and pivots*; (4) *sideslips*; and (5) *eddy turns and peelouts*. Each of these maneuvers either moves the raft in a new direction, or rotates the raft around its pivot point.

As you begin to learn about these maneuvers, think of how they'll work when they're done on moving currents, and visualize the two components that make up each one: the raft's *momentum* and *angle* in relation to the current. Some maneuvers—like ferries and eddy turns—rely heavily on current to drive the raft across the river's surface. Other maneuvers—such as turns and side-

Paddle teams must work together to maneuver through rapids.

slips—rely little on currents, but have to overcome them to be effective. The same current that assists one maneuver may hinder another.

RIVER DIRECTIONS: As you read through this chapter, you will see references to things like *river left* and *river right*. Rivers have descriptive directions, just like maps are labelled north, south, east and west. When describing river directions, one of four terms are used: (1) *upstream* is where the current is coming from; (2) *downstream* is where the current is flowing to; (3) *river left* is to your left as you face downstream; and (4) *river right* is to your right as you face downstream. These terms will help you understand the movement of the rafts in the diagrams in this chapter, and will make your descriptions of rapids understandable to fellow river runners.

River directions: the river is flowing from the bottom of the diagram to the top. A is upstream; B is downstream; C is river left; and D is river right.

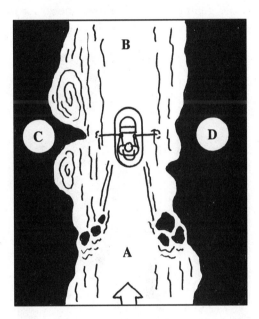

PART ONE: Staying Parallel With The Current_____

The first technique any river runner should learn is how to keep the raft parallel with the current. This not only helps when it comes time to slow the raft down, it continually expands your understanding of river currents, and provides a solid basis for most other river running techniques.

Since rivers rarely flow in a straight line, keeping your raft parallel with the current can be trickier than it sounds. There are bends to contend with, eddies and slack water which try to spin your raft, and obstacles that interfere with your strokes. Still, you can start with a straight, obstacle-free section of

115

river where it will be easier to work on your river running techniques.

To slow a raft on a straight section of river, line up the raft's long axis with the current lines using subtle adjustment strokes. Once properly aligned, the raft can be slowed or accelerated with back and forward strokes. If there are no obstacles downstream, leave the raft on the main current, relax, and enjoy the scenery.

In the next diagram, the current's velocity changes as the main current slips from a swift, deep channel onto shallow, slow shoals. As the raft crosses the interface between faster and slower currents, the slower current drags on the bow at the same time that the faster currents push on the stern. If the raft turns even slightly to the current the river will try to twist it sideways. To avoid getting turned sideways, the rower or paddlers must turn the raft in the opposite direction with well-gauged turning strokes.

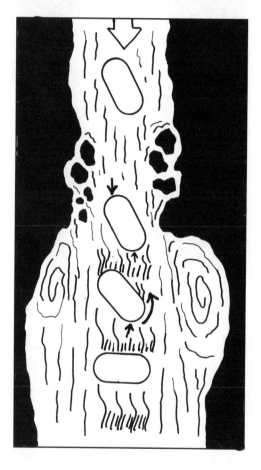

This raft is emerging from a fast chute at a slight angle to the current. As the bow hits the slower water flowing through the waves, the fast water of the chute is still pushing on the stern. As a result, the raft spins sideways as it goes into the waves. If the waves are tall enough, the raft might flip.

Eddies have the same raft-twisting effect as changes in the current, only worse: eddies are flowing in the opposite direction as the main current! The added force of these oppositional currents can frustrate even the best rafters. If it becomes impossible to turn the raft back in the direction of its original course, just let the eddy spin the raft. Then, complete the spin with a turning stroke and realign the raft with the current.

PART TWO: Ferrying

HISTORY: Today's ferrying techniques date back to days when cable-guided ferry barges transported people, horses and wagons across swift rivers. Attached to a cross-river cable by one or two strong cables, these barges could be turned at an angle to the current either by turning a rudder or changing the length of one of two chains. Once the barge was turned at an angle, the current would build up pressure on the barge's upstream side and force it cross-river to the opposite bank.

Modern rafters pull against the current with oars and paddles instead of cables, but they use the same angles and forces to help move their rafts back and forth across the river. Carrying on with the tradition of ferrying, rafters now use these historic techniques to maneuver their craft around riverborne hazards and into safe channels.

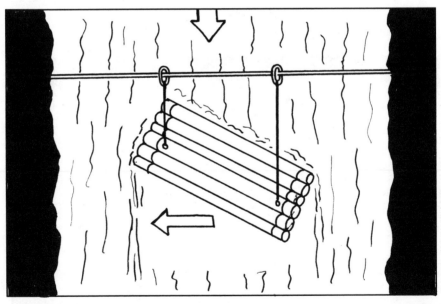

Old-time ferries relied on strong cables and river currents to move back and forth across the river. By increasing the length of one cable, currents would build up on one side of the barge and push it to the opposite bank. Rafters use the same techniques today as the basis for ferrying.

OAR RAFTS: There are two types of ferrying techniques: *back ferrying* and *forward ferrying*. In a back ferry, start off with your bow pointed downstream and align your raft parallel with the current. From this position, begin backrowing. You will feel the raft's descent slow down significantly. Now, begin ferrying toward the left bank by turning the bow 30 to 45 degrees to your right. If you continue backrowing while maintaining that angle, the raft will either slow or cease its descent (depending on the power of the current) and will move sideways toward river left (the left bank as you look downstream). To reach the right bank, simply point the bow towards the left bank and use the same backstroke.

If back ferries sound confusing, just think of one easy concept: *pull away from the danger*. If you want to get away from the left bank, point your bow toward it and pull away... you'll move to river right. If you want to move away from a rock as you approach it, point your bow toward it and pull away. You'll ferry away from the rock in the direction of your stern.

It takes a little practice to really get the feel of back ferrying. But stick with it until it becomes second nature. As you become more attuned to proper angles and trajectory, start experimenting with your oar strokes. Do long, slow strokes work better? Or, do short, fast strokes work better for you? Also try adjusting your cross river speed. The more angle the raft maintains in relation to the current, the faster the boat will move across the current, but the faster it will also proceed downriver.

Now, I hate to disappoint you, but the *forward ferry* is not very compli-

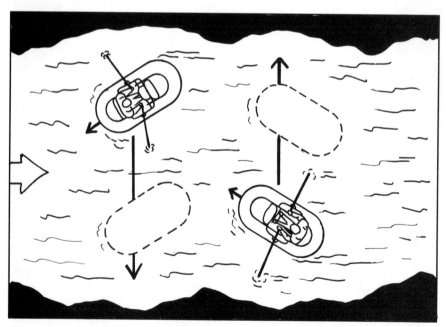

The raft on the left is back ferrying. The raft on the right is forward ferrying.

cated. In fact, the only difference between the forward ferry and the back ferry is the direction of the bow. In the forward ferry simply turn the bow upstream and portegee (push on the oars) to push against the current. Keep in mind that the forward stroke, or portegee, is not as powerful as the backstroke. So, the forward ferry is more difficult to maintain and more energy-consuming than the backstroke. Also, forward ferries can leave the raft broadside at bad times as the oarsperson rotates the raft through one or two 180's to turn the raft into the forward ferry then back downstream again.

PADDLE RAFTS: Ferrying is a dynamic pursuit, where fickle currents do their best to frustrate rafters' efforts. In an oar boat, the rower can feel the changes in current and adjust the raft's ferry angle immediately. Paddlers, on the other hand, must work in unison while ferrying. This makes paddle raft ferries more challenging, yet more exciting.

Ferrying a paddle raft cross-river is identical to oar-boat ferrying. Again, begin the back ferry by aligning the raft parallel with the current, bow facing downstream, and slow the raft's descent with synchronized backstrokes. (Paddlers should stroke in unison and concentrate on the river and their course rather than looking at their paddles.) It is up to the paddle captain to turn the raft 30 to 45 degrees to the current. As the team continues backstroking against the current, the raft will move towards the bank nearest the stern.

The forward paddle ferry starts with the bow facing upstream and uses the powerful forward stroke to counteract the current. The paddle captain steers the raft, and points the bow in the direction he wants the raft to go.

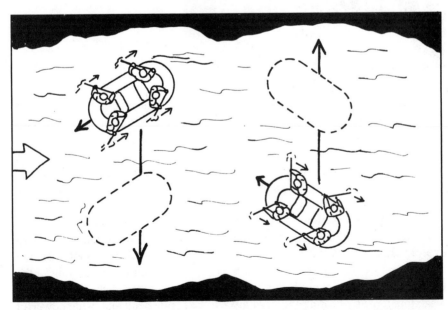

Paddle rafts use the same techniques as oar boats to ferry. The raft on the left is back ferrying, while the raft on the right is forward ferrying.

APPARENT VERSUS REAL COURSE: The first few times you try ferrying your raft in a current, you're likely to notice that it may take a stroke or two to stop the raft's downstream momentum and that it takes a moment before the raft starts moving across the river. Also, even when you execute a ferry properly, you'll notice that rafts *drift* or sideslip more than other whitewater craft. This means that the route you *imagined* your raft would follow won't be the same as the route your raft actually *will* follow. By anticipating the difference between your raft's *apparent* and *real* course, you can adjust early and make the moves you desire.

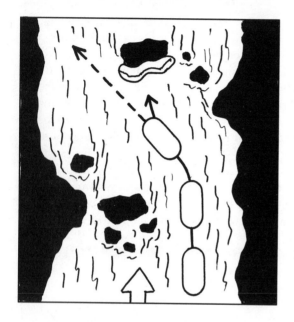

Real versus apparent course: momentum and current will carry your raft further downstream than you might expect when you are trying to execute a maneuver. This raft forgot to account for the raft's drift when it tried to move to the left and wrapped on a rock.

FERRYING AROUND BENDS: Put an unobstructed bend in the sample river you've been using. As you already learned in Chapter Five, currents don't curve around a bend, they flow in a straight line from the inside to the outside of the bend. To compensate for the river's tendency to slam your raft toward the outside of the bend, you should enter bends from the inside corner. From there, it will be much easier to follow the current to the outside of the bend than to fight the current back to the inside of the bend.

Since the current flows straight at the outer bank, you'll actually have to turn the raft at an even greater angle to the inside bank than you would expect. (Remember, you're staying parallel with the current, not with the bank!) First work against the current to slow down, then begin ferrying to the inside of the bend to avoid being dragged toward the outer bank. Oar rafts can make this ferry by tucking the stern toward the inside bend and using powerful backstrokes, while paddle rafts might want to turn their bow inward in order to use the crew's more powerful forward strokes.

120

Ferrying around bends: remember to angle the raft to the current, not to the bank. If there are no obstacles present, start along the inside of the bend and keep pulling toward the inside bank. If there are obstacles there, it will be easier to move toward the outside of the bend quickly.

PART THREE: Turns and Pivots

Turning a raft in whitewater rapids differs little from turning a raft in flat water. In fact, the same turning strokes that were discussed in Chapter Six are used to turn the raft here. Unlike ferrying, turns don't call on river currents for assistance, they just require some powerful oar and paddle strokes. The only time current becomes a factor is when it is piling up on the wrong side of your raft and counteracting your attempted turn.

Rafters should remember that the raft's inertia will keep it turning after the strokes have ended, resulting in a spin. Most turns require little more than one or two quick strokes.

Pivots are nothing more than turns, but are usually used to straighten and narrow a raft's profile when approaching a narrow slot, to align the raft with oncoming hydraulics, or to free a partially snagged raft from exposed obstacles.

As you can see in the *front pivot* diagram, the raft is approaching a narrow slot at a ferry angle. In order to squeeze the raft through the narrow opening between the two boulders, it must be turned parallel with the current so that the bow passes through the slot first. Later in the same diagram, the front pivot straightens the raft into big waves so that it won't flip broadside.

The *back pivot* is great for freeing a raft from a low rock. If the bow gets stuck on a shallow rock, try backing off the rock by pivoting the raft 180 degrees into the current. You can even have passengers shift their weight off the rock to help it spring free. Besides being useful for freeing rafts from shallow rocks, the back pivot works great in tight rapids, where extreme ferry angles are necessary to get around boulders or holes. In fact, there may be times that the back pivot is the only way to make a seemingly impossible move possible.

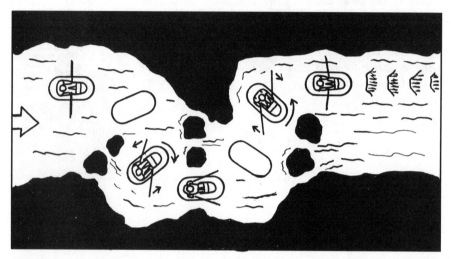

The front pivot: this raft is doing a front pivot to narrow its profile as it squeezes through a narrow slot, then does another front pivot so that it hits a set of waves straight.

The back pivot: this raft is doing a back pivot to help it slide off a rock, then does another back pivot so that it can make a drastic move through a boulder choked section of the rapid.

PART FOUR: Sideslips

In some boulder or hole-riddled rapids there simply isn't enough time to execute a turn or to ferry around an obstacle. In fact, some rapids will wrap or flip any raft that lets itself turn broadside. In these types of situations, a quick horizontal maneuver may be the only way to find safe passage.

The fastest and most efficient sideslipping strokes for paddle rafters are the draw, cross-bow draw, and pry stroke. Done correctly, each of these paddle strokes move rafts laterally across the river in a hurry. Oar rafts can sideslip by planting one blade against the bow and pushing it away from the tube (to move the raft away from the oar), or by planting it a foot or two from the bow and pulling it toward the tube (to pull the raft toward the oar). Since these oar strokes are limited in their application, good oarsmen recognize their shortcomings and try to avoid getting themselves into tight situations in the first place.

Though this crew looks like they're about to run straight into a boulder, they are about to sideslip toward the bottom of the picture by executing drawstrokes on the left side of the raft.

PART FIVE: Eddy Maneuvers

A raft floating along on the main current has a lot of inertia. It carries not only its own weight, but also the force of the main current. So, to stop that raft in its tracks, it takes at least the same amount of braking force working in the opposite direction. One example of incredible braking forces are midstream boulders. If a boulder hasn't been moved for a while, chances are it isn't going to let some measly raft push it out of the way. Another example of braking forces are big holes or reversals. Here, the surface current is moving upstream at the same rate as the downstream current. A raft hitting this surface current broadside might find its downstream progress violently arrested.

What *you're* looking for is user-friendly braking forces. Something that will let you stop without wrapping, flipping, swimming, or losing your composure. What you're looking for is *eddies*.

Eddies are one of the most important features on the river. Their upstream currents can provide enough braking power to gently—or violently—stop a raft. A mild eddy provides a calm haven for weary rafters, a parking area for loading and unloading boats, and a placid platform from which rapids can be scouted. Conversely, large, tumultuous eddies can trap and flip small rafts, and can make any trip across an eddyline difficult.

ENTERING EDDIES: The best way to enter an eddy is to paddle or row into it *high* (upstream, where the maximum current differential is located), and *deep* (directly behind the center of the obstacle). In fact, it is even OK to barely skim the obstacle while entering the eddy. Entering high and deep brings the river's friendly forces into full effect—upstream currents that will brake the raft's momentum and bring its descent to a halt. If you're wondering why you shouldn't enter eddies low, here's an answer: the powerful upstream currents found higher in the eddy begin to disappear downstream. So, a raft entering an eddy low is left with nothing more than its own oar or paddle power to stop its descent and may blow right past the eddy. Somewhere between the eddy's high and low point, the currents are grabby yet forgiving. This midway point can be a nice spot to aim for if you're trying to beach a heavily laden raft, since the stronger upstream currents high in the eddy might drag you past your landing spot.

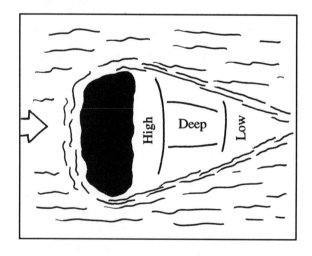

When entering most eddies, aim both high and deep. That is where the eddy is the strongest.

There are two things to think about when entering an eddy: the *speed* of the raft, and the *angle* of entry. Both concepts tie into one goal: to get across the eddy line quickly!

The most important step in entering an eddy is establishing a good *ferry angle* upstream of the obstacle. Since currents *jet* along eddy lines faster than they do either inside the eddy or out in the main current, eddy lines create hydraulic shields that deflect any raft that approaches the eddy with too little angle. On the other hand, any raft that approaches the same eddy line with too much angle will succumb to the main current before it has a chance to cross the eddy line.

To enter an eddy in an oar raft, start your maneuver far upstream by rowing wide of the obstacle. At the same time, angle the stern so that it will point 45 to 90 degrees upstream at the obstacle when you get there. Now, begin backferrying toward the eddy and keep this angle as you pull across the eddy line. Once in the eddy, the upstream currents will pile against the raft, drag it to a halt, and begin pushing it upstream along the eddy.

Paddle rafts can enter eddies the same way as oar rafts by using backstrokes, or they can turn upstream into a forward ferry and use the more powerful forward strokes to drive the raft, bow first, at a 45 degree angle across the eddy line. (Oar rafts can do the same thing by portegeeing.)

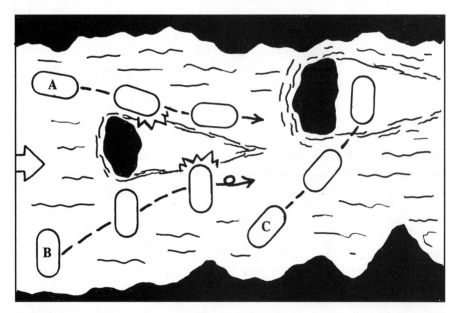

Raft A has tried to enter an eddy with too little angle and was deflected downstream by the eddy line. Raft B came in with too much angle, and missed the eddy because it was caught on the main current. Raft C approached the eddy with a 45 degree angle and made a perfect entry.

Speed is one of those vague terms that varies from person to person, and eddy to eddy. The key to entering an eddy is to get across the eddy line—fast! The slower you try to cross an eddy line, the more likely you are to miss the eddy altogether. Then again, if you enter a small mid-river eddy too fast you're likely to blow out the other side. So, the key to eddy success is matching your speed with the eddy's power, and to choose an angle that will quickly expose your raft to the eddy's upstream current and drag it to a halt. (Note: in weak eddies, a few extra paddle or oar strokes might be necessary to drive the raft upstream and bring it to a halt.)

STAYING IN EDDIES: Once you've made it into an eddy, look around. Are you at a standstill, or are you still moving? Since eddies have their own sets of currents, they will carry your raft upstream toward the confluence with the main current. Since this confluence marks the most powerful transition point between the eddy's current and the main current, you'll probably want to relax in the calmer waters deep in the eddy. To stay in the heart of the eddy, use small correction strokes or lean the raft against the wall or boulder that formed the eddy and hold on.

MORE EDDY TIPS

To prevent travelling all the way through small midstream eddies, enter them extremely wide. Continue stroking until your raft stops, or do a little turn to square up in the eddy and prevent flying across it. If you need to enter a huge, boiling eddy, with a big eddy line, stroke full speed across the eddy line at 90 degrees with lots of momentum. Don't eddy out on the eddy line! Keep rowing until you feel that you're safe.

EXITING EDDIES: There are three ways to exit an eddy: (1) ferry across the eddy line, (2) *peel out*, and (3) exit downstream. Downstream exits are only used in mellow eddies with weak currents—all you have to do is paddle or row downstream until the eddy releases your raft. The first two exits—ferries and peel outs—take a little bit of know-how, and some finesse.

Ferrying out of an eddy is little different than ferrying across the main channel, except that the transition between currents tends to take novices by surprise. The moment the bow or stern hits the main current, the raft will try to spin downstream. To avoid spinning out, anticipate the main current, build up some upstream momentum as you work the raft to the top of the eddy, and cross the eddy line pointing more upstream than usual (10 to 25 degrees to the main current). When the raft enters the main current, use some extra powerful strokes to drive the side of the raft sticking out in the main current upstream. Once you're totally free of the eddy, you can ferry across the river as usual.

A *peel out* is an exciting maneuver which spins the raft downstream as you exit the eddy. To start your peel out, accelerate the raft upstream and across the eddy line just as with the ferrying exit, but point the upstream end of the raft 30 to 45 degrees to the main current. As the raft crosses the eddy line, the main current will pile against the upstream tube and spin the raft to face downstream.

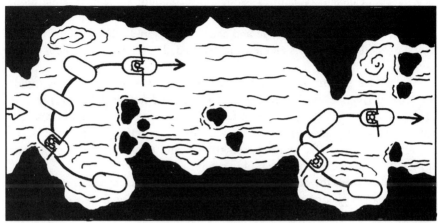

The raft on the left is ferrying out of its eddy to get around the obstacles downstream, while the raft on the right is executing a peel out.

CAPSIZING FORCES: Whether ferrying or peeling out of an eddy, rafters have to contend with strange currents swirling about the eddy line. The overlapping currents found here not only slide horizontally past each other—speeding up and throwing your maneuvers off—they drive downward, building within themselves strong *capsizing forces.* On large volume rivers, giant eddy fences can generate enough capsizing force to suck down one side of the raft and flip it.

Even on mild rivers, these capsizing forces can wreak havoc. When a raft exits a fast moving eddy, its upstream tube is exposed to the main current. Here, the main current drives against the upstream tube, then *under* the raft. As it does, it tries to drag the upstream tube under with it. Unsuspecting passengers can be tossed overboard as their tube plunges downward, and powerful currents can be strong enough to flip the whole raft.

Whether entering or exiting eddies, rafters can avoid tilting and flipping by shifting their weight to the far side of the raft, away from the diving current. In other words shift passenger weight *upstream* when entering eddies, and *downstream* when exiting eddies. Once a vulnerable tube has been unweighted, the river has little chance to do any harm.

PART SIX: Heading Downriver

Heraclitus once said, "You cannot step twice into the same river, for other waters are continually flowing on." Few words capture river running's mystique as eloquently as those. With each bend in the channel, rivers reveal new facets of their personalities—sometimes tranquil, sometimes tumultuous. And even the personality of individual rapids transforms as water levels rise and fall, or as streambeds erode and shift. While rapids shift freely from one mood to another, the skills and techniques needed to read and run them remain constant.

To novice rafters, unfamiliar with the distinctive components of rapids, whitewater rivers exemplify nature in chaos. Liquid furies. But to the seasoned river runner, rapids share common features, each one a road sign to routes of safe passage. *Reading rivers* is the art of interpreting those road signs, recognizing the pitfalls of ill-chosen routes, and envisioning the maneuvers that will be necessary to float rapids safely.

While reading the rest of this chapter, keep three important concepts in mind: First, think of rowing as a means of changing your raft's speed and direction in relation to the *current*, not in relation to solid obstacles such as rocks or cliffs. Second, always have a *contingency plan* in case you miss a stroke, spin off a rock, or lose an oar. Finally, remember that whitewater is ever changing and that your ability to *adapt* is more important than learning the names or categories of each technique. If you keep these mental footnotes handy, the following techniques will make more sense and your boating success will increase.

PART SEVEN: The "SAFE" System™

Rafting is a surprisingly systematic endeavor, with regular routines that simplify the way in which we run rivers.

On your first outing, you may find yourself preoccupied with all facets of rafting techniques. Oars may feel awkward, paddle commands might make little or no sense, and currents may drag you unwittingly toward obstacles. However, these fledgling frustrations will soon disappear, leaving your mind open to the real task at hand... *reading the river.*

Before running any whitewater rapid, rafters can follow a pre-set game plan called *"The SAFE System™."* The SAFE system is an easy way to evaluate any rapid, and provides a safe and simple approach to whitewater travel. It is based on four steps:

(1) **SCOUT** rapids fully before entering them. This can be done from either bank, or, if there is an eddy or slow pool, from your raft.

Make sure that every trip member observes the entire rapid from a variety of angles, looking both upstream and downstream. Also, select visual guideposts—such as uniquely shaped boulders—that will guide you as you're running the rapid. Finally, remember that rapids look different when floating toward them in a raft than they do standing alongside them on the bank.

(2) *ANALYZE* the rapid and your group's ability to run it. Where are the obstacles? Where are the safest channels? Is there a safe line through the rapid? Which way will you swim if you fall out? Is your team and equipment capable of running the rapid safely?

(3) *FORMULATE* a plan. Which route will you follow? What is your backup plan? What maneuvers will you have to execute? Should you portage instead? Should a rescue team be stationed along the banks?

(4) *EXECUTE* your plan. Run the rapid, carry the raft along the bank, or line the raft to safety.

SCOUTING: Unless you know what is around a bend or over a horizon line, or you feel that you have the skills to pull to shore in an emergency, scout! Pull ashore well above the lip of rapids and long before strong currents drag your raft places you don't want to go.

Starting from your landing point, walk all the way to the base of a rapid,

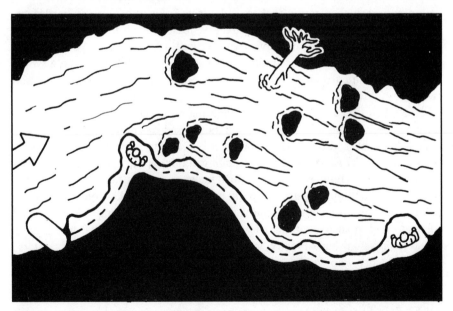

When confronted with a rapid that you are unsure of, scout it from top to bottom, making sure that you can see all of it from different angles.

129

or all the way around a bend, so that you can see the entire section of river you'll be running. A lot of times, this may take some scrambling to reach the best vantage points, but the clear lines of sight are usually well worth the extra effort! While scouting, make mental notes of easily recognizable landmarks and distinctive hydraulics—if you decide to run the rapid, you can use them as signposts to tell you where you are and where you need to turn. Remember that rapids are areas of *falling water* and that your landmarks might not be visible from upstream. Keep looking over your shoulder as you walk back to the raft to see if your landmarks disappear. If they do, walk downstream again and pick new ones.

ANALYZE: By now you have learned about most every type of hydraulic and obstacle you'll see in a typical rapid. You learned that tongues and wave trains signify safe channels, while sharp ledges, roostertails and undercuts are hazards to be avoided. It's now time to apply your knowledge of river features—together with your knowledge of raft maneuvers—to analyze the rapid before you.

When scouting a rapid look for two things: obstacles and safe routes. On smaller rivers the hazards will probably be solid obstacles, like rocks or logs. Large volume rivers, on the other hand, might not have any solid obstacles that cause you concern, but can have minefields of keeper holes and menacing haystacks that can spell the demise of a raft and crew.

To find safe routes, try walking upstream from the bottom of the rapid and play *connect the dots*. Can safe routes be connected, or are they broken up by major hazards? (The more broken and twisted the route is, the harder the rapid will be.) Your goal is to discover at least one *clean line* through the rapid—one that you can maneuver without putting yourself or your crew in serious danger. If you are scouting a particularly difficult rapid, note where you can exit the current if you flip, and where *not* to be if you find yourself swimming.

Once you find a runnable line through the rapid, ask whether your team's skills and equipment are up to the demands posed by the river. If not, take a look at the bank and figure out whether it is better to portage or line the raft.

FORMULATE: If you think you *can* run this rapid, run it mentally first. Let your mind imagine each move you'll make as your raft descends the rapid from top to bottom. Again, keep in mind the landmarks you scouted out before, and correlate them with moves you'll make in the rapid. As your mind comes to each maneuver, think of what could go wrong and what you'll do in the event of a mishap. Finally, discuss your plan with your fellow rafters, especially those who will be in your raft. If there's any chance that you'll have problems, station rescuers at key points along the bank who can assist you. (More on that in the safety and rescue chapter.)

EXECUTE: By the time you get back in your raft, you have already run the rapid mentally. Now it's time to do it for real!

The entry into the rapid is the most critical maneuver. Unless you have to punch a big hydraulic right at the top of the rapid, consider approaching the lip as slowly as possible to glean a last glimpse downstream. It might even be helpful to stand up in the raft in order to gain a better view. Remember that the rapid is going to look quite different from your new vantage point—especially if the rapid is steep—and that you're probably going to have pre-rapid butterflies.

As you enter the rapid, relax and look around. It is amazing how many rafters experience tunnel vision in whitewater, emerging wet and excited in the pool below, but totally unable to remember what just happened upstream. Run the rapid methodically, sticking to your main plan, and adjusting it whenever the river proves to be too cunning a foe. Make each move by adjusting your raft's momentum and angle just as you learned earlier in this chapter, and be ready to celebrate your trip when you reach the safety of the pool downstream! If all goes well, you'll have plenty of reason to rejoice!

When you are on the river, be "SAFE": Scout, Analyze, Formulate, and Execute your run through rapids!

BAILING: Standard-floor rafts hold an amazing quantity of water. Whether it all pours in from one giant wave, or accumulates after many splashes, the extra water makes the raft heavier and less maneuverable.

Every standard-floor raft should have at least one bail bucket securely stored and available for quick use. In pool-drop rivers (rivers with calm pools following short, steep rapids) it is usually easier to wait for a calm eddy than to bail the raft in the middle of a rapid. On rivers with continuous whitewater, on the other hand, stopping may be difficult or impossible, so fast, effective bailing becomes very important.

In an oar raft, it's nice to have a *swamper* along—someone who will bail while the rower concentrates on the oars. Without a swamper, the rower has to set the oars down in order to bail out the passenger compartment. In paddle rafts, the bow paddlers should be the *last* people selected to bail out a raft since they are important to the overall control of the raft. Appoint the middle paddlers to handle the task. Make sure that each time the bucket is to be filled the swamper securely stores their paddle, pushes the bucket toward the floor to fill it as quickly and fully as possible, and holds the bucket tight when dumping the water back into the river.

Bailing helps keep standard-floor rafts light and maneuverable.

HIGH SIDING: Highsiding can give your raft an edge over boulder-cluttered rapids. Many rafters call high siding *rock siding*, which is perhaps an easier way to visualize this technique.

When a raft snags sloped rocks or shallow boulders, a crew can usually free their raft by shifting their weight to the side of the raft which will swing free, pushing off the rock with their feet, bouncing up and down, or by using pivot strokes to loosen the raft. If the current is strong enough, though, the raft may keep sliding up the obstacle while the lower tube dives deeper into the main current. Left to its own device, the river will bury the lower tube and pin the raft against the obstacle, causing a *wrap*.

To avoid a wrap, the entire crew *highsides* by leaning on the downstream tube (the tube riding up on the rock). This unweights the upstream tube, allowing its tremendous buoyancy to lift the tube free of the river's currents. Done successfully, the crew can then pivot the raft off one side of the rock before the river has a chance to pin it in place.

High siding works equally well when a raft gets caught in a large hole. In holes, the upstream surface currents combine with the downward current of the falls to try to flip the raft upstream. To avoid flipping, crew members can lean over the downstream tube and highbrace. Then, while keeping their center of gravity low in the raft, the crew can try paddling the raft laterally out of the obstacle. (The crew's low center of gravity helps them stay in the raft if it bucks wildly or spins suddenly. Also, if the raft does spin, all crew members will need to quickly scamper to the downstream tube again.) If the raft is caught in a wide, powerful hole, it can take considerable patience and fortitude to bust free!

This raft has slid up onto a rock, and the upstream tube is about to dive underwater. To avoid a wrap, the crew is highsiding.

THE DIG: Powerful hydraulics—like holes and breaking waves—can halt, spin, and flip a raft before you even knew what hit you. If you can't avoid such traps you need to punch them straight, hard, and fast! In an oar raft, this means that the rower should portegee all the way through the hydraulic, or turn the raft downstream and backrow through. Paddle teams can get the edge on big hydraulics by putting their strongest paddlers in the bow. The bow paddlers should reach deep into the back of breaking waves, or over the top of curling holes, and dig their blades into the solid body of water downstream. This will give the bow paddlers a firm grip on the current that can pull them through the hydraulics. Also, if all paddlers lean slightly forward, throwing their weight at waves and holes as if these watery objects were tackling dummies, the raft might gain just enough extra momentum to bust through some of the biggest hydraulics.

LOWERING CENTER OF GRAVITY: Some rivers generate waves and holes of mind-boggling proportions. Rafters seated high on a tube are in a precarious position—just one giant splash away from a swim. On occasion, the only way to stay aboard the raft is to keep your body well inside the passenger compartment with your weight low.

There are three important elements of getting paddlers low in a raft. First, when dropping your weight toward the bottom of the raft, don't let your legs slip under the thwarts, and don't sit or kneel on a standard floor—these moves are an invitation to an injury when the raft bucks or hits rocks. Next, use your outside hand to hold the paddle, and keep your paddle low and toward the outside of the tube—this will stop the paddle from swinging wildly and hitting your neighbor. (Tall rafters can still paddle even when seated low in rafts.) Finally, turn your inside shoulder—not your head—into the raft. This will prevent heads from knocking together, and will keep your vision clear so that you can anticipate your next move.

BEACHING: Rafts must be pulled ashore when bank scouting, stopping for lunch, portaging, or when taking out. So, knowing how to stop and secure the raft to shore is as important as maneuvering the raft on the river.

In a one-person oar raft, beaching can be quite a feat. Unless the river is calm near the bank, the rower must slowly approach the shore, free up a line, and tie the raft off before it gets away. In paddle rafts, beaching is usually handled by an agile bow person who can stow her paddle and deftly jump ashore.

Proper beaching technique involves *six steps:* (1) maneuver slowly toward shore so you won't bounce off the bank, and keep stroking to counteract the current once at the bank; (2) securely stow paddles or oars; (3) grab the bow line and unravel it; (4) the bow paddler or rower jumps ashore with the rope just *before* the raft hits the bank (not *after*) the raft hits the bank!; (5) if the person now on the bank is strong enough, and the raft is not too heavy or moving too quickly, she can simply pull back on the rope to get the raft to pendulum into the bank. A superior alternative is to belay the raft by quickly

This crew is entering a huge hole. So that no one falls out, the guide has had the paddlers lean in and get low.

wrapping the bowline once or twice around a rock, tree, or other solid object. (*Never* wrap the rope around your wrist, back, or any other part of your body!); (6) if the raft simply won't stop, quickly reboard the raft, recoil the rope, and store it safely so that it doesn't pose a hazard downriver. In paddle rafts, the belayer can also release the rope and follow the raft downstream along the bank.

PART NINE: Honing Your Skills

In time, things like oar strokes, whitewater maneuvers, and reading rapids will become second nature. As your basic skills improve, you may find yourself longing for wilder rapids, or contentedly returning to the gentle rivers you have become accustomed to. No matter what your aspirations, you can vastly improve your rafting skills by looking at the river you're on *right now* in a very different light.

Up until now you have been taught to look for the safest, easiest routes through rapids. At the same time, you learned that many rapids have several runnable channels. Now it's time to shun the obvious passages, and to test your skills by *using* the river to challenge yourself.

Rather than taking the cleanest line through a Class II or III rapid, look for an imaginary slalom course, using boulders, holes, or logs to mark your serpentine route. Ferry back and forth around boulders and try to connect the eddies behind rocks, stopping in each one as you go. Soon you will be able to put the raft exactly where *you* want it to go, rather than just going wherever the *river* carries you. With just a little bit of practice, your skill level will skyrocket, preparing you for greater challenges to come.

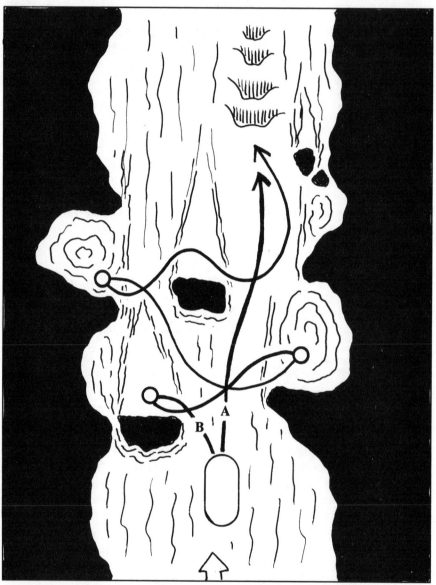

To improve your rafting skills, first find a familiar rapid. Then, instead of following your usual route (A), look for a more challenging route (B). Slalom around boulders and hydraulics, and catch all of the eddies.

9

SAFETY AND RESCUE:
Keeping Your Head & Gear Above Water

Risk is a constant companion in whitewater travel. Nonetheless, many veterans scoff at this danger, bragging about how few times they have flipped or swum in their careers. That would be like a skier saying, "I've skied for 17 years and have only fallen once!" Sounds pretty silly when you think about it.

Today's rafters find themselves in a unique paradox. Equipped with top quality equipment and a wealth of intellectual know-how, modern rafters are able to tackle rapids which would have sent previous explorers scurrying toward the riverbank in search of portage routes. Also, the techniques that took our predecessors many years to learn can now be acquired by zealous novices in just a few weeks or months.

The rush toward more exciting and difficult whitewater has carried with it greater risk and increased perils. The difference between a Class III and Class V swim can be astounding, yet many newcomers find themselves on expert runs without even having flipped a raft in whitewater before. And fundamental rescue skills—such as those necessary to retrieve a wrapped raft

---

SAFETY AND RESCUE

Safety and rescue procedures—like rivers themselves—change from moment to moment, and from situation to situation. Since any river outing presents unique sets of risks and hazards, no book of this length can describe all of the procedures followed on raft trips, or all of the rescue techniques available to rafters. Still, safety and rescue should be of paramount concern to any rafter.

Before attempting rivers which push your skills to their limit, take a course in river rescue from one of the certified Rescue 3 instructors or guide schools listed in the appendix, read books like Les Bechdel's and Slim Ray's River Rescue, *and follow the basic guidelines in this chapter. Take the time to practice new safety and rescue skills at home or on easy rivers. You'll soon find that with proper skill, knowledge, and judgment, most river outings are safe, fun, and exciting.*

or pinned swimmer—frequently elude the eager novice while he moves on to harder and harder rivers.

As in any outdoor sport, uncontrolled risk invites calamity. Accordingly, safety should be the primary concern on any river outing, whether it involves a peaceful scenic float or a heart-pounding Class V descent.

PART ONE: Pre-Trip Preparedness_____

PRE-TRIP PREPAREDNESS: One of your most important pre-trip considerations is to select a river which your entire group is capable of doing. Using the weakest members of your party as a reference point, pick a river that is within your *entire* group's skill level. Though this may sound silly at first—many outfitters carry paying passengers down rivers which they would never get to paddle or row by themselves—it really isn't. Outfitters know their rivers intimately, can anticipate most hazards, and have adequate rescue provisions for the less lucky members of their trips.

There are scores of outstanding guidebooks, maps, and other resources to assist you in your search for the ideal river. Be sure to adequately research the location and distance between put-ins and take-outs, the time it will take to run the river, the classification and location of major rapids, and the recommended water levels for safe trips. Pay particular attention to road access and shuttle information—important factors on any trip since shuttles frequently consume a lot of valuable time and daylight. Also keep in mind that any guidebook is only a reference source, and that rivers change constantly. Seek out the recommendations and advice of more experienced rafters who's first-hand knowledge of the river exceeds that of any guidebook author.

The next step in your pre-trip agenda is to survey water levels and local weather forecasts. Even gentle streams become angry, dangerous torrents at high water, and bone-chilling winds or driving rains can dampen even the liveliest rafting spirits. A number of governmental agencies provide phone recorded river level readings and weather reports. Another source of information is your local whitewater shop or an outfitter located near the river. Check out the names of national agencies monitoring river level information in this book's appendix, and ask them how to contact the agencies nearest you. Then, keep this information handy for future outings.

TIME ON THE RIVER: Rivers flow—dams notwithstanding—on their own schedule. Still, veteran rafters can *guesstimate* how long a trip will take by comparing the current's average velocity to the distance between the put-in and take-out. Beginner to intermediate rafters can avoid this kind of guesswork by simply consulting a guidebook or a knowledgeable rafter to find out how long a particular trip usually takes.

Once on the river, rafters can try to beat the clock by paddling faster than the river's average flow, but that expends a lot of energy and cuts down on

SHUTTLES

The river shuttle is one of those necessary evils that accompanies any river trip, and no matter how many times you do them, there will still be room for screw ups. Yessiree, shuttles have been botched by novices and veterans alike!

Plan your shuttles well in advance. Consult a guidebook for directions, and double check your information against any maps you can find: AAA road maps, National Forest maps, USGS maps... whatever. If you're not going to be doing the shuttle personally, give the real drivers the right directions, and make sure they understand them. (You'd be amazed how many times shuttlers turn the wrong way, get lost and wind up asking directions at the nearest mini-mart!)

Add shuttle time to your river time when planning trips. Some rivers might only have ten miles of water between the put-in and take-out, but a full day of shuttle driving. I call the road miles-to-river miles comparison the shuttle-to-fun ratio. Unless you're hard core, pick rivers with low shuttle-to-fun ratios, like rivers that carve serpentine canyons while the road bee-lines for the take-out. Also, take into account time consuming factors like mountainous terrain and stop signs. What looks like a fast and easy shuttle route on a map might be slower than a mule train once you're actually on the road.

Besides worrying about mileage and travel time, rafters should pay special attention to their gear. Strap your raft tightly to trailers, and take special care to prevent chafing. Unless you've got lots of van space, you should also check the local weather forecast. If it predicts cool evening weather, have some warm, dry clothes waiting at the take-out, and find some shelter for the non-shuttling members of your group.

Last, but not least, figure out what you're going to do with your car keys. As one possessed of little—if any—short term memory, I can attest to leaving car keys in the dumbest places imaginable. But now, my misadventures can become your lessons. Don't put your keys in an ammo can or dry bag... if you flip, your keys might end up in the bottom of the river. Next, don't hide your keys under a rock or bumper. Clever crooks know that rafters hide keys near their vehicles, and will spend a half-hour trying to find it. Finally, don't give your keys to your best friend, girlfriend, or spouse. If they lose it, it'll be grounds for divorce. Leave non-essential keys at home, and keep your car keys on your person in a zippered or velcro-sealed pocket. That way, whether you flip, wrap, or tick off your best friend, you'll still have your keys.

Note that if all of this is too complicated, you might be able to hire someone to worry for you. That's right... there are people who make a living off of running shuttles. Local government agencies, outfitters, chambers of commerce, and local paddlers can tell you where to find professional shuttle drivers. And they're usually pretty reliable.

Well, drive safely, and I'll see you at the mini-mart!

the quality of the rafting experience (unless, of course, you're racing). Also, rivers tend to hold time-consuming surprises for the wary and unwary rafter alike—an unseen snag can puncture a tube and delay your take-out, or an unexpected rise in water level might increase the river's difficulty, leading to more scouting or portaging.

To make sure that you have enough time to safely enjoy your whitewater trip, *expect the unexpected* and leave enough time to handle ordinary mishaps. Start early enough to insure your arrival at the take-out in daylight, and leave enough time to run your shuttle.

PRE-TRIP DISCUSSION: Before leaving the put-in, take some time to gather the group and select a group leader. Discuss the day's itinerary, expected hazards, what order the group ought to travel in, and the signals that will be used to communicate between boats. (See the appendix for suggested signals.)

PART TWO: Equipment

Top quality equipment often makes the difference between an enjoyable river excursion and whitewater fiasco. On the other hand, you don't have to dump all of your hard-earned money into the finest gear available. Instead, it is simply important to utilize equipment which is designed to withstand the rigors of whitewater use.

In addition to all of the rafting equipment and personal gear described in Chapter Three, rafters should carry an assortment of essential safety gadgets—*carabiners, knives, whistles, prussiks, pulleys, throw bags, static ropes, web slings,* and *first aid kits.* If you're fortunate, they'll just collect waterspots while you enjoy the river. But if an emergency arises, their presence will bring on a sigh of relief and peace of mind.

CARABINERS: Aluminum-alloy carabiners are truly the river runner's *multi-purpose tool*: they can be used to clip in gear, attach lines to rafts, and can be substituted for pulleys in an emergency. Experienced river runners carry two or three carabiners clipped to the shoulder or waist of their life jackets so that they'll be readily accessible when needed. However, it is important to keep the carabiners tucked flat against the life jacket with the gates *facing inward* to prevent injury or accidental clipping into stray ropes or branches.

KNIVES: It is not at all uncommon for knife-wielding river guides to get some nervous stares from first-time rafters. I mean, it sort of makes the guide look like some kind of semi-psychotic para-militarist. However, the river knife is another essential safety tool for guides and recreational rafters alike. They can be used to cut the floor out of hopelessly pinned rafts, and can quickly sever a rope before it puts you or a fellow rafter in danger.

Rescue gear: make sure that you have everything you need to make your rafting trips safe and enjoyable.

Quality river knives have solid sheaths of plastic or stiffened leather and can be worn on the chest or shoulder of your life jacket for quick access. If you have a thumb released sheath, check the thumb release frequently to make sure your knife will still be there when you need it.

WHISTLES: It is encouraging to see and hear more whistles in use today than ever before. They are real attention-getters in almost any situation, and can be used to signal an emergency by giving three short blasts.

PRUSSIKS: A prussik is a short loop—about four or five feet long—made of five to seven-millimeter kernmantle rope. It can be used to tie off rafts, or to set brakes in Z-drag rescue systems.

When making your own prussiks, decide whether you'll want to wear them around your waist like a belt. If you will be wearing the prussik belt-fashion, measure your waist with your life jacket and rafting clothes on, then double your waist width and add one foot to get the length of rope you'll need. Next, tie the ends of the rope together with a double fisherman's knot to form the loop (see the appendix). Now the prussik is ready to be worn around the waist like a belt, and clipped in with a carabiner.

PULLEYS: A pulley is one of those items you're going to wish you had the first time that you wrap your raft. Pulleys are tremendously handy friction-reducing tools that can be used in Z-drag rescues (discussed later in this chapter) to increase the efficiency of the system. For river use, select sturdy aluminum-alloy pulleys designed to accommodate half-inch (eleven millimeter) ropes.

THROW BAGS: Throw bags—also known as throw ropes, rescue ropes, and rescue bags—are remarkable rope-retaining tools designed to freely spool out rope when the bag is tossed to a swimmer. It simplifies the rope throwing process and makes it easier for swimmers to see the rope coming—especially when the bag is filled with brightly colored, high-floating rope. When not in use, the throw bag neatly stows rope out of harm's way.

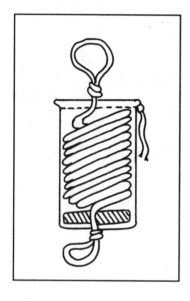

A throw bag is an important rescue tool. It usually contains brightly colored, high flotational, sturdy rope, and is much easier to toss than coiled ropes. When thrown by a rescuer, the rope feeds out gradually.

STATIC ROPES: Wraps and entrapments are two of the biggest perils facing whitewater rafters. Either situation demands a rope with superior strength and minimum stretch. High quality static lines have incredible tensile strength—far more than found in most throw bag ropes. Rafters should carry at least 100 feet of neatly stored half-inch (eleven millimeter) static rope for unwrapping rafts and freeing stranded or trapped swimmers.

WEB SLINGS: Web slings—made of one or two-inch-wide nylon webbing—are used as anchors in Z-drag systems (discussed later in this chapter), can be used as rappel anchors, and provide make shift harnesses for vertical extrications. By carrying a few slings of varying lengths (ten feet to twenty feet long) in your rescue kit, you'll be prepared to set up anchors in most any type of canyon environment.

FIRST AID KITS: A first aid kit should be standard equipment on any river trip. Minor injuries are inevitable, even on easy rivers, but can often be treated immediately by someone trained in first aid. Take the time to consider the type of trip you're undertaking and the location of the nearest medical assistance when assembling the first aid kit. Also, consult the appendix in this book for a partial list of suggested items to fill your first aid kit.

PART THREE: Group Travel

LEAD AND SWEEP RAFTS: River trips are safer when two, three, or more rafts join in. The extra rafts and passengers can provide assistance in emergencies, and can make the difference between a successful rescue and a disaster. In groups of three or more rafts, it will be helpful to choose a *lead* boat to run at the front of the pack, and a *sweep* boat to bring up the rear. The lead raft usually contains the most experienced and knowledgeable rafters, acts as a scout or probe in rapids, and renders assistance to other rafts when pulling over to scout. The sweep boat also contains highly experienced rafters, but lags slightly behind the pack so it can render assistance if a problem arises.

GROUP SCOUTING AND RESCUE: Once ashore, scout rapids together as a group, and follow the *SAFE*™ plan (Scout, Analyze, Formulate, and Execute). Try to get everybody involved and listening to the group discussion even though one or two individuals may be responsible for many of the decisions. If any rafter is unwilling to try a rapid, let that individual walk, line, or portage around it.

In easy rapids, a rescue plan is rarely needed. However, more difficult rapids demand special consideration and extra precautions. Position a couple of rafters with throw bags at key points along the rapid to render assistance if a flip or swim is possible. If the rapid is too difficult to be run safely, scout out the riverbank for a portage route or lining route. Practice *redundant safety*, which simply means that you should have both a main plan and a contingency plan for everything that could go wrong.

It is helpful to have the whole group scout together when scouting rapids. That way, each member of the team can decide whether they want to run the rapid or walk around it, and everyone can discuss the game plan.

PART FOUR: *Portaging and Lining*

Rapids evoke a broad spectrum of emotions—from excitement to outright fear. Your mind's inner voice usually provides a good gauge for your chances of success. For those of us who like to ignore our *mind's* inner voices, we can listen to our *bodies*—a sudden desire to urinate, or inability to spit are pretty good indicators that the rapid's going to present a heck of a challenge.

Always keep in mind that portaging and lining are commonplace on difficult rivers, and present viable options whenever rafters choose to avoid running a particular rapid.

One of the key considerations in running or portaging rapids is how *everybody else* in the group feels. If you're rowing your own raft, you can usually run a rapid without upsetting anybody else. But if you're a paddle captain, you're going to have a tough time avoiding a mutiny if you decide to *go for it* in a marginally runnable Class V+ rapid against your crew's wishes.

Before you line your raft around a rapid, secure or remove any gear that might break loose. Next, attach long ropes to both the bow and stern and scout out a foot path along the bank that won't snag the rope. When you're ready to go, give the raft a slight push out toward the current. With two people manning the ropes, adjust the raft's angle the same way you would if you were in the raft. If the raft will be running steep falls or sticky holes, keep it moving fast and pull hard on the downstream line to prevent it from

Portage Route

When confronted with a difficult rapid, you usually have the option of lining or portaging around it.

being held. In long, powerful chutes, try tying just one length of rope to the bow. Have one person hold the raft in place above the chute while the belayer walks the end of the rope downstream to the midpoint of the chute. When the belayer is ready, the upstream person can let the raft go. As the raft zips through the channel, the belayer runs downstream until he reaches a point where he can pull the raft to shore with the rope.

Since there are so many complexities involved in lining rapids, portaging can be a less strenuous option for lightly loaded rafts. Terrain permitting, all the raft team has to do is hoist the raft and carry (not drag) it to a safe pool below the hazards.

PART FIVE: Self-Rescues

River-based rescues fall into two categories: *self-rescues* and *assisted rescues*. In self-rescues, rafters are essentially left to attend to their own well-being, while in assisted rescues, land and water-based rescuers contribute to the relief efforts with throw lines, extra boats, and physical support. In both types of rescues, one aspect of river safety reigns supreme: people come first!

SWIMMING: Swimming a rapid, much to the surprise of many beginners, is nothing like swimming in a lake or pool. Strong currents can overwhelm and quickly fatigue even experienced swimmers. However, once swimmers understand the forces involved—either by swimming easy rapids, or from prior experience—they can relax and rationally set out upon swimming to safety.

Unless you intentionally jumped into the river, your first reaction to swimming will be one of *surprise*. Most of the time you'll pop back to the surface instantly, cussing the cold and aiming your lips toward waterless airspaces. In these situations, survey the river and banks the moment your vision clears, and look downstream for calm pools and major hazards. Hold onto your paddle unless releasing it increases your chances of a quick rescue. If you are near your raft and it is still upright, pull yourself back into it from the upstream side to avoid getting caught between the raft and an obstacle. (Sometimes it is better just to get into the raft as fast as you can without worrying whether you're on the upstream or downstream side!) Even overturned rafts may be mounted by swimmers and paddled back to shore in easy rapids. It is important, however, to beware of the pitfalls of holding onto a raft when you are swimming. While it provides tremendous flotation and visibility for other rescuers, it can pin or crush you if you get trapped between the raft and an obstacle. Be prepared to abandon your boat if you will be better off swimming to safety.

RE-FLIPPING RAFTS: If your raft is equipped with *fliplines*, bow, or stern lines, it is possible to climb atop the overturned boat and re-right it. One

Your first swim can come as quite a surprise!

type of flipline is a small bag with ten to twelve feet of thick nylon rope. The bag attaches to a D-ring or to the rowing frame, and is sealed with a velcro closure when not in use. The moment you need it, you just open the bag, pull out the line, and throw it across the raft's floor. Next, climb up on the floor on the opposite side of the raft using the rope to help you. Stand up on the edge of the raft, pull back on the flipline, and lean backward until the raft flips back over.

In serious whitewater, you might want to pre-rig a one-inch nylon webbing flipline tightly across the floor *underneath* the raft. (Secure the webbing to the rowing frame or to D-rings with a cord that will break free if you hit a snag.) With the pre-rigged flipline, you won't waste precious time getting the flipline in place or worrying about it floating off the floor before you swim to the far side of the raft. Instead, just grab the line, pull yourself up onto the floor, and use it the same way you would use bagged fliplines.

The final way to re-flip a raft is to insert your paddle's T-grip into the lacing of your self-bailing raft. You won't have as much leverage as you would with the fliplines, but this technique will work fine on small self-bailers.

Whenever you re-flip a raft, keep in mind that you will end up right back in the river. Be careful not to fall backward into rocks, and consider staying on the floor if staying aboard is safer than swimming the next rapid. Finally, unless there's a big pool just downstream, be prepared to quickly re-board the raft before the next rapid.

What happens if your raft doesn't have fliplines, you're not paddling, and you're not in a self-bailer? Well, you can loosen a bow or stern line and tie part of the rope to a side D-ring or rowing frame. Once the rope is tied in place, it can be used the same way as any other flipline. Keep in mind, however, that the extra rope is a real hazard. Do everything possible to avoid becoming entangled in the loose coils!

Righting a raft: use fliplines tied across the far side of the raft to help pull the raft back over again. If the raft is heavy, it may take many people to flip it back upright.

ACTIVE SWIMMING: If you find yourself too far from your raft or rescuers to do a fast self-rescue, you should be prepared to actively find a way to the safety of an eddy or the bank. Start off by getting yourself to the surface. (Now, I don't really expect you to ask yourself what the first goal is—your lungs will remind you in a hurry!) In violent hydraulics it can be pretty difficult to find the surface. Relax for a second and look around. Head toward the light or follow the bubbles. When you know you're heading in the right direction, keep a cool head and tight lips until you can breathe again.

Once back at the surface, aggressively spot and avoid hazards and prepare to swim toward shore when an opportunity arises. Swimmers in shallow, boulder-strewn rapids should lay on their backs, feet held high and pointed downstream. By assuming this *human shock absorber* position it is possible to fend off rocky collisions with your feet, and to use backstrokes and leg kicks to ferry yourself toward safety.

With your feet floating ahead of you, a new hazard presents itself—foot entrapments. To avoid the perils of foot entrapment, never try to stand up in rapids. Instead, wait until the current has subsided or you are in the calm of a gentle eddy.

In any swimming situation, let the river dictate your actions. In deeper, more powerful rapids, you may be better off turning onto your stomach and swimming aggressively toward shore. In steep, bone bruising rapids, the *cannonball* position—pulling your knees into your chest—may be a good short-term way to protect your limbs (and other vital parts) from injury. Always strive to keep enough air in your lungs. Swimmers should breath only in the calm troughs between wave crests, and should turn their head to the side to avoid inhaling any spray or foam.

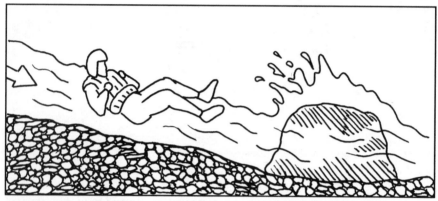

When swimming a rapid, you can use your legs like giant shock absorbers to avoid painful collisions with obstacles. Keep your legs and feet near the surface, but ball up if you're going to go over a steep drop. When an opportunity arises, swim actively toward safety.

HOLES AND DAMS: The upstream surface currents of large holes and lowhead dams can recirculate swimmers indefinitely, and once caught in these traps, your lifejacket may not have enough flotation to float you above the aerated water. Accordingly, holes and dams sometimes demand special techniques for quick escapes.

Keep in mind that most holes are too small to be keepers. So, if you find yourself stuck momentarily in the backwash, relax for a second, breathe when you can, and try to swim sideways out of the hole. If you can't escape sideways, remember that the falls contains a powerful downcurrent which can be used to push you under the hole and out. Swim right into the falls, ball up in the cannonball position, and hang on for the ride. If you come up on the boil line, be sure to swim aggressively downstream to avoid being recirculated.

Lowhead dams contain the most deadly of all holes, and the most difficult to escape. *Don't run them!* If you ever *do* find yourself swimming a dam, you may recirculate in the backwash many times. Try to save your energy and work your way toward shore. Swimming into the falls may be enough to push you out under the backwash, but be prepared to make many attempts at self-rescue. Above all, *don't give up!*

STRAINERS AND SWEEPERS: Some of the worst hazards facing swimmers or rafts are downed trees (sweepers) and boulder sieves (strainers) which don't impede the current entirely. Sweepers can snag life jackets and hold a swimmer underwater, while strainers can wedge swimmers into tight subsurface pockets.

If you find yourself swimming toward one of these hazards, try to swim around it with all the power you can muster. If a collision with a downed tree or log is inevitable, turn onto your stomach and face downstream, concentrating on the approaching log or tree. A split moment before you reach the log, begin kicking with your legs and pull your body *over* it *head first* using any handholds you can find. Give it all you've got! If you can't make it over the log, try hanging on until you can be rescued. If you absolutely have to go under the strainer, first feel for snags with your legs. Remember, going underneath a strainer is the last thing you want to do! Only do it as a last resort.

PULLING SWIMMERS INTO RAFTS: When a strong rapid bounces just one or two passengers out of an upright raft they usually surface right next to the raft. If the swimmer can be rescued without endangering the rest of the crew, follow these simple guidelines, each of which comprise a quick series of motions:

(1) *Act fast! Get the swimmer into the raft before the situation gets worse.*

(2) *Have the swimmer move upstream of the raft to avoid getting caught between the boat and rocks. (It may be safer to get the swimmer aboard fast than to move the swimmer to the upstream side of the raft.)*

(3) *Have just one or two passengers assist the swimmer. Keep everyone else paddling or rowing to maintain control of the raft.*

(4) *The rescuer should stand up in the raft in front of the swimmer with her knees braced against the main tube for support. Then, with the swimmer facing the raft, the rescuer should grab the shoulders of the swimmer's life jacket and lean back into the passenger compartment and pull, lifting the swimmer out of the water. (It is usually much easier to pull in the swimmer if the swimmer kicks his feet underwater and pulls up on an available rope or strap.)*

(5) *Keep rowing or paddling—don't gloat over the rescue. There may be more rapids just downstream.*

(6) *If a quick rescue imperils the rest of your crew, wait until it is safe before trying to help the swimmer.*

PART SIX: Rope Rescues

Throwropes—also called *rescue ropes* and *rescue bags*—can provide life-saving umbilical cords linking swimmers with rescuers, but it takes a lot more than just aiming and tossing a throwrope to carry out a good rescue. It takes frequent practice to land a throwrope right where a swimmer can reach it, and it takes keen knowledge of currents and river forces to finish off a rescue once a swimmer actually grasps the rope.

GETTING ROPES TO SWIMMERS: Before throwing a rope to a swimmer, evaluate the situation. The most effective rope rescues are those that were anticipated before the swim. By stationing rescuers where the swimmer actually has an opportunity to see a throw bag coming, rescuers have a chance to establish the *first goal* of rope rescues: *eye contact* with the swimmer. By stationing a rescuer slightly downstream of where a flip might occur, the swimmer has a chance to get back to the surface and clear their vision before the rope toss is made. Then, with a strong yell from the rescuer *(ROPE!!)*, the swimmer has a chance to look at the rescuer and see the rope coming.

The rescuer's *second goal* also involves proper bank positioning, this time taking into account the power of the main current and downstream obstacles. Position the rescuer so that her first toss angles *45 degrees upstream* toward the swimmer. That way, the current can actually *help* push the swimmer

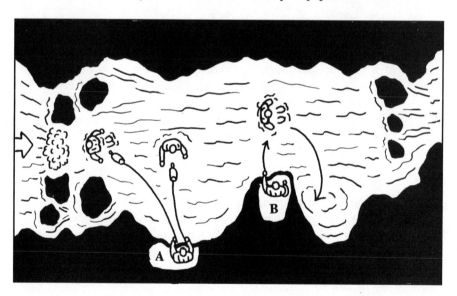

Position rescuers where they'll do the most good. Here, rescuer A can toss a throwline 45 degrees upstream toward the swimmer after a flip, and can get in a second toss before the swimmer heads downstream. Rescuer B can pull the swimmer into a calm pool before he floats into a dangerous boulder sieve.

toward the rescuer as the rope is pulled in. (Also, by throwing the rope upstream to the swimmer, the rescuer may have a chance at a second toss if the first one misses the mark.) If there are calm currents or gentle pools below a likely flip spot, the rescuer can use the rope to pendulum the swimmer into shore. Never, however, pull swimmers into a worse situation than they're already in. Make sure that the rescue path is free of boulder sieves, sweepers, and other hazards that might be best avoided by letting the swimmer swim a few more yards downstream.

The rescuer's *third goal* is to actually get the rope *to* the swimmer. Depending on your dexterity, and surrounding obstacles like overhanging cliffs or branches, your best toss may be underhand, sidearm, or overhand. Though it helps to be adept at all three types of throws, most rescues are done with an underhand toss. When aiming your throw, try to land the rope *at* or *just downstream* of the swimmer. That way, the swimmer can reach the rope, even if it is a few feet away. (If you aim upstream of the swimmer, the slower surface current will slow the rope's descent while the swimmer accelerates downstream in the deeper, faster currents.)

Swimmers have to be able to help themselves just as much as the rescuer helps them. Presuming that the rope reaches the swimmer, the swimmer must be prepared to grab the rope with one or both hands and turn onto his back, face up. (It is important to grab the rope, not the bag!) In this position, the swimmer's body will plane toward the surface and offer less resistance to the current. Swimmers should never wrap the rope around their hands, limbs, or bodies!

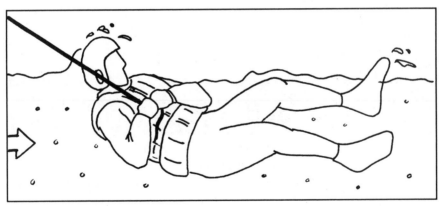

Swimmers should hold the rescue rope over their shoulders and lay on their back. That way, they'll plane toward the surface and have an air pocket over their face. Never wrap the rope around your wrist, arm, or body!

BELAYS: Once the rescuer and swimmer are holding either end of the rescue rope, it is time to work the swimmer toward shore. Both people should pull the slack out of the rope and prepare for a powerful jolt as the rope pulls tight. Now, there are two ways to pull the swimmer ashore: the rescuer can pull the swimmer in from a stationary position with a *static belay*, or can run downstream with the swimmer in a *dynamic belay*.

In a *static belay*, the rescuer pendulums the swimmer toward the shore from a stationary point on the bank. The rescuer can step on the end of the rope if he's worried that it will pull free, or can use a belay anchor, such as a tree stump or boulder. In using a belay anchor, the rope is wrapped one-half to one full turn around the anchor. (If you wrap the rope more than once around the anchor, it will take longer to unwrap it.)

In strong currents, a *dynamic belay* is better since it reduces the counteracting forces which could jar the rope from the swimmer's hands. In a dynamic belay, the rescuer walks or runs down the bank with the swimmer, pulling him in gradually with light rope pressure. This technique, as you can imagine, only works if there is an open corridor along the river bank.

There are a few more tips that will make rope rescues easier. First, don't pick a rescue position too high above the river as this will make the working length of rope both shorter and less versatile. Second, use the best type of throw you can. Depending on where you're standing, the throw bag or rescue rope may have to be thrown underhand, overhand, or sidearm.

The rescuer can use a static belay (A) or a dynamic belay (B) to assist the swimmer. In case a dynamic belay becomes necessary after a static belay has already started, never wrap the rope more than one turn around an anchor.

PART SEVEN: River Crossings

It is sometimes necessary to walk rafters across shallow rivers without a rope. This can be done solo in gentle currents, or as a team in stronger currents. No matter which technique is used, the same basic concepts apply:

all shallow water crossings are premised on maintaining *three points of contact* with the riverbottom, and are done slowly and methodically to avoid foot entrapments. Also, one crossing method may outweigh another depending on the speed of the current and the depth of the rivers.

SOLO CROSSINGS: When crossing a river by yourself, use a long, sturdy paddle, oar, pole, or tree limb as a brace. (The pole—together with your two feet—provides three points of contact.) Face upstream and jam one end of the pole into the river bottom and tilt it 30 degrees back toward your shoulder. At the same time, brace your shoulder against the pole and lean your body 30 degrees upstream against it. Now, maintaining this 60 degree triangle, you can slowly sidestep your way across the river, moving one point of contact at a time.

When doing a solo crossing, use an oar, long paddle, pole, or a sturdy branch to brace yourself. The pole and your feet provide three points of contact with the riverbed. By leaning forward and moving just one point of contact at a time, you are much more stable than you would be otherwise.

GROUP CROSSINGS: The most basic group crossings are mere variations of solo crossings: the solo crosser carries someone *piggyback* from one bank to another or a second individual follows the lead person across the river pressed tightly against his back and the back of his legs.

If more people are to be added to the group, each new person can step toward the outboard shoulder of the person in front of him, effectively forming a *wedge* formation. A *line astern* formation works by placing additional people directly behind the point person. The secondary people add stability to the system by pressing down on the point person's shoulders, effectively increasing the pressure on his feet and the river bottom.

If there are three people in your group, arrange yourselves in a triangle and lock your arms around each other's shoulders. With the heaviest person on the downstream end of the triangle, facing upstream, the group can lean into each other and form a pyramid. With one person moving their feet at a time, the group can work their way across the river.

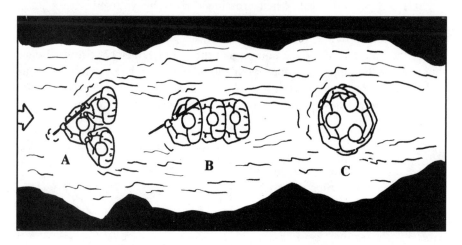

Three ways to cross a river with a small group: group A is standing in a wedge formation; group B is using a line astern formation, and group C is using a triangle formation. Each technique relies on the downward pressure exerted by each individual to stabilize the entire group.

Another way to shuttle people across the river without a raft is with a *fixed horizontal line*. The fixed horizontal line is a rope which is stretched taught just a foot or so above the river. The crosser simply stands upstream of the fixed line, holds the rope against his waist, and walks sideways across the river. If something goes wrong, all he has to do is somersault over or swim under the rope to break free. Since there is always a possiblity that the crosser could snag a life-jacket buckle or carabiner on the line, the line shouldn't be anchored on both banks. Instead, use belay points on both banks, or just tie one anchor off while belaying from the opposite bank.

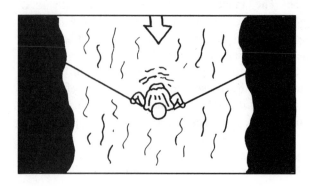

A horizontal line supports the crosser, but allows him to dive over or under the line in an emergency. Don't anchor the ends of the rope—you may have to let one end go if the crosser gets caught on the rope.

PART EIGHT: *Other Rope Rescues*

There may be times when a swimmer is caught against a midstream boulder and a throwrope or boat-based rescue is simply impossible. If someone has to reach the swimmer to render assistance, one technique that might work is the *strong-swimmer rescue.*

The strong-swimmer rescue is a paradox in rescue procedures—it increases the risk that the rescuer could be hurt or drowned by placing the rescuer *inside* a rope-loop while working in the current. Nonetheless, there may be times when nothing else works and the increased risk is worth a victim's life.

The strong-swimmer rescue requires—at a minimum—a swimmer, a belayer, and a strong rope. A large, *very loose* loop is tied into one end of the rope and placed around the rescuer's chest. (The loop must be loose enough to push free if the rescuer runs into any trouble.) Once in the loop, the rescuer can be pendulumed to the victim from the far bank (this only works in narrow streams), or lowered downstream to the victim from an upstream boulder or island.

A slightly safer alternative to the strong-swimmer rescue is an offshoot of the fixed-horizontal line (just discussed in Part Seven). In rescue situations, the

Strong swimmer rescues: the rescuer can be pendulumed down to the victim from the bank, or can walk downstream from an island.

fixed-horizontal line can be rigged looser than usual so that the rescuer can make some *downstream* progress as she works her way out into the main channel. By slowly letting rope out from one of the belay anchors, the rescuer can walk downstream while leaning her waist against the line, and can be set free in an emergency by somersaulting away from the line or having a belayer release one end of the rope.

PART NINE: *The Telfer Lower*

The *Telfer Lower* combines many of the rope tricks you just learned, but adds a raft as a rescue platform. The raft, in turn, is controlled by shore-based rescuers through the use of tag lines and fixed ropes. Since it is so complex, it is rarely used—especially if a speedy rescue is necessary. However, it can provide one way to get to a wrapped raft or stranded rafter when time isn't a critical factor.

The Telfer Lower requires, at a minimum (1) an anchor line, (2) three carabiners, (3) two tag lines, and (4) a belay line. The anchor line is a fixed rope that crosses the river eight to ten feet above the surface, and twenty to fifty feet upstream of the rescue site. (By angling the anchor line slightly downstream toward the rescue site, the river will help push the raft toward the site with little help from shore.) From this anchor line, hang a chain of three interlinked carabiners. Next, attach two tag lines to the middle carabiner, with one leading to each bank. Finally, add a belay line. This long, sturdy rope runs from the raft, up through the lowest carabiner in the carabiner chain, and back to the raft.

To operate the system, the shore belayers pull the tag lines until the raft is positioned upstream of the rescue site. Then, the rafters aboard the rescue raft use the belay line to lower themselves to the rescue site.

There are many ways to set up a Telfer Lower (the belay rope can be run to shore and manned by a shore belayer, two canoes can be used in place of a raft, and various types of friction brakes can be used to make the belay system more efficient), but each one takes a lot of planning and engineering skill. Accordingly, make learning a Telfer Lower one of your Sunday projects. Get a copy of *River Rescue* (by Les Bechdel and Slim Ray, Appalachian Mountain Club Books), and try to set up the system on an easy river with some friends. Better yet, take a course in Swiftwater Rescue from Rescue 3, where you'll learn all the nuances of the system. Then, when the right calamity presents itself (hopefully, *never*), you'll be able to set up the Telfer Lower quickly and efficiently.

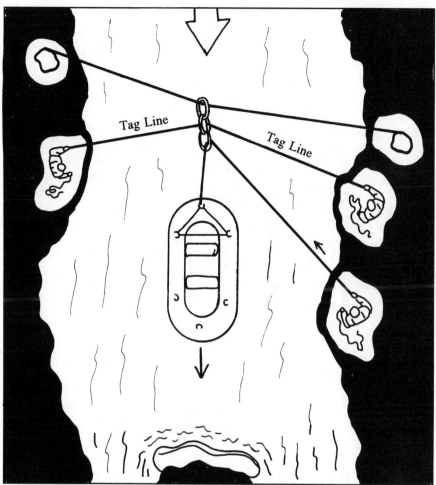

An example of a Telfer Lower. In this example, the raft is being belayed down to the wrapped raft from shore. It is also possible to set up the system such that the rescue raft's descent is controlled from the raft itself by having one of the rafters hold the free end of the belay rope.

PART TEN: Wraps

WRAPS: A wrap is one of those river ordeals that you'll never forget. It provides an exciting opportunity to apply all of your rescue skills and ingenuity, or leaves you tapping your booties together and chanting "there's no place like home, there's no place like home, there's no place...."

When a raft wraps around a rock or obstacle, many tons of water hold it securely in place. Overcoming such forces takes muscle, sturdy equipment, and a bit of streamside engineering.

Some river runners look at wraps as an outstanding opportunity to whip out all of their rescue paraphenalia, blanket the landscape in nylon ropes and metal devices, and set up intricate raft retrieval systems. While some wraps require just that type of action, it is usually more efficient to select the most basic system that will retrieve the raft quickly without any complication.

*"We might be here a while. Let's send out for pizza!" (PS: this is a **wrap**.)*

SURVEY THE SITUATION: Before setting up any ropes, survey the scene. Which bank is the raft facing? What obstacles await downstream once the raft is freed? How much of the raft is left showing? How accessible are anchor points on the raft and along the banks? Will the raft be easier to remove in one direction than another?

Next, appoint someone to direct the rescue operation. The director should be a member of the shore crew unless the only one who knows how to unwrap the raft is still sitting in the middle of the river. By putting one person in charge, rescuers can work together as a team under the guidance of one coach. Finally, keep in mind that the rescue process set out below is flexible and should be tailored to meet the needs of your situation.

THE ANCHORS: Start the rescue operation by securely attaching one end of a strong rope to the raft. (Don't use your throw bag rope on a severe wrap, unless that's all that you have available. It could easily snap under stress and injure a rescuer.) If the raft is left in a precarious position after all of its passengers washed free, reaching the raft could be very difficult. Proceed with great caution and choose the approach that is lowest in risk. That might mean that you'll have to set up a horizontal line, strong swimmer rescue, or even a Telfer Lower to reach the boat. Once at the raft you may be able to stand on the obstacle holding it in place or sit on the exposed tube. If an anchor point is submerged, try to have an assistant hold on to the rigger to avoid getting pinned or swept beneath the surface.

Some raft rescue systems develop a tremendous amount of force—more force than most D-rings and handles can withstand. Since these attachments have a tendency to unexpectedly blow free during raft rescues, consider other anchoring options. In self-bailing rafts, try tying your rope around an exposed tube by threading it through the floor's drain holes; in standard-floor rafts, ropes can be tied to thwarts or multiple D-rings; and on oarboats, ropes can always be tied to the frame.

BASIC ROPE SYSTEMS: The first way to pull a raft loose is to simply join your fellow rafters in a riverside version of tug-o'-war. The tug-o'-war develops only a 1:1 mechanical advantage, but can pull lightly wrapped rafts free. A variation on this is the *vector pull:* rather than pulling on the end of the rope, the end is tied to an anchor point and a second rope is attached to the center of the first rope at a 90 degree angle. When the second rope is pulled, the same 1:1 power ratio is transferred to the raft.

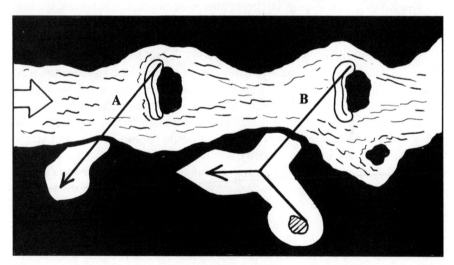

The tug-o'-war (A) and vector pull (B) provide two basic ways to unwrap a pinned raft. Neither system generates any mechanical advantage.

To double the power of your pulling system, anchor a couple of carabiners or a pulley to the raft and run the rope through them. Then, with one end of the rope tied to an anchor point on shore, you can pull on the loose end of the rope and create a 2:1 mechanical advantage.

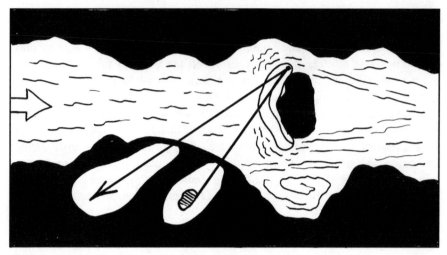

To set up a 2:1 system, run the rope from an anchor, to the raft, and back to shore. For every pound of pressure exerted on the end of the rope, two pounds of pull will transfer to the raft.

Z-DRAGS: The Z-drag is one of the most popular raft rescue systems available. In a simple Z-drag system a 3:1 mechanical advantage is developed, while more complex Z-drag systems can generate much greater leverage.

It takes little more than some strong rope to build a rudimentary Z-drag system, but carabiners and pulleys cut down on rope friction any time the rope makes a turn. (If you don't have carabiners or pulleys, use a figure-eight or butterfly knot in their place. These knots are shown in the appendix.)

The first step in setting up the Z-drag involves anchoring the rope to the raft's thwarts, frame, or D-rings just as you would for tug-o'-wars and vector pulls. At the same time, tie a sturdy tubular webbing sling or rope around a shore-based anchor and clip in a carabiner and a pulley (if they're available).

Next, tie a figure-eight or butterfly knot in the rope between the raft and the anchor loop. Since this knot will move toward shore when you start pulling on the rope, it is important to set the knot close enough to the raft so that it won't jam into the shore anchor. (If you're standing on the shore far from the raft, you might want to tie the figure-eight or butterfly knot *before* you anchor the rope to the raft.) If you have another carabiner and pulley handy, clip them into this knot.

Now it's time to complete the system. Take the rope's loose end and thread it through the shore anchor carabiner or pulley, back through the figure-eight or butterfly knot, and back to shore. If you've done this correctly, the system will form a backwards Z. To operate the system, just pull the free end of the rope.

Some rescuers add a *brake prussik* (shown in the appendix) to the shore

160

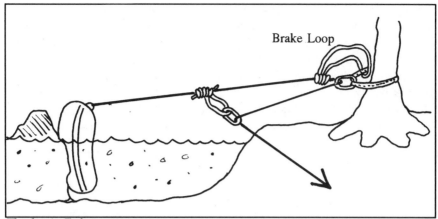

The basic Z-drag system.

anchor loop. The brake prussik lets rescuers re-rig the system if a knot approaches the anchor loop, and stops the rope from travelling backward through the system. Second, additional lines to the raft can be used to ease the burden on the Z-drag. A *rollover line* can also be used to help tug the raft free. The rollover line runs over the top of the exposed tube, down around the back of the raft, and attaches to the submerged D-ring or thwart. When pulled from upstream, this rope helps the raft dump water and lessens the pressure on the Z-drag.

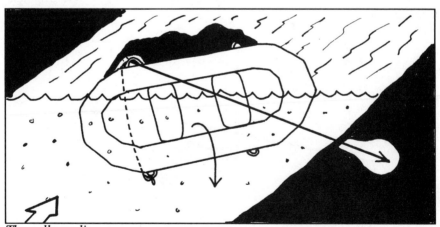

The rollover line.

Z-drags can be rigged in many ways. By adding a 2:1 pull to the system, the mechanical advantage grows to 6:1, and by doubling the Z-drag, the mechanical advantage grows to 9:1. If nothing works—including one of the high advantage Z-drag systems—it may be time to relieve the resistance caused by the floor. In self-bailing rafts with laced-in floors, cut the floor line and let the floor flap open. This may make the raft much easier to pull free. In standard-floor rafts, cut a hole at the point of greatest pressure, but beware of the consequences of doing this: the whole floor might tear out. Although tubes could arguably be deflated to assist in the rescue, this lets water enter the tubes, which eventually damages the raft. The deflated tubes are also more likely to conform to the obstacle and make the wrap even worse.

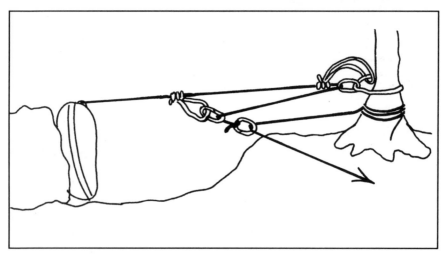

By adding a second line, the mechanical advantage of this Z-drag has increased to 6:1.

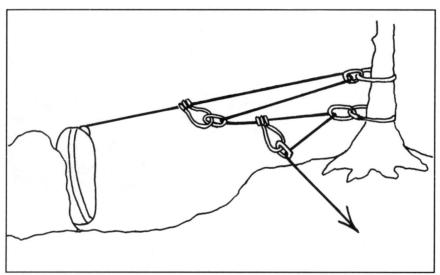

In this double Z-drag, the mechanical advantage is 9:1.

PART ELEVEN: First Aid

FIRST AID: As with any other form of outdoor recreation, rafters may get injured during a river trip. Fortunately, small cuts, bruises, or bouts with poison ivy are about as bad as any first aid provider will see. In any event, it is important to be prepared for any type of first aid situation, from broken bones to near-drownings.

Guides and private rafters alike should take the Red Cross basic first aid and CPR courses and should strive for higher levels of first aid certification. Rafters should know their physical limitations before embarking on a trip, and should inform others of medical conditions that may affect patient care decisions. Also, a first aid kit should accompany rafters on every trip. On longer wilderness ventures it is not only important to *have* every item necessary to handle first aid care, but to know *how to use* them effectively.

HYPOTHERMIA: The same water that provides a thrilling rollercoaster ride for rafters can become a dangerous enemy for swimmers or underdressed passengers. Hypothermia—a cooling of the body temperature—can happen whenever a swimmer is immersed in water for any length of time, or when cool air and spray drain the body's ability to stay warm. Hypothermia affects a rafter's judgment, and can be life-threatening in its advanced stages. So, it is important to avoid hypothermia with proper preparation, and to know how to reverse its effects once hypothermia sets in.

Warm clothing, adequate food consumption, and constant activity provide the first line of defense against hypothermia, but one quick swim can drain even the heartiest rafters of internal warmth. If a rafter winds up in the river, get him out quickly. Water can drain body heat 20 to 30 times faster than air, making even a short swim in very cold water dangerous.

It is important to know hypothermia's warning signs, and how to treat victims once these signs are present. In the initial stages of hypothermia, victims may shiver vigorously, act cold, and appear pale. Treatment is easiest and most effective at this stage. Get victims away from the river, into dry clothes, and near a source of heat, such as a warm car or a campfire. If nothing is available, walk victims along the bank until the cold and shivering go away. Left untreated, victims will progress into the next stage of hypothermia.

As the body's core temperature drops to 90-95 degrees fahrenheit victims may become confused, clumsy, and sluggish, and shivering may slow down. Their speech may become slurred and their eyes dull. By the time these symptoms appear, the body has lost its ability to rewarm itself, and the basic treatment regimen won't work—an external source of heat is necessary. In a fix it may be necessary for a couple of people to climb into a sleeping bag with the victim and establish full body skin-to-skin contact, letting their body warmth gently warm the victim. If a strong fire is available, seat the victim close to the heat with a backdrop of blankets or sleeping bags for insulation. Whatever is done, it has to be done *before* the victim loses any more heat.

As the victim's core temperature drops further, his muscles will become rigid, the patient will become unconscious and may suffer a cardiac arrest. Immediate evacuation and hospitalization is mandatory in this situation.

A well-prepared paddle team tackles the whitewater of Idaho's Payette River.

10
ADVANCED RAFTING:
Rafting on the Cutting Edge

How many times have you stood above a rapid, shoulder to shoulder with fellow rafters, saying things like, "I'm going left of that hole, then to the right of the big boulder, then back to the center of those waves?" With minor variations, I've heard myself talk like that hundreds of times.

Subtle as it may seem, the myopic thought process going into scouting rapids was always two-dimensional, locked into directions like upstream and downstream, left banks and right banks. It actually took kayaking to turn me onto the missing link in my knowledge of rafting techniques... whitewater's third dimension.

Whitewater's third dimension is the river's vertical world. A world of steep waves, sharp holes, exposed rocks, and swelling boils. Up to now you have thought of many surface features as *obstacles*—things to be avoided or overcome. But now you can begin to think of these things as natural tools. Tools which provide an extra link with gravity, friction, or hydraulic forces. Tools which enhance your ability to out-maneuver a tough rapid, and tools which can make seemingly impossible rapids runnable.

In this chapter you'll also go beyond rafting's third dimension to look at the techniques and mindset necessary to raft difficult rivers. You'll discover specialized techniques for running everything from waterfalls and narrow chutes to giant waves. To the novice and intermediate rafter, a lot of these concepts will sound insane. After all, who in their right mind would *intentionally* slide their raft over rocks, drop off the lip of waterfalls, or surf holes to stop and scout a rapid?! But to the advanced rafter, these techniques not only exist, *they work*! If you're willing to step beyond conventional wisdom, and to use every part of the river to its fullest potential, you'll walk away with a broadened perspective of your raft's capabilities... and possibly your own.

PART ONE: Preparation

Class IV and V rivers present challenges rarely found on gentler streams. Whether these challenges manifest themselves as endless boulder labyrinths or minefields of boat-swallowing holes, the consequences of human miscalculations or the failure of inferior equipment can be catastrophic. Accordingly, Class V rivers mandate that guides, passengers, rafts, and all supporting equipment be up to the rigors the river will present.

Expert rafters can paddle some incredible rivers! (Photo by Mike Doyle, courtesy of Beyond Limits Adventures.)

Without the benefit of a professional guide, any rafter preparing to run a Class V river should already have one thing going for them... the skills and confidence borne of many hours on the river. Not just skills well suited to a particular river or set of rapids, but skills which will translate well in any river situation: the ability to quickly read and run confusing currents; full knowledge of the Z-drag and other rescue systems; the ability to quickly re-right a raft; experience in swimming rapids; and an understanding of emergency medical procedures.

A Class V rapid is *not* the place to learn about advanced rafting. Instead, practice flipping and re-flipping rafts in Class III rapids with safe pools. Swim Class II rapids, trying to catch eddies by swimming back and forth across the current. Do everything *that* could happen in a Class V rapid in a controlled setting—and get *good* at fast rescues—long before your first Class V adventure.

In addition to the obvious skills needed to survive difficult whitewater, advanced rafters should be in good physical condition. By being in shape your body will withstand the stresses of powerful rapids. You'll have the strength to power swamped rafts around in pushy hydraulics, the ability to hold your breath during long swims, and the dexterity to leap to the high-side if your raft collides with a menacing boulder.

Finally, advanced rafters should surround themselves with top-quality equipment. Today's self-bailing rafts and catarafts provide an enormous safety margin for intrepid river travellers, while oars, paddles, helmets, life jackets, throw bags, and rescue gear stand up to the rigors of the most demanding rapids. Still, rafters should check and re-check their gear for flaws. Spare equipment should be carried whenever possible in order to replace whatever breaks down, and enough rescue and first aid gear should be carried to meet or exceed the needs of any emergency situation. This means carrying extra throw bags, static lines, carabiners, pulleys, expeditionary medical kits, and much, much more.

STOWING GEAR: The combination of extra gear and raft-flipping rapids can be lethal. Catching a foot in a loose rope during a wrap might be all it takes to turn an adventure into a disaster. Pack gear as lightly and compactly as possible, remembering to leave safety gear readily accessible. Lash it tightly to the raft in places that won't interfere with the positioning or movement of rafters. (Remember that things like high siding, beaching, and cross-bow draws require extra floor-space.) Also, try to avoid carrying solid items—like ammo cans—in the passenger compartment if possible. Soft-sided dry bags may work just as well, and won't rearrange valuable body parts in the event of a collision.

TYPE OF RAFT: Almost any type of raft can be used on Class V rivers, but some rafts are better suited to extreme conditions than others. As already mentioned, self-bailing rafts and catarafts increase your level of safety during difficult descents. Their ability to shed water quickly makes them much more nimble in long rapids than their non-bailing cousins.

The choice between a self-bailing raft and cataraft is mainly one of personal preference. Catarafts tend to stall less in big holes, but require much more hardware (frames) to operate. Self-bailing rafts can be paddled and can hold a lot of gear, but aren't as agile as some catarafts. The best thing rafters can do is to choose the craft they are most skilled and comfortable operating. That way, when things get out of hand, the added confidence will give you just the edge you need.

Insofar as the paddling versus rowing option goes, a lightly loaded self-bailing raft can be easily portaged by a small team of strong paddlers, and can even be deflated and carried through narrow ravines or tree-lined trails. By adding a frame to that same raft, portaging and lining becomes much more difficult. The frame will not only add weight during portages, it can snag rocks if the raft flips when lining, and will make it more difficult to fit the raft through narrow passages. Frames also add one more piece of equipment that can fail even if all else goes well. If you are catarafting, the frame is essential. However, catarafts are usually lighter and less bulky than rafts to start with, so some of the cataraft's frame disadvantages fade.

Again, don't let my opinions shape your own! Only *you* know the rivers you'll be attempting, and only *you* know your own skills and preferences. Listen to them and you'll be much better off.

THE CLASS V ATTITUDE: The first sentence of the definition of Class V rapids says, *"Extremely long, obstructed, or very violent rapids which expose a paddler to above average endangerment."* Scary, huh?! You bet! Try rowing a long Class V rapid—even after scouting it thoroughly—and you're likely to be on the edge of your seat until you're resting safely in a pool below.

Class V rapids take both a different mindset and a different approach. First, don't stare at one or two objects in the river, such as a big rock or wave. You'll end up getting tunnel vision and lose sight of everything that is going on around you. Strive to broaden your peripheral vision and expand your senses. Relax, take a couple of deep breaths above the rapid, and try to breathe normally once in the whitewater. You'll have a much better feel for the rapid, and be able to react better if things go wrong.

Next, don't just sit on your butt and ride the raft like a golf cart. Put more pressure on your legs and feet, and flex with the raft. If you're rowing, keep your butt off the seat so that you're ready to highside in a flash. In a paddle raft, do the same so that you can lunge into cross bow draws or switch quickly from easy forward strokes to radical farback strokes.

It is important to never give up trying to navigate your raft upright through a rapid until it flips or wraps. If you're suddenly confronted by a big boulder or the largest hole of the day, it is often better to keep maneuvering rather than to look for a handhold. Your last ditch effort might provide just enough momentum to bust through a hole, or just the right move to slip through the tight spot unscathed.

Finally, don't just run a Class V rapid in one mad dash, dissect it into bite-sized portions. Rather than blasting downstream, use a zig-zag approach. Jump from eddy to eddy, concentrating on the next eddy as you head downstream, then regrouping and reassessing your plan once you arrive in the eddy. Use powerful ferries in the main channel to counteract the current, and avoid turning broadside to the current. Using this piecemeal approach to rapids, you'll have more control, more time to react, and additional time to mold your strategies around the demands of the river.

PART TWO: Helpful Hydraulics

WAVES: The same gravitational forces that pull a kayak down the face of a wave—allowing the kayaker to *surf* in place—act on a raft. By pulling your raft against the current on the upstream face of a wave—or in the trough between two waves—the raft will stall out dramatically. This is not only fun, it can buy some extra time to execute maneuvers.

The first time you use a wave to slow down, keep your raft parallel with the current. This will give you an extra second to make your next move. Once you get used to the feel of stalling on a wave, try turning your raft slightly, set a ferry angle, and backferry. The wave will magnify the intensity and trajectory of your ferry—in fact, by using medium-sized waves (not waves large enough to flip your raft), some seemingly impossible ferries can be achieved.

By ferrying on the up-stream face of small waves, your raft will ferry across the river faster than usual.

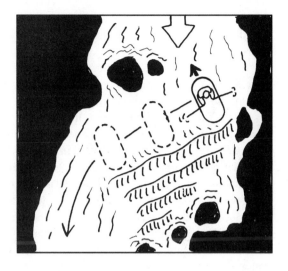

Waves can also act as *turntables*, making turns much easier. As your raft approaches the crest of a wave, the bow and stern become unweighted, and for a split second the raft will spin easier than it does in wave troughs. Since a turn started in the trough between two steep waves often produces nothing until the raft reaches a balancing point on the tip of the wave anyway, start your turns high on the wave to save a lot of unnecessary effort.

It is much easier to turn on the crest of a wave than it is in the trough between waves.

Once you get comfortable with wave moves, it will be easy to use them on other vertical features—large pillows, surging boils, and small breaking waves. Gravity acts as a maneuver turbo-charger in all these situations. Provided you don't flip broadside (keep most of your crew's weight toward the downstream tube), the usefulness of these hydraulics will be much appreciated.

HOLES: Now, turn your angle of trajectory downward. Rather than slowing your vertical ascent on the face of waves, control your rate of descent through holes and reversals.

Since few small holes meet the textbook definition of a *keeper* (most provide an easy escape route at one end or the other) they can be surfed in place or cross-river just like waves. In fact, small holes sometimes present the only stopping point in the midst of a long rapid.

The same concepts you just learned for wave surfing apply equally well—with some minor modifications—to hole surfing. As you approach a hole, look for the direction of its *kick*—the direction it will toss your raft as you plow into its backwash, then be prepared to highside in order to keep the raft upright. If you think that impeccable highsiding is all that stands between you and a swim, you probably shouldn't run the hole in the first place.

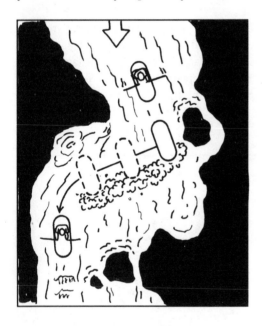

Small holes can be surfed to stop your raft or to move across the river. Holes that lay at a slight angle to the main current have a current that will kick your raft toward the side that reaches the furthest downstream. Be prepared to highside at any moment, and don't try this trick in big holes!

EDDIES: You have already acquired the basic skills needed to enter and exit eddies. You have also learned that eddies house a variety of useful currents—some of which flow upstream, some of which swirl downstream faster than the main current, and some which suck downward. Now you can

170

expand your knowledge of eddies and tap into these currents for your own benefit.

It is possible to make some pretty dramatic stops or turns using eddies. Try entering an eddy high and deep with a lot of momentum. As you cross the eddy line, present the downstream tube broadside to the eddy's upstream current and lean on the downstream tube (stay low in the raft so you don't fall out as the downstream tube dives downward). The raft will scream to a gut-wrenching halt. If you're peeling out of an eddy, try leaning over the downstream tube—the raft will snap around faster as it crosses the eddy line.

In well-protected eddies, slamming across the eddy line into the upstream current might be impossible. An example of an elusive eddy is one that has many nearby boulders which prevent the rafter from turning the raft at a ferry angle. Since the raft can't be turned 45 or 90 degrees to the current, a fast and powerful entry technique is required.

Oar boats can frequently muster the energy to enter these types of eddies by backrowing early, then pulling into the eddy at the last possible second. Paddle rafts, on the other hand, have to coordinate many paddlers to overcome their inertia. They too can start slowing the raft down ahead of time with forward or back ferries, then ferry the slowed raft into the eddy at the last moment.

When it is impossible to set the proper angle to enter an eddy, try slowing your raft down ahead of time. If you are moving slow enough by the time you're next to the eddy, you can quickly pull across the eddy line.

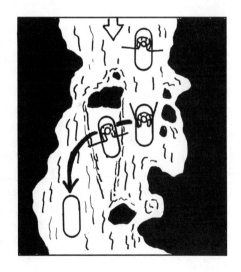

Aside from entering and exiting eddies, eddies can be used to slingshot rafts cross river, or to spin the raft 180 degrees.

A raft that begins ferrying in the main current will find its lateral momentum greatly magnified by conveniently placed eddies. As the raft crosses the eddy, the eddy's upstream current will hurl the raft upstream against the main current faster than when it entered the eddy. The turbocharged effect of the transition from one side of the eddy to the other and back into the main current is very exciting, and can make some big, powerful moves possible. Try practicing it in a familiar rapid until you can get the raft to make S-maneuvers back and forth across the river.

S-turns: eddies can be used to accelerate your raft when you are ferrying across the river. Approach the eddy at a ferry angle and keep ferrying through the eddy. You will exit the far side with more upstream momentum than when you entered. (By linking eddies, you can actually use S-turns to climb upstream!)

PART THREE: Boulders and Slots

BOULDERS: Early in my rafting career I treated solid obstacles as enemies—the nemeses of ill-fated rafters. I respected and avoided rocks and boulders, and portaged rapids that were too boulder-choked to be considered runnable. It took a bona fide Class V rafting adventure to change my perspective of these notorious river features.

In some instances, shallow rocks and boulders provide midriver brakes when there are no eddies to be found. By running the raft onto partially submerged boulders (pay attention to your highside and don't pivot sideways), the raft can be drug to a halt, then spun off the boulder to continue downstream. Even if you don't want to stop completely, you can use the boulder to help make quick turns. This can be a real boon in the middle of a long Class V rapid! Also, shallow, wet boulders might provide the only feasible route through an otherwise impossible rapid. If the main channel is hopelessly boulder-choked, it would be senseless to try to raft it. On the other hand, wet boulders can be *boofed* with some momentum. In *boofing*, stiff, slick-bottomed rafts are paddled or rowed full speed across the tops of wet boulders and into the safety of the eddies below.

LOWSIDING: Lowsiding is just the opposite of highsiding. While highsiding throws your body weight against an obstacle to keep a raft from wrapping, lowsiding throws your weight away from obstacles to get you through tight squeezes. In the lowsiding diagram, the raft is too wide to fit through a narrow chute. However, by seating the crew on one side of the raft, the other tube rides up out of the water and slides over the obstacle.

On some rivers, the only way to run narrow chutes may be to let some air out of the thwarts. Without the rigidity of fully inflated thwarts to keep the tubes their normal distance apart, the raft can flex inward and run slots slightly narrower than otherwise possible. Of course the trade off for this technique is a more flexible raft that might be harder to control.

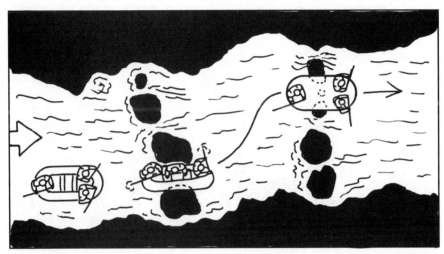

This paddle team is negotiating a difficult rapid. To make it through the first narrow slot, the team has to lean to one side of the raft (lowside). Next, the team boofs over some barely submerged rocks to avoid the boulder sieve.

PART FOUR: *Waterfalls and Steep Drops*

Though I've hammered rafts over scores of waterfalls, I've yet to figure out a way to suppress the butterflies I get staring out over a thundering, foam-spewing horizon line. In fact, all that has stood between me and pre-drop hysteria was the right choice of runnable waterfalls and the techniques described here. They haven't stopped me from being eaten alive in a couple of big drops, but they have increased my confidence in my raft and have gotten me through a couple of close calls.

SCOUTING: The first key to successful waterfall descents is knowing which falls *not* to run. Check out the face of the falls. How far does it drop?

Does the falls pour freely off a ledge or slide downward at an angle? Are there rocks in the falls that are going to throw the raft off course before it even hits bottom? A tall free-falling waterfall might flip your raft end over end, while a slanted falls might feel like little more than an exciting carnival ride. Next, check out the hole at the base of the falls. Is it free of boulders and debris? Will the raft have enough momentum to break through the backwash, or will the river be too powerful? What if I'm swimming? Can I break free of the hole or will it be a keeper? Judge all these features carefully before you decide to run any waterfall, and always have a rescue team set up in case anything goes wrong.

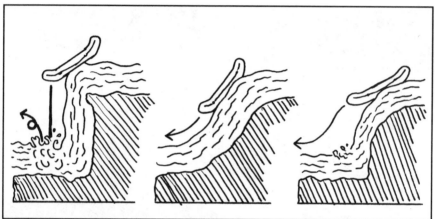

Three types of waterfalls: The waterfall on the left drops steeply over a ledge. If it is tall enough, the raft will flip. The middle waterfall is a slide. If there isn't a keeper hole at its base, or sharp rocks in the face of the falls, the slide may be runnable. The waterfall on the right forms a rounded dome. Unless it is tall, the raft will kick outward and away from the waterfall instead of pencilling straight down into the hole. (Note: rafts usually flip in big falls.)

PLANNING: Ask yourself how you're going to know where to enter the falls. After all, you're going to see nothing but a big horizon line from your raft. Pick distinctive landmarks along the bank that will help tell you where your line is "I'll enter ten feet left of that big boulder." Other useful signposts are obvious hydraulic features ("We'll nick the right of that hole with our left tube, then drop over the falls."), or downstream landmarks that can be used as a gunsight ("Paddle straight toward the tree.") No matter what you use to point your way, make sure you can see it from upstream or it won't do you any good! Walk upstream and look back down at the falls from a distance. Is your landmark still visible? If not, consider picking another one.

If you're about to run a large waterfall, figure out when the best time is to stop maneuvering and hold on. Keep in mind, however, that even the strongest grip won't do you any good if you quit paddling twenty yards above the lip of a waterfall, plop over it sideways, and flip in the hole. Figure out the last place you can take a power stroke, and, if you can, keep adjusting your raft's direction right up to the lip of the falls. If you're a paddle captain, get your crew down inside the raft a second or so before you do and steer the raft until the last possible moment. Also, make sure your handhold is easily accessible—it'll be much harder to find with your heart in your throat!

If you have a heavy crew, consider leaving some paddlers ashore. Smaller crews can unload passengers or gear from the bow compartment to help the bow snap up and away from the falls quickly.

TAKING THE PLUNGE: After you've tightly lashed down any loose gear and set out on the main current, begin visualizing the falls. Build up as much speed as possible to launch the raft out over the lip of the falls (this is called *ski jumping* or *airplane jumping*), and line the raft up so it drops down the falls towards the safest landing. This might require a straight descent in some falls, and a diagonal descent in others.

Paddle as fast as you can over waterfalls so that the bow blasts through the hole. This is called ski jumping.

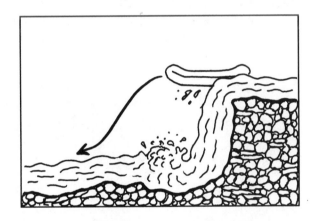

Oar rafts are particularly dangerous in large waterfalls. Rafts flex and torque as they dive over the lip of sharp drops, and stop violently at their bases. All of this energy is transferred into the only mobile objects in the raft—passengers and oars. In response to this, oarsmen have developed two techniques. The first technique involves letting go of the oars and holding onto the frame like a scared barnacle. It works for keeping you on the raft, but subjects you and your passengers to the whims of wildly swinging oars. Hence, the development of technique number two.

In the second technique, the rower plants both feet firmly on the frame's footbar and leans as far back as possible. The oars are shipped with their handles facing the stern, and the rafter's ability to anticipate the raft's gyrations gives him the balance to stay aboard. If there is a chance of getting tossed forward or losing an oar, try grasping the handles and frame together

175

Rowing waterfalls: (1) lean back, hold onto the oars; (2) balance on the seat and prepare for a jolt! It takes experience to avoid falling out of your seat!

Paddling waterfalls is tricky business—only run those that you know are safe. One way to run falls is to sit low in the raft (this is a self-bailer), press your shins against a tube or thwart, and hold your paddles outside the passenger compartment. Hang on! (Photo by John Hall/AAA Rafting.)

in each hand and hold on! Overall, the key to success is keeping your butt just off the seat so that it doesn't snap upward and catapult you overboard.

Paddlers have the same concerns as rowers—flying bodies and equipment—except that in paddle rafts, flying paddles replace flying oars. To minimize these hazards, paddlers should sit low in the raft, hold their paddles outside of the raft, and grip a handhold or grabloop with their inside hand. In self-bailing rafts, paddlers can sit right on the floor with their shins pressed against the thwarts to prevent them from sliding under the thwarts, while paddlers in standard-floor rafts have to sit higher off the floor or risk injury to their lower back.

PART FIVE: Low and High Water Techniques

Low water trips demand a special style of river running—one that won't leave you high and dry on a gravel bar trying to bribe fishermen to help you out of the canyon. Rivers change at low water—the river moves slower and has less push, there are more obstacles to avoid, and there may be many shallow channels to select from. Slow currents decrease the possibility of a wrap, but constant maneuvering might drive you crazy.

There are many ways to make low water rafting enjoyable. Start by picking a river that actually has enough water in it to float your raft, not one that is bone dry. Even if you are forced to line or portage a few rapids, pool-drop rivers are more fun at low water than rivers with continuous gradients since the pools between drops hold water. Low water trips are also easier when you use small, sturdy rafts—ones that fit through tight slots and are easy to pull over shallow bars. Finally, think about your feet. Sooner or later you'll ground out and have to pull your raft free. A solid pair of tennis shoes or hiking boots—even if worn over neoprene socks—will save your feet from the inevitable bashing of slippery rocks and hidden potholes.

When running rivers at low water your primary goal is to spot and stay on the deepest channels. Here are a few hints that will make your task easier:

1. *Look for slick surfaces or long, even waves amongst smaller, choppier waves. These features reveal deeper, more forgiving channels.*
2. *Use the deep eddies behind big boulders to make cross-river maneuvers around shallow shoals. When a shallow bar is impossible to avoid, build up some momentum to help you slide over it and into deeper water.*
3. *Lowside to lessen the amount of floor actually touching the water. The unweighting of one tube might be just enough to get the raft*

through a narrow slot,

4. *Don't be afraid to spin or pivot your raft to and fro. Since the raft will inevitably snag rocks and shallow obstacles, pivots might get your raft off the rock before you have to jump out and pull the raft free.*

BIG WATER: When rivers bloat and swell after heavy rains or big snowmelts, their moods can become downright cantankerous. The current speeds up while eddies disappear, and holes become deeper while waves surge higher. It takes a dedicated crew with level heads (figuratively speaking, of course—my friends have oval heads, just like yours!), and strong river skills to match wits against big, powerful currents.

High water runs take some additional safety precautions. First, every passenger should be a good swimmer and experienced in self-rescue, and there should always be rafts close by to help out in rescue situations. Next, it is safer to run rivers with nearby roads and easy evacuation routes in case the river turns out to be too dangerous. Rafts should be big enough to survive the river's hydraulics—the same raft that works late in the Summer might feel like a helpless cork during the peak of Spring runoff. Rig fliplines onto the D-rings and install hand holds inside the passenger compartment. Additional fliplines can be run under the raft and cinched tightly to the D-rings. Consider using longer, more powerful oars on oar boats, and enough paddlers to power a paddle raft.

On the river, the techniques used during high water are the same as those used during any river trip, only more exact: keep paddles and oars moving to keep your senses well-tuned to the river's moods; keep the bow pointed

High water excitement!

squarely at waves and holes, not necessarily square with the current; keep standard rafts bailed; and portagee or paddle hard through waves and holes to avoid stalling out in their troughs. If you find yourself on a collision course with a mightly hydraulic, maintain your momentum and hit it straight on. Also, don't try to pull off dramatic ferries in front of big haystacks or holes—you're likely to drift broadside into the hydraulics and flip.

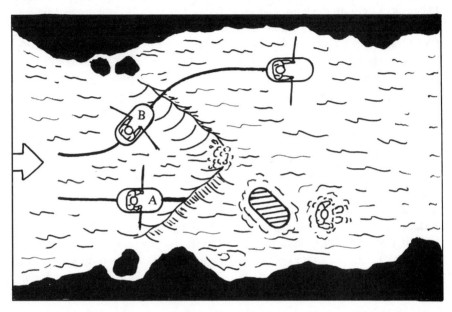

When hitting big waves, drive straight at the wave. Here, raft A had to turn at a slight angle to the current to hit the wave. Raft B stayed parallel with the current and flipped when it hit the wave broadside.

High water rafters need to know when to quit paddling and when to get down and hold on. You are much more likely to spend time highsiding in gaping holes during highwater runs than you are during ordinary trips, so your ability to recognize the need for body weight shifts will really help out.

Another difference between high and low water rivers involves scouting. During high water, rocks and shoreline landmarks might be invisible or moving too fast to be of much help. However, things like individual holes or waves become more significant and can provide just as good of signposts as riverside landmarks.

No matter what you do, *avoid rivers at flood stage!* Flooded rivers are unpredictable and dangerous. Powerful downcurrents can hold you under for dangerous periods of time, and tree-lined banks can pose a serious threat to swimmers attempting to escape the river's grasp. If the river has water in it now, it will have water in it another day. But if you run it now, you might not be around to run it another day!

PART SIX: A Quick Course in Steep Creeking_____

THE ART OF READING AND RUNNING: When I first started rafting I scouted *everything*! I didn't care whether it was Class II or Class IV, I wanted to see exactly what I was getting myself in to, and which way I was going to go once I was in it. Later on, as my river reading skills developed, I spent less time on the bank and more time in my raft. Piloting a raft through Class II and III rapids became as familiar as piloting my feet along rocky forest trails. But Class IV and V drops still kept me ferrying toward the bank.

While shoreline scouting is the best way to go in *any* rapid, it isn't always possible. In fact, on some really high-gradient, steep-walled rivers, bank scouting might be plum out of the question. So, a whole new set of river reading skills has to come into play. Skills which will let you read blind drops without actually seeing what's going on up close.

One of the best examples of reading a blind drop is the perfect horizon (shown in the next diagram). There is nothing above the drop which hints of a safe passage route, but downstream of the drop there is a clear line of standing waves. As you learned in the hydrology chapter, these waves usually show up wherever the current flows clear and unobstructed. So, if you had to place a bet on where to run the drop, the best bet would be to head straight for that part of the drop that leads into the waves.

Check out the diagram below, and try to match it with a drop you've seen before. Still scout whenever possible, but keep these ideas in mind for the time they're really needed.

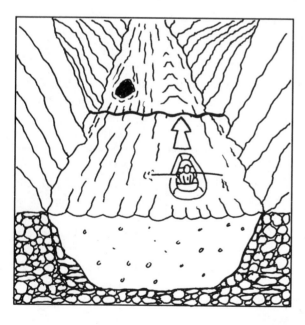

There may be times when you are forced to run a rapid that you can't scout. Look for clues—like a clean set of standing waves—to mark the best point to approach the horizon line, and be prepared to alter your course quickly.

TWO-MAN TECHNIQUES: Rafting with just two paddlers in a small raft—known as paddling *R-2 style* or *R-2'ing*—is an exciting and challenging way to run rivers. The technique excels in small, steep creeks, but works well anywhere when done by skilled paddlers. When R-2'ing, both paddlers must act together to accomplish moves. This can take a sixth sense, a keen knowledge of your partner's paddling traits, or strong communication. On bigger, more powerful runs, a well-honed sense of balance also helps.

Technically, there are three ways to paddle R-2 style: side-by-side in the central compartment; end-to-end in the bow and stern; or diagonally in the bow and stern. However, with the advent of small rafts specially suited to the demands of R-2 paddlers, the diagonal formation (sitting as you would in a tandem canoe) is becoming the most popular seating configuration.

In the first R-2 formation, paddlers sit side-by-side in the central passenger compartment. This puts the pivot point in the center of the raft and makes both turning and power strokes easier.

The second R-2 technique—developed by rafters to meet the special demands of narrow, technical rivers—is sometimes called *sweep boating*. In sweep boating, the paddlers sit in the bow and stern and paddle over the ends of the raft. Specially mounted footcups—mounted sideways in tandem in the bow and stern compartments—keep the paddlers aboard. The sweep boat formation narrows the raft's profile considerably and distributes the paddlers' weight more evenly along the raft's long axis. This lets the raft slip over wet rocks and slink down incredibly steep and narrow rivers.

To maneuver the R-2 from the sweep position, the bow paddler lines the bow up into narrow slots and the stern paddler keeps the boat straight. Once

An R-2 (two man raft) can negotiate tight channels with ease.

in a steep drop, the stern paddler may discover a drawback of sitting in the stern—it is a proverbial catapult. To avoid getting launched forward in steep drops, the stern paddler either has to get low, or the paddlers have to switch to the side-by-side formation.

In the final R-2 configuration, the paddlers sit in the bow and stern but paddle over the side tubes the same way two canoers would paddle a tandem canoe. This method regains the forward and backpaddling power found in the side-by-side configuration and gives paddlers a more stable seating position.

HAVE YOU DRIVEN AN R-2 LATELY?

It's almost inevitable. In our whitewater schools, we'll introduce rafters to every kind of inflatable river boat imaginable: big oar rafts, paddle boats, catarafts, inflatable kayaks... the works. But in the end, the odds-on favorite to win our students' hearts is the R-2. And for good reason. This sporty little raft is as irresistible as an MG convertible, or a Jeep with the top down.

The explanation for the R-2's appeal is more than just high performance. True, the R-2's speed and agility are real crowd-pleasers: it can turn faster, catch tighter eddies, slide through narrower slots, handle lower flows, and even run smaller rivers than its bigger inflatable cousins. But just as appealing are the R-2's easy logistics.

Low-volume R-2's inflate in a snap, are a breeze to rig (no rowing frames to hassle with), and are a pleasure to lift and carry (many only weigh about 50 pounds). For rafters, this means that put-ins and take-outs have never been faster. Even better, instead of having to hunt up an entire paddle crew, you only have to find one partner to run an R-2. The R-2 gives rafters a taste of the simplicity that kayakers and canoeists have always enjoyed.

Another key to the R-2's popularity is its low price. Since these craft require less material, some models retail in the same range as good whitewater canoes and kayaks. That can make the R-2 a perfect first raft for beginners who regularly run smaller rivers, and a good second raft for those who already have a full-sized boat.

Taken together, the R-2's high performance, easy logistics, and low price make an appealing combination. But there's one more thing that probably wins over more hearts than anything else: these boats are just plain fun to drive!

— **Bill Cross, Director**
Running Wild Whitewater School

11

SINGLE TO MULTI-DAY TRIPS:
Carrying Your Toys

Rafts provide the ultimate form of wilderness travel for those who wish to explore the outdoors without sacrificing their dependence on material luxuries. Despite rafting's *float-and-bloat* reputation, the sport maintains its dignity, for even the most brazen, self-reliant river explorers depend on rafts to carry passengers and gear down the world's great rivers.

Knowing how to load and safely take advantage of a raft's cargo-carrying capabilities is a skill which must be learned. In some ways, loading a raft with gear—whether for a one day jaunt or a three-week expedition—is truly an art form. On multi-day trips there may be sleeping bags, tents, kitchen equipment, portable potties, food, water, first aid boxes, and a plethora of other equipment crammed into one boat. Keeping all this gear damage-free and dry takes some preliminary planning and some technical know-how.

PART ONE: What to Carry

Long before you start your raft trip, consider what you'll need to bring. Will you be on the river one day or five days? Will a few pairs of shorts and t-shirts comprise your entire wardrobe or will you need lots of clothing to stay warm? Do you plan to take small, easy to prepare freeze-dried meals, or do you plan to cook exotic riverside feasts? No matter how long a trip you plan, or what type of conditions you expect to encounter, the mere fact that you'll be *rafting* will change the type of food and equipment you'll have to carry.

Let's start with some simple presumptions. They may not always be correct, but they work:

1) *No matter how hard you try, the river is going to work its way into your gear cache, and even the best packed gear is going to get jostled and bounced repeatedly.*

2) *The more gear you carry with you, the heavier and less maneuverable your raft will become.*

By planning for your wardrobe, camp gear, and food needs as if everything might get wet, you'll be able to formulate ways to keep your gear dry and make your trip as comfortable as possible.

PART TWO: *Waterproof Containers*_____

OK. *I lied.* Even though improperly packed gear is destined for a soaking, a number of modern technological wonders have made rafting drier and more enjoyable than ever. You really *can* keep your gear dry on the river.

In days gone by, rafters tried to keep the river out of their gear by packing it into sealed tins or by stuffing everything from river wear to bagels into plastic trash bags, tying the bags closed, and avoiding waves. Nowadays rafters can choose from a long list of items specially designed to keep their gear dry and safe.

Dry bags are durable, specially designed waterproof sacks. When properly sealed shut—usually with foldover or zip-lock closures—dry bags keep their contents totally dry. Most of the time. For items that must stay absolutely dry, seal them in small plastic trash bags *before* inserting them in dry bags. Smaller items can be separated into sandwich and freezer size zip-lock bags before dropping them into dry bags. Not only will this help keep small things dry, it will make finding them in camp much easier.

Dry bags are used to carry clothes, sleeping bags, personal items—anything that needs to stay dry. When properly sealed, they are waterproof.

Some items—such as loaves of bread, patch kits, or camera gear—need to be stored in hard-sided dry boxes so they won't get smashed or eat their way through the soft sides of dry bags. Inexpensive surplus army ammunition cans, called *ammo cans*, perform this function quite well. Durable o-ring seals render them totally waterproof, and the ammo cans are available in a variety of sizes. Their only drawback is their sharp, square corners, which can easily injure passengers in the event of a collision. To avoid injuries, glue neoprene or foam to the outside of ammo cans or invest in high quality plastic waterproof boxes. These *dry boxes* are frequently lighter than ammo cans, are available in a broader range of sizes and shapes, and often have pre-cut foam inserts which can be customized to protect your valuables. The trade-off for all of this, of course, is added cost.

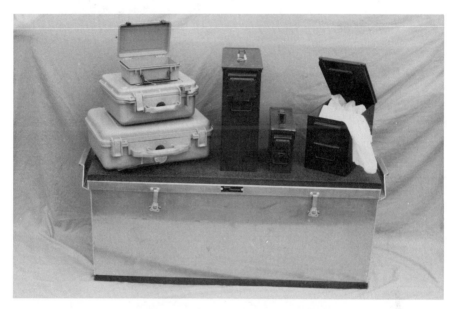

Fragile gear and food—such as cameras or bread—can be stored in waterproof ammo cans and dry boxes. O-ring seals around the inside of the lid keep water out when the box is clamped shut.

PART THREE: *Stowing Gear Safely*

Veteran rafters take great pride in their ability to pack a raft. They can take piles of oddly shaped items and fit them neatly within the raft like so many pieces of a puzzle. Some of you might be wondering why you can't just throw gear aboard and run a mile of rope around it. The answer is *some day you're gonna' flip*. That's right! Sooner or later all the gear standing high *above* the tubes will be hanging far *below* the tubes as your upside-down raft floats downriver. And, the longer it hangs there the more likely you are to lose it. So, rig the raft as if you're actually going to flip, and keep in mind some standard principles:

1. *Keep the raft's center of gravity low: lash all gear down with a low profile, and keep heavier items lower in the raft.*
2. *Keep the raft balanced: store heavier gear toward the center of the raft with lighter items toward the ends.*
3. *Leave open spaces: leave room for passengers' legs and room to bail. If you are rowing, make sure you have room to ship your oars and to lean backward during your strokes.*
4. *Protect your gear and your raft: rather than laying gear directly on the floor—which can result in broken and torn equipment—use a suspended cargo platform to support everything. Also, keep hard-sided and sharp-cornered items away from the flight paths of bouncing passengers, tubes, and floors. These can do a lot of damage when ricocheting through wild rapids! (If you are packing light gear into a self-bailer, you may be able to load some gear directly onto the floor.)*
5. *Organize your gear for efficiency: put commonly used items toward the top of the pile, and rarely used items toward the bottom. Label dry bags and containers with duct tape and waterproof magic markers to remind you where everything is.*
6. *Lash everything down tightly: make sure every item is securely fastened to the raft, whether encased in cargo nets, tarps, or merely tied down with ropes or straps. Buckled webbing works great for this purpose since it is available in many lengths, and can be cinched tight without having to learn how to tie special knots. Use the best anchor points available—on a self-bailing raft, gear can be strapped to D-rings, floor drain holes, or even to foot cups, while on standard rafts the D-rings and thwarts provide the main anchor points. On any oarboat, the rowing frame provides a great anchor for lashing gear down.*
7. *Don't overload your raft! If you don't really need an item, consider leaving it at home.*

12

RIVER CAMPING AND COOKERY:
Life at the Riverside Inn

Camping and rafting make great travel companions. In fact some of my less adventurous friends have gone so far as to say that the river is little more than a hassle between campsites—a liquid highway to be travelled before the next park. Though few rafters might agree that river running is a hassle, many rafters would agree that camping is a ton of fun.

Riverside camping has a special air about it. There are no RV's parked in the next space, no pop machines or laundromats nearby, and, if you're lucky, no humans for miles around. Everything that's in camp was put there by Mother Nature or floated there in your raft. But that doesn't mean that river camping demands a Spartan existence.

Rafts can carry lounge chairs, lanterns, thick ground pads, spacious tents, and much, much more. River camping can be as simple an experience as dropping your sleeping bag out under the stars, or as luxurious as playing guitars and drinking exotic concoctions whipped up in battery powered blenders. The choice is yours.

PART ONE: Clothing and Camping Equipment

In the equipment chapter, you learned a lot about river wear... dry suits, wet suits, paddle jackets, booties. While that stuff works wonders on the river, there is nothing so delightful as slipping into warm, dry clothes at the end of the day.

On overnight camping trips, just keeping items like clothing, tents, and sleeping bags totally dry can be a challenge. So, water absorbent items like cotton shirts, canvas tents, and down sleeping bags become obvious invitations for long, damp nights in camp. Polyester and nylon fleece clothing works as well in camp as it does under your dry suit—it dries quickly and will keep you warm even when wet. Synthetic sleeping bags—filled with Hollofill, Quallofill, Polargaurd, or other space age insulators—also work well even when damp.

Whatever you decide to take on your trip, keep in mind that you'll need to pack clothes and sleeping bags into dry bags. Don't carry personal items too large to stuff into a dry bag, and don't show up at the put-in with so much gear that you'll have to compromise your comfort by leaving some at home.

PART TWO: Site Selection

Some canyons offer a wide variety of terrain and campsites, while others contain few if any hospitable camping niches. It is nice to find out about campsites before undertaking a raft trip. Peruse the local guidebooks for camping opportunities, or ask some friends who have run the river what to expect. If the river is unexplored, check topographic maps for broad valleys that may offer level, comfortable sites. There may even be a government agency which pre-assigns designated campsites to river travellers. If you are able to find out about campsites ahead of time, try to preselect sites that fit your travel plans. If the trip is two days long, pick a site mid-way so that both river days are enjoyable.

Whether or not you've learned about campsites before leaving the put-in, make sure that you're looking for a feasible site in daylight. There is nothing more petrifying, disheartening, or dangerous than travelling downriver after dusk! If the riverbank offers many ideal settings, you're in luck. You can choose campsites that will be sunny early in the morning or late in the day; campsites that slope gently into the water, or involve a short hike away from the river; and campsites which offer shade or unobstructed vistas.

One thing you certainly don't want is a riverside campsite that might disappear if the river comes up! If there is any chance that the river will rise—whether from heavy runoff or dam releases—pick a site high above the

Riverside camping can be as luxurious as shown here, or as simple as some backpacking trips. (Photo by Doc Loomis)

waterline that offers easy escape, even in the dark of night. Unload small rafts in the evening and carry the gear and rafts up onto the shore. Tie the rafts off securely to solid anchors such as large trees or boulders and leave some slack in the line just in case the river gets too high. If you've prepared for a rising river, you'll only need to check your raft and gear occasionally as the river rises through the night. And even if the river comes up a few feet, you can spend the remainder of the night resting peacefully as the river roars many yards away.

There's one other thing to think about when you make camp for the evening: *wind*. If you've spread your paddle jackets, dry suits, t-shirts, and hats all over the rocks so that they can dry out, they might not be where you left them come morning. Canyons have a way of focusing and amplifying local air currents, especially late in the afternoon. Make sure you secure all of your belongings each time you *make* camp so that you'll still have them each time you *break* camp.

THE ENVIRONMENT: Conscientious rafters strive to minimize their impact on the riparian environment. Thick grassy banks, or beaches lined with delicate shrubs, are especially susceptible to human harm. On the other hand, broad sandy beaches and pebble strewn bars can camouflage and erase your presence soon after your group leaves. Pick a site that has been used many times before or one that won't record your presence, and treat it with respect.

One trick to preserving the habitat is to use nothing but freestanding gear. Utilize tents that don't have to be staked out, and kitchen tables that can be set up without having to rely on rocks or logs.

PART THREE: Fires

One of the great joys of camping is sitting around the campfire. Campfires are soothing, enchanting, hypnotic. They also provide a valuable source of heat on cold trips, and can be used for cooking if necessary. Still, campfires can leave unsightly scars on the landscape. In today's world, it is probably best to save the campfire for designated campgrounds, to use gas powered stoves for cooking, and to savor the warmth of friendship and the great outdoors rather than relying on a fire for that warmth.

If you must have a fire, you can minimize its effect on the surrounding ground by using a fire pan. The fire pan is a large metal pan with high sides specially designed to accommodate small logs or charcoal briquets. Place the pan on the shoreline below the high water mark so that burn marks from stray coals will disappear with the next freshet. Fill the bottom of the fire pan with a thin layer of dirt or sand before adding firewood to avoid burning through the pan, and set the pan on rocks to avoid scorching the ground. You are now ready to enjoy a great fire.

Camping gear can lessen your impact on the environment. Shown here are a roll-up table, portable chairs, a firepan (frees you from building a fire on the ground), briquet starter, and dutch ovens. Many rafters only use gas powered stoves since any kind of campfire can break free.

Check the pan in the morning to make sure that the coals have totally cooled. Next, sprinkle them with water and shovel them into an ammo can so they can be packed out. The ashes can now be used at the next camp to line the bottom of the pan, and each time the ashes are re-burned they shrink. Eventually the ashes will be little more than light dust, making packing them out with you easier.

Fires built without pans are more difficult to clean up, and it takes a little more forethought to hide their marks. First, locate the fire much as you would one in a fire pan—below the highwater mark. Next, use rocks that will be easy to toss into the river channel the next morning. Don't build the fire near immovable boulders or trees that will bear blackened scars for many years to come. Finally, build the smallest fire practicable. That way you won't have half-burnt logs laying around camp the next day. When the morning comes, douse the ashes with water and dismantle the site. Spend some extra time restoring the ground to its natural condition... or better.

THE RIVER SAUNA: If I haven't talked you *out* of building a great fire, I might as well talk you *into* building a river sauna. A river sauna is just as it sounds... a sauna built along the river. If that doesn't conjure any mental images, think of it as a sweat hut. A steamy teepee. These ingenious contraptions spell instant relief for weary rafters, and make a memorable impression on anyone who has ever tried one.

The river sauna starts with a big waterproof tarp and some imagination. Pick a site near the river, use paddles, tables, or whatever is available, to build a small, tent-like structure with the tarp. The structure should be fully enclosed, with a sealable flap entrance, and barely big enough to fit you and your friends inside. Since you are going to be trapping steam and warmth inside this makeshift hut, the tighter and smaller it is, the better it will work.

Now, how do you add steam to the sauna? Well, that brings you back to the fire. Put a dozen or so clean, round, brick-sized rocks in the fire when you first start building it. As the fire burns, these rocks will heat up and begin glowing. Once they're red hot, take them out of the fire with a shovel or some sturdy sticks and carry them over to the sauna. Put the rocks in a sandy hole, a big steel pot, or a steel can in the middle of the sauna, and keep a pot of cool water nearby. To get the steam going, just dab water on the rocks. In seconds your claustrophobic hut will transform into a dreamy chamber of soothing vapors.

To get the most out of your sauna experience keep a few more things in mind. Keep the tarp sealed shut unless you're entering or exiting the sauna, getting short of breath, or getting too hot. Each time you open the tarp, all the steam escapes and you have to start over again. Pick sauna sites with clear paths to the river. (The river gives overheated steambathers a chance to cool down.) Next, choose your rocks carefully. Round igneous rocks without cracks give off a lot of heat and aren't prone to cracking. Moist, misshapen rocks can explode violently. If you can't tell your igneous rocks from your sedimentary stones, your best bet is to pick round rocks many feet above the highwater mark. Also, try mixing up the size of the rocks. Smaller rocks give off more heat, but big rocks stay warm longer. Finally, keep the rocks clean. There's nothing worse than mixing noxious smoke with steam when your lungs are wide open.

PART FOUR: Human Waste

Sooner or later you're going to have to answer the call. So, what are you going to do? I've admittedly dashed behind a thousand trees in my day, but I don't profess it to be the best way to do things. With ever increasing numbers of river runners flocking into the world's great canyons, your business might just make things a little unpleasant for somebody else.

In earlier days, environmentally conscious rafters carried an eighteen-inch ammo can (known as a *rocket box*) for bathroom purposes. The can was lined with a new plastic bag each night, and provided a convenient—though not exactly comfortable—place to deposit human waste. In fact, one of the rocket box's discomforting propensities was to leave a pair of reddened dents in your cheeks by the time you were done, well, ...you know. And it was for that reason that these primitive toilets were dubbed *groovers*.

Today, federal law prohibits landfills from accepting human waste in plastic bags. Since you should still carry a portable latrine in order to carry all human waste out of the canyon, it will take a little forethought to bring your wilderness practices into compliance with the law. Fortunately, there are a few alternatives from which rafters can choose.

One alternative is to continue to use your ammo can, sans the plastic bag. Some federally controlled rivers now have *scat machines* (high tech ammo can dishwashers) that are specially designed to do your dirty work. For those of you who still insist on plastic bags, there are reusable plastic bags which can be taken to RV dumps when the trip is through. (Fittings for RV hoses make cleaning of these bags easy.) Finally, rafters can use chemical holding tanks which are also designed to be emptied at RV dumps. The chemical holding tanks are the easiest to use, but are also the bulkiest and most costly.

To find out what *is* permissible on the river you're going to raft, contact the nearest federal agency. If one of the described latrines are required, check out the appendix and contact one of the portable toilet manufacturers about their products.

Now, getting back to our primeval heritage... if neither a latrine or a legal dump station is available, dig a single hole for your group six to eight inches deep at least 100 feet from the river and dispose of all human waste there.

HUMAN WASTE

Here are some tips from the National Forest Service to make human waste management a bit easier:

1. Separate daily sewage into several smaller containers to make it more manageable rather than using a single, sealed container.

2. Sand and paint the inside of ammo cans to make emptying and washing easier.

3. Use a washable liner in the ammo can or bucket.

4. Use non-formaldahyde odor killers like Pine-Sol, dry Clorox, or kitty litter to reduce odors.

PART FIVE: Cookery

Rafting—like any other form of outdoor recreation—burns calories. And if you're anything like me, much of your time will be spent figuring out how to restore those calories while keeping your taste buds amused. After a long day on the river, a tasty meal provides a soothing transition into the lazy hours after dusk, while bountiful lunch spreads will give you all the energy you need to get you down the river.

Riverside meals can be simple or elaborate, depending on your budget, available kitchen paraphenalia, carrying space, and gastronomic preferences. They can be simple one pot meals, cheese and salami, or extravagant banquets. In reality, these meals are only limited by your culinary creativity.

MENU: Menu planning begins long before you make your first lunch stop or reach your first night's camp. In fact, it starts before you get to the local supermarket. Nevertheless, planning your river menu is only slightly different than planning your menu at home. You are only limited by carrying space, refrigeration, and cooking utensils. Select a menu that will make everyone happy, and get everyone involved in selecting meals, either by having them list items they do and don't like, or by having people rotate menu responsibilities for each day they're on the river.

Try to plan meals around the length of the trip, your level of patience, and the amount of cookware available. On lengthy trips, select durable, long lasting foods that won't spoil quickly. Most perishables are bulky and only last a few days in a cooler, while dehydrated food items save weight and last the longest.

If you are a patient cook, and have lots of kitchen gear, you can make some pretty fancy entrees. But if you'd rather relax and keep things simple, consider easier meals like one pot stews, pasta dishes, and mexican dinners. Also consider the season and weather. Do you *really* want to stand outside slow simmering that special stew in the middle of a rainstorm?

PACKING YOUR FOOD: Food storage is dependent on the length of your trip, the number of people on your trip, and the amount of food you're carrying. On a short one-day jaunt, with no more than a handfull of rafters, you may be able to get by with string cheese, apples, and high energy bars packed into a small dry bag. More hearty eaters may pack along a cooler—stored either in a rowing frame or cooler frame—to carry cold beverages, fresh meats, and more. On multi-day journeys, even the chilly compartment of a cooler might not be enough to keep food fresh and edible. In this case, some creative menu planning and packing becomes necessary.

River runners tend to be an inventive and resourceful lot when it comes to packing foods. The tricks of the trade are many. Since eggs break easily, they can be broken ahead of time and stored in plastic bottles, ready for use in your morning omelette. Durable fruits and vegetables—such as potatoes, apples, watermelon and cucumbers—can be stored in tough bags and are easier to keep fresh and undamaged than other types of produce. Even canned meats, powdered milk, and freeze-dried items can be used to replace fresh goods—they'll last longer, and they come in their own protective containers.

COOLERS: Ice chests are the most valuable tool for rafters in need of portable refrigeration. Packed generously with ice, a sealed cooler can keep perishables fresh for days.

To maximize your cooler's efficiency, use it wisely. Since the cooler warms quickly when opened, try to keep the lid shut at all times when it is not being used. By separating your meals ahead of time, designating certain coolers for use early or late in the trip, you can avoid opening and closing coolers at every food stop. (Put a piece of duct tape on top of the cooler listing its contents or which day it is to be used.)

Pre-freeze your meats and use block ice if it is available. To avoid a big pool in the bottom of the cooler, drain the meltoff from the ice blocks daily or use frozen plastic milk jugs full of water—as the water melts inside the jugs it provides a fresh source of drinking water instead of just another mess. On really long journeys, consider packing the cooler with dry ice. The dry ice is much colder than regular ice, and, if you pack every spare inch of the cooler with newspaper and keep it tightly sealed, the dry ice will last for days. Another trick to keep your cooler cool is to cover it with wet rags or other gear to shield it from the sun's warming rays.

One common misconception is that coolers are waterproof. Evenly tightly strapped coolers can let water in if the raft flips or gets stuck in big hydraulics. Consider tying the cooler shut with bicycle inner tubes or strong bungee cords, and seal the food inside the cooler in individual plastic bags.

Coolers are great for carrying perishables, and *can* carry everything if there isn't much food to be hauled downriver. But sometimes food has to be divvied out among other containers—dry bags, ammo cans, and waterproof boxes. Some items—like canned beverages—don't even need to be stored in containers. They can be packed neatly away just like any other item in the raft.

SORTING: On trips longer than a couple of days, labelling and sorting meals becomes more important, especially if there is more food than can be packed into the available cooler space. In this case, the coolers only carry perishables, while goods with long shelf lives get divvied out among dry bags, ammo cans, and waterproof boxes. The problem with this is that food-finding gets confusing... fast!

Rather than guessing where your food is before every meal, or flipping open every lid in search of one or two items, carefully divide your food between containers and label them ahead of time. One handy trick is to put all parts of one meal in one big tupperware container or plastic pickle barrel, and to label the container with a waterproof pen, or put all of one type of food (e.g., cereals, rice, pasta, or oatmeal) in one container and label it accordingly.

THE KITCHEN: Just about any manually powered tool you have in your home kitchen will work in your riverside kitchen. In fact, the kitchen list included in the appendix is little different than what you'd expect to see in your own cupboards and drawers. Stoves are different than those you find at home. There are many wonderful camping stoves on the market today, with

194

The fully equipped river kitchen. (Photo by Doc Loomis)

stoves powered by white gas, propane, and butane leading the market. Though all of these fuel burning stoves work fine, some rivers restrict the type of fuel rafters can use in camp. So, it might be helpful to find out about local regulations well in advance. To make camp cooking even easier, there are things like roll-up kitchen tables and aluminum kitchen boxes designed especially for rafters.

Once in camp, set up the kitchen away from the gear pile. That way, people won't constantly pester the cook and make off with important ingredients before they hit the pan.

DUTCH OVENS: One remarkable cooking tool is the *dutch oven*, or the *DO*. The dutch oven is a cast iron or aluminum pan and lid that dates back to America's colonial days. It was first invented by Paul Revere and manufactured in the United States. Later, when Holland fur traders acquired a lot of these ovens to use in trading with Indians, this American invention got a *Dutch* name.

Dutch ovens are designed to absorb and spread heat evenly. (Because of this, some purists shun the aluminum ovens since they heat and cool faster and don't disperse heat as well. Non-purists don't worry about this. They applaud the aluminum oven's lighter weight, and avoid heat fluctuations by shielding the oven from the wind.) A typical 10" diameter oven holds about 4.5 quarts, while a 12" oven holds 7 quarts. Almost all ovens have short legs to raise them above the ground, and a raised lip around the lid to hold coals. They work by placing charcoal briquets, or coals from the fire, evenly along the top of the lid and below the pan, creating a hot cooking environment inside.

Before you use an iron DO, you must season it by melting a tablespoon of shortening inside the pan. (Aluminum DO's don't require seasoning.) Remove the DO from the heat after the shortening liquifies and rub it into the pan and lid until it disappears, leaving just a shiny, slick surface. Keep doing it until it will take no more, then wipe clean. Another method is to wipe the inner surfaces with cooking oil and bake the DO in your home oven for 20 minutes. (If you ever have to re-season the DO, just scrape off any rust with steel wool and repeat the seasoning process. Clean the DO with mild soap and water only.)

Once you're ready to cook with your DO, place your food inside (you can cook anything, from stews to fresh-baked brownies, pan pizzas to pound cake) and close the lid. Place the DO over a firepan to avoid scarring the ground and line coals along the lid near its edge. Coals that go beneath the DO should be laid about one inch from the edge.

The number of coals you use depends on what you're cooking. A ten or twelve inch oven will hit about 375 degrees with about 25 briquets. If you're making a stew, divide those briquets evenly among the top and bottom of the oven. But if using the DO to bake something, put about 3/4 of the briquets on top and 1/4 on bottom. It's always better to underestimate the number of coals that go beneath the pan since the lower coals can quickly overheat the oven.

Once you start cooking, periodically turn the lid a quarter-turn, but avoid lifting it. Opening the oven will let all the heat out and make cooking much more difficult. Even without lifting the lid, experienced dutch oven connoisseurs can tell when their meals are done just by the smell alone.

DISHWASHING: Rancid dishes—much like those that are sitting in my kitchen sink right now—are a sure invitation for a host of gastric maladies. It's far better to clean your dishes daily than to risk losing your appetite over a stomach bug.

One of the time tested ways to clean dishes is what I call the *three bucket technique*. Starting with three buckets or large pots, pour pre-boiled water into each bucket. (Boiling the water ahead of time decreases the risk of contamination.) Put some biodegradable soap in bucket #1, pure water in bucket #2, and two teaspoons of chlorine bleach in bucket #3. Now, start out by scrubbing your dishes in the first bucket, rinse them off in the second bucket, and disinfect them by dousing them in the third bucket. To keep your hands happy and soft, you may want to wear some rubber gloves. Also, replace heavily soiled water with fresh water. When you're all done, strain the solid waste from the buckets and pack it out of camp in an ammo can. The residual water should be dumped in a small hole, deep enough that animals won't try to dig it up, and far away from the river.

WATER: It is disheartening to think that almost every raftable river poses a potential risk to humans if used for drinking water. Even the clearest streams can carry industrial pollutants, dangerous bacteria, and a nasty little bugger called *Giardia lamblia*. Nonetheless, it is important to maintain your level of hydration by drinking enough water every day. So, fresh, safe drinking water demands some special attention. Especially on long rafting trips.

The most obvious way to guarantee fresh drinking water is to carry your own supply. Large two to five-gallon jugs can be strapped onto your raft, and may carry enough water to last a couple of days if used sparingly. If you're going to be on the river longer than that, or if there will be many people on the trip, one of the methods of producing your own safe, potable water will have to be used.

There are three common ways to treat water for most living organisms. The first way to kill living organisms is to boil the water for 10 to 20 minutes. (For every 1,000 feet you gain above sea level, add one minute of boiling time.) The next method is to use chemical purifiers such as halizone, iodine or bleach. Halizone and iodine tablets come with instructions for proper dosages. However, if you're using tincture of iodine (2%), use 5 drops per quart of water and let it sit 30 minutes. (Double the time if the water is cold, and double the dosage if the water is cloudy.) Bleach is generally added to water at the rate of eight drops per gallon, and takes about 30 minutes to kill living organisms. None of the chemical treatments are foolproof, and each requires some patience and caution. Remember that it takes a little bit of time to kill the organisms, and that just one drop of untreated water can spoil the whole batch.

The third water treatment method—filtration—is the only one which can remove pesticides, solvents and other artificial contaminants as well as living organisms. Portable filtration units (water filters) actually strain water through microscopic pores in the unit's filter element, and eject potable water out the tail end of the system. Rafters should carry large enough water filters to supply adequate water for everyone on the trip, and should carry replacement filter elements in case one clogs or breaks.

GARBAGE: Low impact camping means carrying everything out of camp that wasn't there when you arrived. *Everything!* Garbage can be carried out in plastic buckets with air tight lids, in large ammo cans, in onion or potato sacks, or in plastic bags stuffed into dry bags. Even empty coolers can be used to haul garbage. Don't just strap trash bags to the raft. They're likely to burst open on the river and negate all your finest environmental intentions.

13

ONE STEP FURTHER:
Rafting Alternatives

Adventurous rafters can expand their whitewater horizons far beyond the limitations imposed by everyday river running. For those willing to accept new challenges, there awaits new rewards. In this chapter you will learn three new ways to look at rivers. First, you will learn the basics of planning and carrying out exploratory trips. Next, you can read about the growing sport of raft racing. Finally, there is a whole section on playboating—an exciting endeavor that pits your skills and wit against the river's most exciting hydraulics.

PART ONE: River Exploration

Exploring an unnavigated river can be an extraordinary experience. Some rafters feel an irresistable draw to these types of trips, much the same as some travellers prefer forgotten backroads over popular highways. In many ways, exploratory descents mark the apex of all whitewater endeavors. Such trips provide the ultimate test of rafters' skills, judgment, and river prowess since many aspects of these adventures start as unknowns. First descents can combine the reverence of traversing untouched wilderness with the personal challenge of negotiating unnavigated canyons.

THE RESEARCH PHASE: Few exploratory descents—successful ones at least—take place without an enormous amount of preparation. In fact, pre-trip planning can take longer than the trip itself, beginning weeks, months, or even years ahead of time. By learning ahead of time everything there is to know about the river and surrounding terrain, many of the risks inherent in wilderness exploration, or running untested rapids, can be minimized.

Any exploratory descent should begin with a survey of all available information resources. Start with a copy of the region's best guidebooks, review paddling magazines, paddling newsletters, and call around to local whitewater clubs. It is quite possible that your exploratory trip is really a second, third, or twentieth descent! Next, check out topographic maps. For North American paddlers, the United States or Canadian Geological Surveys maintain detailed topographic maps covering any river you can find, and these maps are a rafter's single most valuable resource.

When purchasing topographic maps, select the smallest scale possible. Large area maps (with a scale of 1:100,000 or 1:250,000) usually offer too little detail to help much at all. However, smaller-scaled maps—particularly the 1:24,000 or 7.5" maps—are quite useful. Many of these maps have contour intervals of 20 to 40 feet, which can at least forewarn of the presence of large waterfalls.

Begin reading the map by looking at the width of the blue line denoting the river. Is it a *thick* blue line, indicative of a large volume river, or is it a *narrow* line, indicating a small stream? Next, note the contour intervals (change in altitude between lines) and the mileage scale. Look at the section of river you wish to explore and break it down into half-mile or one mile sections. Now, by counting the number of times the contour lines cross the river in a one mile section, and then multiplying by the contour interval, you can get the average gradient in feet per mile. (See the next diagram.)

Knowing how to interpret gradient is important. Many popular streams drop 10 to 100 feet per mile. More extreme whitewater rivers drop 100 to 200 feet per mile. And on rare occasions, rafters can descend rivers with gradients exceeding 200 feet per mile. Always keep in mind that even low gradient rivers might descend very gradually, then drop many feet all at once over unrunnable falls!

One way to figure out whether your venture is worth the risk is to compare the river's gradient to the canyon's surrounding terrain. If the land adjacent to the river shows closely spaced contour lines, the river is in a canyon. This can be a genuine hazard if there are waterfalls, severe whitewater, or unrunnable rapids. A narrow canyon with a steep gradient is

Topographic maps reveal a lot about a river. This map has a contour interval of 40 feet (elevation rises or falls 40 feet between contour lines) and a scale of one inch per mile. By counting the number of times the contour lines cross the river per mile, you can see that this river drops 80 to 120 feet per mile. At the top of the diagram, broadly spaced contours reveal a valley (A). There is also a tributary that drops over a waterfall (B) one mile from its confluence with the main river (C). The combination of steep gradient and towering cliffs at the bottom of the map (D) spell danger for river travellers.

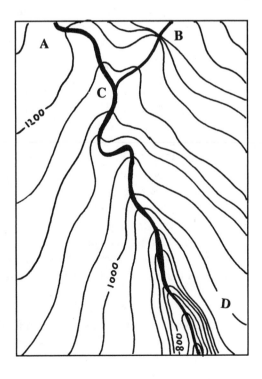

not the place to be unless you've scouted everything out from the air or land ahead of time! However, put that same steep river on a map showing widely spaced contour lines traversing the adjacent land and it may be possible to portage anything.

While looking at your map, look for obvious escape routes in the form of broad contour lines departing the river's edge. Note obvious landmarks such as giant peaks, cliffs, or major tributaries that will be visible from the river. These will let you monitor your progress. Also figure out the total mileage between put-ins and take-outs to get a rough estimate of your expected river time.

Topographic maps are your guidebook during exploratory descents, so take good care of them. Keep them securely fastened and stored in waterproof containers when not in use, and keep a duplicate set on another raft in case one set of maps gets lost or destroyed.

Now that you have an imaginary picture of the river, it's time to gather more information. If you can, go to the river and scout as much of it as you can see. Many first descents started with long, arduous hikes along canyon rims to view the rapids below, or with airplane and helicopter flights over the river to view hidden corridors. Talk to the locals—fishermen, hunters, and hikers—and glean whatever information they're willing to share with you. Also check with local paddling clubs to see if someone else has done some of your homework for you.

The final research stage is to obtain information on water levels. While the mental picture imparted by that thick blue line might be accurate, a gauge will tell you a lot more. Check with the local Geological Survey office, weather services, or water districts to see if the river has a gauge, then monitor the river level periodically. The Geological Survey can also provide historical watershed and drainage area information and flow data. When combined with information on local weather patterns, and a Water Supply Outlook (available from the USGS), this information gives a strong indication of the river's reaction to things like rain and snowmelt.

SELECTING THE CREW: In North America almost anything that *could* be rafted *has* been rafted. Accordingly, it is usually the most difficult and challenging rivers that remain unexplored. To meet that challenge it takes a team of rafters who are compatible in both their personalities and tenacity.

When putting together an exploratory team, it takes much more than a positive mental attitude to confront and survive unknown dilemmas. Each team member should be comfortable with treacherous whitewater, and they should bring to the team a solid set of wilderness skills and useful technical abilities. By including rafters with medical expertise, rock climbing skills, or intimate knowledge of the adjacent terrain, the team will have a broad range of useful skills, and will be more prepared to handle difficult situations.

EQUIPMENT AND SUPPLIES: Since you'll be traversing unknown canyons, portaging with greater frequency, and relying much more on your equipment then ever before, it is imperative that your equipment be of top quality and in excellent shape. Take some time before the trip to double check your raft. Pump it up tightly and check for leaks. Repair any loose seams and seal any noticeable abrasions. Examine oars, frames, paddles, and any other gear you plan to bring, for flaws. If an irreparable defect shows up, don't chance bringing the item along!

The most important part of assembling the equipment for the trip is trimming weight. It is far easier to portage a light raft than one fully loaded with expendable luxuries. That *doesn't* mean that you shouldn't bring all of the gear that is—or may be—*necessary*! You will be relying more on your gear now than ever before, so bring everything that is essential to the success of your trip. However, leave the unnecessary frills at home. Try trimming extra clothing by using layers of polypropylene clothing and waterproof outershells. Instead of carrying many tents, bring a large tarp and ground pads. And when planning the menu, think more like a backpacker. Bring freeze-dried food, one burner stoves, and single pots rather than large stoves and fresh foods.

SAFETY: One place you don't want to shave weight is in your safety gear selection. Bring extra safety gear (climbing ropes, carabiners, throw bags, etc.) in case an emergency arises. Also carry a fully equipped expedition first aid kit along with a detailed medical handbook. The more remote and dangerous the trip, the more you should consider carrying a radio and learning how to use it. Also, notify rangers, family and friends of your itinerary before you leave, including your expected time of return. That way, if something does go wrong, a search party can be sent to find and help you.

GETTING TO THE RIVER: Many first descents and exploratory trips have been overlooked simply due to the difficulty of access to put-ins or take-outs. If you're willing to carry your gear long distances over adverse terrain, you may just find a whitewater paradise awaiting at the end of the trail.

There are many ways to carry rafts to the river. In self-bailing rafts with laced-in floors, remove the floor and divide the load between two or three team members. One strong person can carry a floor or set of tubes many miles draped over his shoulders! Another way to carry the raft is to use the *burrito roll* (shown on the next page). Start the burrito roll by laying on oar (or four or more long paddles) lengthwise down the center of the raft. Roll the raft around the oar lengthwise as tight as possible and strap the roll closed. This will leave a long, thin bundle that can be carried on the shoulders of two or three rafters.

Keep in mind that additional gear—sleeping bags, river wear, safety gear and food—has to be carried to the river. If the hike down to the put-in is only a mile or two long, consider spending one day hiking back and forth to transport everything to the river. On the other hand, if you only have time to make one hike, load your gear into backpack-style drybags. They carry a heavy load and won't interfere with carrying the raft on your shoulders.

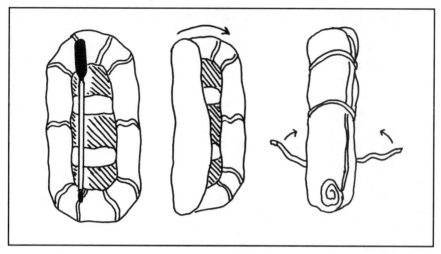

The burrito roll: place on oar or some paddles lengthwise in the deflated raft; roll the raft tightly around the oar; keep the bundle tightly rolled with three or four straps. The burrito roll can be carried on the rafters' shoulders.

Finally, for those of you who have too much gear or a little extra money, your hike to the river can be made easier by loading rafts on wheeled deer carts, pack animals, or even helicopters.

RUNNING THE RIVER: Whenever you're in a new canyon or on an unknown section of river, run more conservatively than you would otherwise. Make sure your gear is loaded down with bombproof straps or knots. Take a moment to ask yourself "what if..." before running blindly around a bend or over a horizon line. On remote rivers, a mistake could be costly, and a serious injury could go untreated for days. Don't let paranoia overcome you, but take a slight step back from your normal river bravado. By the time you reach civilization, the descent will take on heroic proportions anyway.

PART TWO: Racing

Raft racing is a dynamic and exciting sport for competitors and spectators alike. From downriver to slalom races, and from rescue competitions to river orienteering events, the thrill of running rivers is magnified when every move becomes critical. In the desire to go fast and minimize errors, racers become totally focused. All the skills learned before—from raft control to route finding—come to a head. Sound skills shine, while deficiencies become blaringly apparent.

It is in this process that another aspect of raft racing appears: rafters who

Slalom events really test your paddling skills! (Photo by Doc Loomis)

make good racers make good river runners! The same precision that goes into running gates carries into running rapids, and, despite philosophical differences as to what river running is all about, racing and recreational rafting accent each other magnificently.

TYPES OF RACES: Raft races have varied over the years as much as the rivers which have hosted them. Today, most races involve one or more of these events: *slalom, giant slalom,* and *downriver races.* Some international rafting competitions add rescue, running, and orienteering events, but these rarely show up in North American races.

Slalom competitions are the most dynamic and fascinating of the rafting events. Based on standardized canoeing and kayaking events, raft slaloms entail maneuvering rafts through a series of gates while racing against the clock. Slalom racers balance speed with perfect technique since each tapped pole or missed gate adds significantly to the rafters' final time.

In regular slalom competitions, there may be as many as 21 gates set up over a short section of river. Once in the gates, the action is fast and furious. Rather than progressing downstream at tremendous speed, rafts have to maneuver back and forth from gate to gate, sometimes turning into eddies to drive through upstream gates. Giant slaloms—especially those held during the same competition as the slalom events—have fewer gates, slightly longer runs, and demand less drastic moves than in slalom events. While precision maneuvering remains critical in the giant slalom, raw speed becomes a bigger factor in the final outcome.

Downriver races—also know as *wildwater races*—are the purest forms of raft racing. They are the sprints and marathons of the whitewater world, with no poles, gate judges, or penalties. They are purely races against the clock, where the fastest overall time wins. It takes both physical conditioning and solid river reading skills to compete effectively in the downriver race. The idea is to maintain fast, powerful strokes throughout the race, while sticking to the fastest currents.

Rescue events are the most exciting to watch, and pour gallons of adrenaline into the hearts and veins of the participants. In a sample rescue event—roughly patterned from the rescue event used in the 1991 Costa Rica Rally—there are four gates, four raft paddlers, and one designated swimmer. The paddlers sit in the raft at the starting line while the designated swimmer stands on the opposite bank. At the sound of "go!" the raft team paddles across the river and through gate #1. The swimmer then dives into the river and climbs aboard the raft before it enters gate #2. Before negotiating gate #3, the paddlers must exit and flip the raft, then negotiate gate #3 upside down. Between gates #3 and #4, the team rights the raft, climbs aboard, and paddles through gate #4. The clock finally stops when all of the paddlers reach a designated point along the bank.

RACING TIPS: A whole book could be written on raft racing, including chapters on technique, physical preparation, and equipment. But, in many ways, racing merely builds upon the techniques, fitness, and equipment one already possesses. The key to improving your racing results is to hone these techniques, strive to build the muscles and wind for competition, and to choose the fastest rafts available.

Before any race begins, spend enough time to learn all the rules and study the course. If you're on a paddle team, discuss and analyze the course together so that the moves can be executed without waiting for a paddle command. Look for the strongest currents, currents that will assist you with turns, and for the fastest route from gate to gate. Finally, form an indelible mental image of the course so that you can imagine every stroke ahead of time.

DURING THE RACE: Since the racer's goal is to make the run as fast and penalty-free as possible, it can be difficult to relax at the starting line. Before the starter says *go*, set your oar or paddle in the catch position so that you can make the first stroke immediately. Keep your grip relaxed so that you don't waste any energy, and keep a vision of the course in your head.

Paddling and rowing during a race is no different than at any other time. However, paddlers should concentrate on executing short, fast, and powerful strokes, and should keep their heads up to widen their field of vision. Since the tail end of the forward stroke delivers little energy to the raft, chop it off and begin each stroke's recovery phase sooner than usual. Rowers should strive for fast stroke rates and smooth oar motions. To save energy, use the large, strong muscles of the back and legs, don't lift the oars too high out of the water after each stroke, and let only the blade dip beneath the surface during the stroke.

In slalom events, the fastest way to run the course is to keep the raft running *smoothly* from gate to gate. This means avoiding momentum-draining corrective strokes and choppy turns, and running minimally offset gates with subtle drawstrokes or sweepstrokes to shift the raft's position. When making turns, turn *above* or *in* the gates so that you don't have to struggle to change the raft's direction after the gate. Also, as you enter each gate, figure out which pole you should run closer to, watch the poles and your raft's tubes to make sure there are no touches, and always concentrate on the next gate downstream.

WILDWATER RACING: Prepare for wildwater races the same way you do for slalom races: review the rules, check your starting time, and scout the river. Find the fastest currents and the cleanest route through rapids and choose a course with the straightest line and the fewest maneuvers. An ideal course will require no backpaddling and few, if any, turning strokes.

When running the river, avoid eddies, holes, and pockets of shallow, slower moving water. Although wave trains generally signify fast water, run the shoulders of waves rather than their peaks. (The peaks will increase your vertical motion, slap your raft around, and make it tougher to paddle, all of which will slow you down.) If you're doing really well, you may even catch up to the raft in front of you. Plan to overtake the front raft carefully. Don't waste energy trying to pass the raft in slower water. Pick a broad, fast channel with even currents, announce your intentions, and only pass when legal.

PART THREE: Playboating

Rafting has long been a way to get from point A to point B. Even advanced river running does little more than connect clean routes and eddies in an effort to reach the take-out in one piece. But playboating can change all that.

Other whitewater boaters—kayakers and canoers—have long known that waves and holes can provide an endless source of amusement and challenge. Whether gently gliding their craft down the face of a wave, or doing 360's on the shoulders of a hole, playboating develops and hones boating skills while connecting boaters with some of the river's most exciting hydraulics. Now that rafters have self-bailing rafts and catarafts, they too can join in the fun.

EQUIPMENT: A self-bailing raft or cataraft is a must for playboating. With a standard-floor raft, the river will flood the passenger compartment and become difficult to maneuver. Bare paddle rafts make better playboats because they have no dangerous frames or oarstands to collide with if the raft flips. However, frames work fine on paddle cats since they are harder to flip.

Before jumping onto a wave or into a hole, double check all of your gear. Make sure there are no loose items or ropes, and make sure that each person is fully outfitted with helmets, insulating outerwear (you *will* swim sooner or later!), and life jackets.

NECESSARY SKILLS: Before you think about playing around on waves and holes, learn to distinguish forgiving hydraulics from perilous keepers. By knowing what the river is likely to do to your raft ahead of time, you'll be able to anticipate the river's actions and adjust accordingly. Since flips are common when playing, you must be comfortable re-righting a flipped raft and swimming out of holes. Finally, you should be adept at maneuvering your raft in powerful hydraulics.

PLAYING ON WAVES: Surfing a river wave with a raft relies on the same gravitational forces that drag a surfer down the face of an ocean wave. But while the surfer is streamlined and light, the raft is heavy and creates a lot of surface drag. So, to surf a wave, the rafter must overcome the friction created by the raft.

Start off by picking a medium-sized wave (about two to four feet high) just downstream of an eddy. Try to leave the eddy with an upstream ferry, slide over to the middle of the wave, and line your raft up parallel with the current. As you hit the trough of the wave, slow your raft down by pulling it upstream. As you do this, you should feel the raft stall. Work hard to keep your raft straight, since any change in the raft's angle relative to the current will throw the raft off the wave.

To keep the raft stalled in the wave's trough, rudder with paddles or oars and stroke upstream just enough to keep the raft from slipping free. Don't overpower your strokes or the raft will bury in the trough and get pushed off the wave.

To further improve your chances of staying on a wave, center the raft's weight over the trough. For paddle rafts, this might mean unloading the bow compartment. Also, use your most powerful stroke. For oar rafts, this means that backsurfing will be easier since it relies on the more powerful backstroke, while paddle rafts will have an easier time forward paddling against the current.

PLAYING HOLES: Small holes make perfect play spots since their backwash creates natural raft catchers and eliminates the need to keep perfect angles like you would on waves. In holes, all you have to do is stabilize your raft, then focus your attention on spinning maneuvers, bronco riding, and eventually busting free of the hole.

The techniques used for entering holes are similar to those used on waves, with some minor changes. To reach the hole, start parallel or just upstream of the hole and ferry across to it with a steep upstream angle. As you reach the hole, drive the raft upstream over the backwash and into the trough.

What you do at this point depends on the size of the hole. In large holes it can be dangerous to turn the raft broadside since this gives the river a better shot at flipping you. So, strive to keep the bow pointed upstream. Hole size will also tell you whether to shift your body weight to the highside (the downstream tube) or the low side (the upstream tube). In very small holes, the only way to stay in the hole is to lean upstream into the trough. However, in

Playboating teaches rafters many skills that can't be learned when simply floating downriver. (Photo by Doc Loomis)

medium to large-sized holes, the upstream lean is a sure invitation for a flip. So, lean downstream (highside) in stronger holes.

Once you're in the hole, wait a moment until things feel stable then think of what you want to do. The longer you sit sideways in the middle of the hole, the more likely you are to take on water, stall out, or flip. So, move toward the shoulder of the hole and try to spin. Let the bow snag the downstream current passing the shoulder of the hole and turn. At the same time, try to rotate the stern back into the middle of the hole. Voila! Your first *180!* Next time, try to spin the raft *360 degrees* by spinning the bow and stern all the way around. If the river is deep, safe, and has a big pool below in which to reclaim your gear, you can even paddle right into the falls, lean forward, and shoot the raft straight up in the air. This maneuver—called a *pop up* or *endo* is fun once in a while, but can slam unsuspecting paddlers into the boulder or ledge. Use it sparingly!

EXITING HOLES: When you finally get weary of surfing a hole, exit by backpaddling downstream over the backwash or by slipping sideways over the shoulder of the hole. If all else fails, have someone on shore toss you a throw bag and pull your raft free.

THE SECOND SEASON

Long before you started flipping through the pages of this book, I'd already spent countless hours convincing my friends I wasn't nuts. While they were at home sleeping late, shovelling snow off their driveways, and watching Sunday football games, I was on the river. While they were adjusting their thermostats, I was donning my drysuit. I was an addict alright. A full blown river fanatic. But rafting down my favorite stream through the heart of the Winter was as natural to me as Summer paddling was to my friends. It was whitewater's second season. And perhaps its best season.

For the well prepared rafter, Winter is a magical time of year to float rivers. It is a time to explore transient storm-fed streams or to view favorite Summer runs in a whole new light. However, enjoying these Winter whitewater trips requires a keener judgment and a little more preparation than do Summer runs. Here are some tips to make your trip safe, comfortable, and fun:

1. Select shorter trips so that you don't get caught on the river after dark.
2. Raft rivers that you know intimately and are well within your skill level.
3. Avoid iced over streams and rivers.
4. Pick rivers with short shuttles, and leave warm, dry clothes at the take-out.
5. Dress extra warm, using a dry suit (or a wet suit and dry top), helmet liner, gloves, and thick booties.
6. Keep active on the river, and eat well. Carry some Power Bars or granola to provide a burst of energy if you feel tired or cold.
7. Know how to recognize and treat hypothermia.

As Winter settles in around us, a Pandora's Box of whitewater opportunities opens. Maybe this is your year to shun the remote control, cancel the football party, and head for your favorite river! Your friends will think you're nuts, but only you'll know the joy that whitewater's second season brings!

14
STAY IN SHAPE:
Gear Maintenance and Repair

Rafting equipment is built to withstand abuse—collisions with rocks, chafing from poorly loaded gear, the damaging effect of ultraviolet rays. But owner abuse—poor maintenance, careless storage, or improper use of gear—will greatly shorten the life expectancy of almost every item in your rafting arsenal.

It only takes a little bit of care and common sense to keep rafting equipment healthy and kicking long after the warranties wear out. In this chapter we'll look not only at how to maintain rafts and rafting accessories, we'll explore ways to repair gear once it breaks down.

PART ONE: Raft Care and Repair

I've got to admit that I love a shiny new raft. It looks great on the water, and the extra boost it gives my psyche actually makes me feel like I'm rafting better. New or old, I expect my raft to support gear, bounce off rocks, and surround my crew with a buoyant, resilient, and reliable cushion of immovable air on every trip. Though that sounds like an awful lot to demand of one boat, it really isn't. You can ask a lot of your raft if you're willing to give it some care in return.

There are a multitude of ways to damage or destroy a raft, but most raft damage results from overinflation, tears, abrasion, ultraviolet decay, and water damage. Here are some simple guidelines to follow every time you use your raft:

1. *Don't let oar frames rub against the tubes. Wrap the frame with foam tubing or apply a rubbing strake to the tops of the tubes. Also, check metal frames for burrs, and file them off.*
2. *Rinse sand and dirt from shoes and gear when boarding the raft so it doesn't grind its way into the fabric or valves.*
3. *Don't step on deflated rafts. There may be rocks or sharp objects on the ground that could puncture the boat.*
4. *Carry—don't drag—rafts while putting in, taking out, or portaging.*
5. *When pulling ashore, pull rafts to a point where they won't rock or rub against the bank.*
6. *Don't overload rafts or load gear directly on floors (light gear may be loaded on self-bailing floors).*
7. *Don't overinflate rafts, and check rafts periodically for correct air*

pressure—especially on hot or sunny days.

8. *When transporting rafts, make sure they aren't rubbing against trailer sides or the interior of trunks or truck beds.*

TAKE DOWN AND STORAGE: A surprising amount of damage can occur after the raft trip is over—damage which won't show up until the raft is blown up again before the next outing. To avoid this type of damage, take a few extra minutes after each trip to prepare the raft for storage.

At the take-out, unload all of your gear from the raft and rinse the raft thoroughly with clean water. Next, let the raft air dry by leaning it up on its edge against some paddles or a wall. (If it's raining, this will have to wait until later.) After the raft is dry, gently wipe off any residual dirt and lay the raft back on the ground. If there are wet ropes still tied to the raft, remove them so that the water doesn't damage the boat when it is in storage.

Raft manufacturers recommend that you store your raft completely dry and semi-inflated. By leaving the raft with just enough air to maintain its shape, it is less likely to suffer the fabric stresses and delamination problems that go with rolling up a raft. Deflate the tubes the same way as they were inflated—let air out of each chamber evenly and slowly.

If you are anything like me, you don't own a trailer, and garage space is a precious commodity. For folks like us, storing a raft semi-inflated is out of the question, and rolling a raft for storage is the only way to go. A tight roll can be done at the river as described below, then the roll can be relaxed before the raft is put into a safe storage place (away from direct heat, sunlight, chemicals, and sharp objects). The loose roll lets air circulate freely around the tubes and floor.

ROLLING UP THE RAFT: To start the roll, press or pump all remaining air out of the chambers. Looking down at the fully deflated raft, divide it mentally into three long sections: (1) the left tube and the left part of the floor; (2) the center part of the floor; and (3) the right tube and the right part of the floor. To begin the roll, take the left third and fold it across the floor. Next, take the right third and fold it over the the rest of the raft. Now the raft is rolled up lengthwise like a loose burrito, one-third of its original width. To finish the roll, just begin at one end of the raft and roll it toward the other end like you're rolling up a sleeping bag. When you're done, use a strong strap to hold the roll tightly closed, being careful to avoid chafing.

RAFT REPAIR: I'd like to tell you that you'll never have to use the information on raft repair, but I'd probably be wrong. By just looking at the number of sharp rocks in a typical river, then applying the law of averages, you'll see that sooner or later your raft is going to get a hole.

Semi-lucky rafters get small holes in their rafts just before they reach the take-out. That way they can limp the raft to shore and apply a clean, permanent patch at home under controlled conditions. Truly unfortunate rafters get holes in their boats far from the nearest take-out and have to make repairs

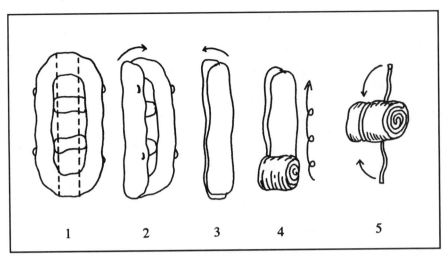

There are five steps to follow when rolling up your raft: 1) mentally divide the raft into three long sections; 2) fold the left over the middle; 3) fold the right section over the middle; 4) roll the raft up from the end; 5) run a strap around the roll to hold it in place.

on the river. These types of repairs are usually nothing more than sophisticated bandaids designed to get the raft downstream. Still, the on-river repair techniques are the same as those used at home. It does, however, take a little bit of patience and imagination to make the on-river repairs work out as well as home repairs.

The first part of repairing a raft is figuring out where the hole is. Though big tears are easy to find, pinhole leaks can be deceptive. In fact, sometimes they go unnoticed for years! The best way to find pinhole leaks is to first listen for the tell-tale whistle of escaping air, then rub the suspected tube with soapy water. The water will bubble once it hits the leak. Once the leak is spotted, it'll be easier to figure out what type of patch is necessary.

THE THREE-STEP PROCESS: An easy way to think about the patching process is to divide it into three stages: (1) select the materials that will be needed; (2) prepare the workplace; and (3) apply the patch.

MATERIALS: Patching materials include glues, solvents, and fabrics which work with your raft's fabrics. There are a number of one and two-part glues available. One-part glues require no catalyst, but can soften and lose their grip in temperatures as low as 150 degrees (which can happen on a hot day). Two-part glues require the addition of a catalyst, but they remain stable at higher temperatures and cure faster. Unfortunately, the working time of many two-part glues is frustratingly short, so you must be prepared to lay down your patch as soon after mixing the glue as practicable.

To figure out what type of glue your raft will need, ask your raft dealer.

Also, buy your glues from your raft dealer—they'll probably be more suited to rafts, and may be of higher quality than those you'll find in a hardware store. When buying glue, purchase small cans and replace them at least once a season. If a can has been opened it may last as little as 30 days, so always have a fresh batch handy.

Solvents are used for thinning glues, cleaning the raft, and for breaking down the raft's surfaces in preparation for receiving the patch. Typical solvents include toluol, which is used on hypalon, neoprene and EPDM rafts, and MEK (Methyl Ethyl Keytone) which is used on PVC and urethane rafts. Note that all of these solvents—and glues, for that matter—are extremely toxic. Only use them in well-ventilated areas while wearing gloves and safety goggles. If you're around raft solvents a lot, consider wearing a breathing mask with an activated charcoal filter.

The fabric used for the patch will be the same as the fabric in the raft. Cut loose pieces of fabric into patches large enough to overlap the edges of the hole by one to two inches. Also, round and bevel the edges and corners of the patch so they don't pull up later. Since really large tears *are* a possibility, it is a good idea to carry along as large a swath of fabric as your repair kit will hold. For additional items to us in making repairs, see the appendix.

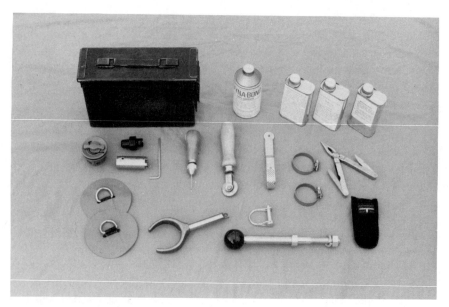

A complete repair kit.

THE WORKPLACE: The ideal workplace is clean and windless, with low humidity and an ambient temperature between 50 to 80 degrees. Set the work place up by laying out all of your tools (listed in the appendix) and preparing the glues, raft surfaces, and patches for use. Lay the loose patch on the tube over the hole and trace it with a pen so that you remember where to apply the glue. If the raft is constructed from hypalon, neoprene or EPDM, sand one side of the patch, and the tube. This will roughen the fabric surface and greatly increase the strength of the bond. Clean off excess grit with a clean cloth (cheesecloth works best) soaked in toluol. PVC and urethane don't require sanding (though some urethane is so tough that sanding or vigorous rubbing with MEK is necessary). Instead, just wipe them vigorously with MEK to soften the coating. Finally, prepare the glue following the manufacturer's directions. If the glues are not pre-thinned, thin them a bit by adding about 20 to 30% of the solvent you'll be using.

APPLYING THE PATCH: There are seven steps in applying patches. Each is set forth below:

1. *Arrange and mark patches so that you'll remember which one goes where.*
2. *Wipe the patch and raft surfaces clean with a clean cloth soaked in solvent.*
3. *Apply a very thin first coat of glue, overlapping the patch outline by 1/4 inch, and let it dry completely. (Use long, quick strokes when applying glue to avoid balling up, and don't touch glued surfaces... body oils will affect the bond!)*
4. *Apply a second thin coat of glue and let that coat dry completely.*
5. *Reactivate the glue by wiping it quickly with a wet solvent cloth. Wait about 15 to 30 seconds.*
6. *Carefully match up the patch and the outline, press the patch against the raft, and firmly press it down with a roller paying special attention to force all air bubbles out from under the patch.*
7. *Clean up excess glue with solvent or a hard eraser, and let the patch dry completely (24 hours).*

PATCHING TIPS: Moving beyond the basics, there are many variables in patching, and some simple tips that make the patching process much easier. Try pre-sanding patch surfaces and pre-thinning glues at home. That way, they'll be ready to go for on-river repairs. To avoid glue splatter, line the outline you drew on the raft with masking tape before you start painting on any glue. This will keep the glue from running rampant away from the edges of the patch.

Really big rips can be particularly tough to repair. In times past, many rafters used an awl and heavy duty thread to sew the tear closed first, using a baseball stitch. Though this is still used periodically, the thread causes an irregularity in the patch, making it tougher to mend the surfaces together flat. If you need to repair a big rip, start by drying out the torn chamber thoroughly. Next, use bias tape or radiator hose repair tape inside the tube to bring the torn edges back together again. Working on a flat surface, lay the tape inside the tube with the sticky side up, and work the rip down against the tape. This will make laying the outside patch much easier. Also, working on the same theory, an inside patch can be used in place of the tape, and applied in the same way as any other patch.

PATCHING SECRETS

On cold, rainy days, it can be frustrating—if not impossible—to apply a good patch to your raft. To make things easier, carry chemical "heat packs" in your repair kit. The heat packs can be laid over the patch to hasten the glue's cure time when the weather is uncooperative.

— Les Bechdel, Author, *River Rescue*

MAJOR REPAIRS: Major repairs include tears near seams and blown baffles. Although it is usually best to leave these repairs to the pros, both types of repairs can be done by experienced amateurs.

Repairing seams or adjacent materials differs little than other patch jobs, except that the seam may have to be peeled away from the raft to make effective repairs to adjacent materials. To save some big headaches, start off these types of repairs by giving your manufacturer a call. Chances are you'll get sound advice and some technical guidance. Next, buy a hot air gun. The hot air gun is used to heat the seams and to loosen the glue.

To begin the repair, hold the hot air gun four to six inches from the seam and warm the seam up very gradually, taking care not to melt the fabric coating. Check the seam every couple of minutes to see if it can be pulled away from the remaining material (use a pair of pliers to grab and pull the seam). Once the seam is pliable, peel it back and proceed with your repair in the same manner as you would for any other patch.

WELDING: As rafting technology evolves, the need for glues and solvents will begin to wane. There are already some hand-held fabric welding units which can be used to make bombproof raft repairs at home. Since welding actually melts the patch right into the raft's fabric, the patch becomes part of the raft rather than just adhering to the raft. If you have a choice, have your major repairs welded to insure that they'll last the life of the raft.

D-RINGS: Hot air guns are also needed to heat and loosen torn or blown D-rings. Again, heat the D-ring gradually to avoid melting the surrounding material, and try pulling the D-ring free with a pair of pliers every couple of minutes. Once the D-ring has been pulled loose, replace it with a similar pre-manufactured D-ring using the same glueing methods as you would to patch your raft.

VALVE REPAIRS: Depending on the type of valve used in your raft, valve repair can be a quick, efficient chore or a real nightmare. However, most of the newer valves are designed for easy replacement, and take nothing more than a few tools and some basic know-how to replace.

Many military-style and AD-1 valves fit into a recessed circular boot on the raft, and are fixed in place with screws. To replace these valves, just undo the screws, remove the damaged valve, and screw a new valve in place.

Halkey-Roberts valves consist of two pieces, and are held in place by screwing male and female parts together. To replace a Halkey-Roberts valve you will first need a specially designed valve tool. This tool fits inside the valve face, and is used to unscrew the outer half of the valve while the repairman holds the valve's inner half in place. When the two halves separate, pull the entire assembly free of the raft. Drop a new female half back into position inside the tube, hold it in place by pinching the tube with your free hand, and use the tool to tighten the male half into the female socket.

If valve replacement makes you nervous, let your local repair shop handle it or give your manufacturer's representative a call.

PART TWO: Oar Maintenance and Repair

You learned in the equipment chapter that wooden oars—unlike aluminum and fiberglass oars—need to be treated and sealed before they're ready for the river. Since water, chipping, and wear from oar locks or clips will slowly eat through oar surfaces, wooden oars need to be periodically treated just as described before. Also, store wooden oars standing upright to prevent warping.

If a wooden oar breaks or cracks, there is still a chance that it can be repaired. Breaks that go straight across the shaft are usually oar killers—throw the oar away or use it for firewood. If you are hopelessly attached to that particular oar, cut the splintered ends away, leaving fresh, squared ends of the shaft showing. Next, drill a vertical hole four inches deep and half an inch wide into each cut end. You can now insert an eight inch by half inch steel pin into the holes. By using a little epoxy glue to hold the pin in place, and then wrapping the oar at the break with overlapping layers of fiberglass, the oar will make a servicable spare on future outings. When using fiberglass, only use epoxy resins since polyester resins may damage the wood.

Diagonal cracks in wooden oar shafts can be repaired much easier. Bend the shaft so that the crack opens up and work some powerful epoxy glue into the crack. After it sets up, the oar will be as good as new.

Even large cracks or splits in oar blades can be repaired with epoxy glue. Cut a rectangular piece of blade out which is 1/4 inch larger than the crack on all sides. Then, carefully whittle and sand down a piece of hardwood identical

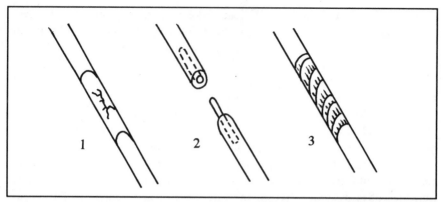

Broken oar shafts can be repaired. Cut the broken section away and drill half-inch wide holes four inches deep into the open ends. Insert an eight-inch long by half-inch wide steel rod into the holes, using epoxy to hold the rod in place. Finally, wrap the shaft with fiberglass.

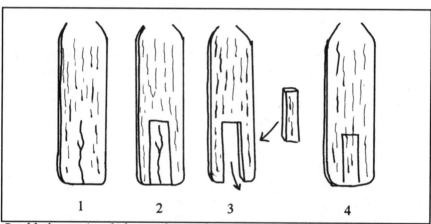

Oar blade repairs: 1) locate the crack or split; 2) cut a block out of the blade completely around the crack; 3) use the block to trace and cut a block from a fresh piece of wood; 4) epoxy the new block in place, and wrap the blade tip with fiberglass.

in size to the open rectangle. Take this new piece of wood and cement it into place with the epoxy glue. To make the repair more bombproof, wrap the blade with fiberglass tape using epoxy resins.

When storing oars (and paddles), don't lean them at an angle in the corner of your garage or lay them on the floor. Prop them up as vertically as possible in an out of the way place. This will keep them from warping or from being carelessly bent and damaged.

Dry suits, wet suits, paddle jackets and booties see an enormous amount of abuse on river trips. Twigs and snags can rip the fabrics, body oils start to stink up your neoprene items, and ultraviolet rays slowly chisel away at the lifespan of nylon.

Neoprene clothing—such as wet suits and booties—should be hand washed with mild soap and water. There are even some special detergents on the market for eliminating the tell-tale neoprene smell that follows many river runners around. Dry suits, on the other hand, demand some special care.

First, never try to zip a rear-entry drysuit by yourself—have someone do it for you. (The zippers are very expensive and can be easily damaged if tugged or bent the wrong way.) Next, take good care of your suit's neck, wrist and ankle seals and cuffs, which are particularly vulnerable to drying, splitting and tearing. Swab the seals with generous amounts of *seal saver* (a food grade silicone) or *303 protectant* before or after each trip. Don't use anything on the seals that contains petroleum, and avoid spilling other solvents on the seals.

If a seal or cuff ever tears, it can be replaced by the factory or by some whitewater shops. If you want to do it yourself, here's how:

1. *Tear off the old cuff, making sure to get rid of all the excess latex and glue.*
2. *Find a container large enough to fully expand the opening where the cuff will be mounted, and stuff it inside that opening.*
3. *Apply a thick coat of Aquaseal (a special glue for use in water) to the outside of the dry suit opening where the new cuff will go, being sure to add an extra 1/4 inch of Aquaseal past the cuff line.*
4. *Stretch the new gasket with your hands and lay it over the glued opening of the suit.*
5. *Hold the seal in place with tape, and let it dry for 24 hours.*

Repair tears to dry suits with vinyl bond—a general purpose glue—and a small patch made of the same material as your dry suit, or simply use a small dab of *Aquaseal* to repair small holes or tears.

WET SUITS: Wet suits start seeing abuse the moment you go to put them on. Neoprene can tear if stretched or pulled too hard, so use care when you're putting it on and taking it off. If a rip does develop, repair it before the tear spreads. The easiest way to repair damaged suits is to use an iron-on neoprene patch (available at dive shops). However, neoprene cement and Aquaseal work better and don't leave an elevated section of material. Both Aquaseal and neoprene cement come in small cans with simple directions for glueing the torn edges back together again.

To keep a wet suit clean and strong, wash it periodically. Use special wet suit detergents instead of harsh detergents, and clean it by hand. It is possible to wash your wet suit in the washing machine on the rinse cycle, but be careful to avoid damage. Once the suit is dry, sprinkle it with talcum powder and store in a dry place.

PART FOUR: Other Equipment

LIFE JACKETS: Life jackets are tough survivors if properly maintained. The key to life jacket longevity is not using it for things like seats, cushions, or rags. Don't sit on them or overpack them in small spaces, and strive to keep them clean. When not in use, keep them away from ultraviolet rays and heat.

PUMPS: Manual pumps have moving parts that work better and last longer when lubricated. Keep the cylinder of hand pumps clean and lubricate them in accordance with the manufacturer's specifications (waterproof grease and boot trailer lubrication work best). Electric pumps will last a lot longer if they're only used to pump rafts up to shape, but they'll die fast if they're used to top the raft off.

15
CONSERVATION:
Preserving the River Resource

"It is worth remembering that, long after we are gone, these rivers will still run to distant seas, and that our daughters and sons will want to stand on the banks, as we have done, transfixed by the magic of a river's music and lulled by its flow.... They deserve their inheritence. Their children do, as well."

— *Paul Vasey, Rivers of America*

I have been fortunate, over these past ten years, to witness the joy, the thrill, and the challenge that only whitewater rivers can bestow. While sliding down a smooth tongue, gliding toward the heart of a rapid, I feel a return to the elements, to primal forces far more powerful than the human spirit. On the river, I gain a deeper understanding of my own roots, and begin to understand humanity's reliance upon water for the sustenance of life itself. And when away from the river, I feel a profound sense of displacement, affecting every aspect of my daily life, as if a part of me had been left at the last take-out.

This sense of interconnectedness has been shared by my predecessors,

Camp 9 on California's Stanislaus River: This was once the put-in for one of America's most popular whitewater rivers. It is now the log-choked backwaters of New Melones Reservoir.

captured in timeless prose for boaters of all generations. John Muir, the grand architect of environmentalism, once professed, "The rivers flow not past, but through us, thrilling, tingling, vibrating every fiber and cell of the substance of our bodies, making them glide and sing." Henry David Thoreau, writing in his Journals, stated, "The river is my own highway, the only wild and unfenced part of the world hereabouts." And Chief Seattle's words have inspired many a follower: "The rivers are our brothers, they quench our thirst. The rivers carry our canoes and feed our children... and you must give to the rivers the kindness you would give any brother."

While contemporary whitewater enthusiasts look upon flowing waters with reverence and respect, others eye rivers as developable resources. A raw product to be harvested, transformed, and sold. The latter group appears in many forms—regional irrigation districts, private utility companies, the Army Corps of Engineers. They come to the rivers not to float and enjoy the wonders of wilderness, but to dam and divert them, shackling eternal waters behind the transient insults of concrete and steel.

I have strained to eloquently capture my own feelings on this latter type of *river use* but have fallen quite short of my goal. So, instead, I have deferred to the poetry of Margaret Hindes, whose beautiful verse I read in William O. Douglas' *My Wilderness*:

Gone, desecrated for a dam —
Pines, stream, and trails
Burned and bare
Down to dust.
Now water fills the hollow,
Water for power,
But the bowl of wilderness
Is broken, forever.

Rivers are the veins of the earth. The lifeblood of the planet. They feed and nourish the land, and rinse away the trivial monuments of man's arrogance, mindless of humanity's misbegotten pride. Rivers are there for all of us to view, to float, and to enjoy. They carry our dreams, and the dreams of future generations.

Whether you raft rivers for inner peace, an adrenaline rush, or financial gain, it is you who can help preserve rivers for everyone. Take the first step by getting involved—from joining your local whitewater club to supporting national environmental groups. Then, let the river's own wealth of inspiration kindle your energies and foster your own desires to preserve free flowing water for everyone to enjoy.

I leave you with these words, passed along by Tanaka Shozo: "The care of rivers is not a question of rivers, but of the human heart."

Put some heart into your rivers and they'll last forever.

RAFTERS (NOT ALWAYS) WELCOME

Next to river conservation issues, few topics stir so much emotion as river access. As rafters, we are reliant on open corridors across lands adjacent to runnable rivers. Without these corridors, we would be unable to partake in our sport.

North American rivers traverse a wide variety of privately and publicly held lands, which has resulted in a complex collection of access regulations and permit systems.

Access to rivers—especially those in more populated regions—may be limited to specific locations. Access easements, public recreation corridors, or commercial access points might be the only way to reach the river without trespassing on private landholdings. If you aren't sure who owns the land or what your rights are, check out the area's leading guidebooks for put-ins and take-outs. Next, verify the guidebook's accuracy by talking to other boaters, land owners, or government officials.

If your river falls within National Forest, National Park, Bureau of Land Management, or other federally owned lands, contact the managing agency in advance of your trip to determine whether boating permits are required. Dozens of popular western rivers restrict rafting only to those rafters who hold permits. These permits are usually granted many months in advance—either by lottery or by putting one's name on a waiting list—so begin planning your trip anywhere from three to twelve months before your actual travel date.

A few state and provincial agencies have jumped on the federal bandwagon by restricting river use to permit holders. Though these agencies usually establish less stringent regulations, they can be equally frustrating—and costly—if you fail to pay the proper access fees or obtain the correct permits.

Rafters are a strong force in the river community. Nonetheless, river access is likely to become increasingly limited as the pressure on our natural resources grows. Accordingly, today's rafters must treat rivers and rafting privileges with respect and care in order to ensure open river corridors for the boaters of tomorrow.

APPENDIX

SAFETY CODE OF THE
AMERICAN WHITEWATER AFFILIATION

(Reprinted with permission of the
American Whitewater Affiliation)

This code has been prepared using the best available information and has been reviewed by a broad cross section of whitewater experts. The code, however, is only a collection of guidelines; attempts to minimize risks should be flexible; not constrained by a rigid set of rules. Varying conditions and group goals may combine with unpredictable circumstances to require alternate procedures.

I. PERSONAL PREPAREDNESS AND RESPONSIBILITY

1. Be a competent swimmer, with the ability to handle yourself underwater.

2. Wear a life jacket. A snugly-fitting vest-type life preserver offers back and shoulder protection as well as the flotation needed to swim safely in whitewater.

3. Wear a solid, correctly-fitted helmet when upsets are likely. This is essential...for...rafters running steep drops.

4. Do not boat out of control. Your skills should be sufficient to stop or reach shore before reaching danger. Do not enter a rapid unless you are reasonably sure that you can run it safely or swim it without injury.

5. Whitewater rivers contain many hazards which are not always easily recognized. The following are the most frequent killers:

A. HIGH WATER. The river's speed and power increase tremendously as the flow increases, raising the difficulty of most rapids. Rescue becomes progressively harder as the water rises, adding to the danger. Floating debris and strainers make even an easy rapid quite hazardous. It is often misleading to judge the river level at the put-in, since a small rise in a wide, shallow place will be multiplied many times where the river narrows. Use reliable gauge information whenever possible, and be aware that sun or snowpack, hard rain, and upstream dam releases may greatly increase the flow.

B. COLD. Cold drains your strength, and robs you of the ability to make sound decisions on matters affecting your survival. Cold water immersion, because of the initial shock and the rapid heat loss which follows, is especially dangerous. Dress appropriately for bad weather or sudden immersion in the water. When the water temperature is less than 50 degrees Fahrenheit, a wetsuit or drysuit is essential for protection if you swim. Next best is wool or pile clothing under a waterproof shell. In this case, you should also carry waterproof matches and a change of clothing in a waterproof bag. If, after prolonged exposure, a person experiences uncontrollable shaking, loss of coordination, or difficulty speaking, he or she is hypothermic and needs your assistance.

C. STRAINERS. Brush, fallen trees, bridge pilings, undercut rocks or anything else which allows river current to sweep through can pin boats and boaters against the obstacle. Water pressure on anything trapped this way can be overwhelming. Rescue is often extremely difficult. Pinning may occur in fast current, with little or no whitewater to warn of the danger.

D. DAMS, WEIRS, LEDGES, REVERSALS, HOLES, AND HYDRAULICS. When water drops over an obstacle, it curls back on itself, forming a strong upstream current which may be capable of holding a boat or a swimmer. Some holes make for excellent sport; others are proven killers. Paddlers who cannot recognize the differences should avoid all but the smallest holes. Hydraulics around man-made dams must be treated with utmost respect regardless of their height or the level of the river. Despite their seemingly benign appearance, they can create an almost escape-proof trap. The swimmer's only exit from the "drowning machine" is to dive below the surface when the downstream current is flowing beneath the reversal.

E. BROACHING. When a boat is pushed sideways against a rock by strong current, it may collapse and wrap.... Even without entrapment, releasing pinned boats can be extremely time-consuming and dangerous. To avoid pinning, throw your weight downstream towards the rock. This allows the current to slide harmlessly underneath the hull.

6. Boating alone is discouraged. The minimum party is three people or two craft.

7. Have a frank knowledge of your boating ability, and don't attempt rivers or rapids which are beyond that ability.

A. Develop the paddling skills and teamwork required to match the river you plan to boat. Most good paddlers develop skills gradually, and attempts to advance too quickly will compromise your safety and enjoyment.

B. Be in good physical and mental condition, consistent with the difficulties which may be expected. Make adjustments for loss of skills due to age, health, fitness. Any health limitations must be explained to your fellow paddlers prior to starting the trip.

8. Be practiced in self-rescue, including escape from (beneath) an overturned craft....

9. Be trained in rescue skills, CPR, and first aid with special emphasis on the recognizing and treating of hypothermia. It may save your friend's life.

10. Carry equipment needed for unexpected emergencies, including footwear which will protect your feet when walking out, a throw rope, knife, whistle and waterproof matches. If you wear eyeglasses, tie them on and carry a spare pair on long trips. Bring cloth repair tape on short runs, and a full repair kit on isolated rivers. Do not wear bulky jackets, ponchos, heavy boots, or anything else which could reduce your ability to survive a swim.

11. Despite the mutually supportive group structure described in this code, individual paddlers are ultimately responsible for their own safety, and must assume sole responsibility for the following decisions.

A. The decision to participate on any trip. This includes an evaluation of the expected difficulty of the rapids under the conditions existing at the time of the put-in.

B. The selection of appropriate equipment, including a boat design suited to their skills and the appropriate rescue and survival gear.

C. The decision to scout any rapid, and to run or portage according to their best judgement. Other members of the group may offer advice, but paddlers should resist pressure from anyone to paddle beyond their skills. It is also their responsibility to decide whether to pass up any walk-out or take-out opportunity.

D. All trip participants should constantly evaluate their own and their group's safety, voicing their concerns when appropriate and following what they believe to be the best course of action. Paddlers are encouraged to speak with anyone whose actions on the water are dangerous, whether they are a part of your group or not.

II. BOAT AND EQUIPMENT PREPAREDNESS.

1. Test new and different equipment under familiar conditions before relying on it for difficult runs. This is especially true when adopting a new boat design or outfitting system. Low volume craft may present additional hazards to inexperienced or poorly conditioned paddlers.

2. Be sure your boat and gear are in good repair before starting a trip. The more isolated and difficult the run, the more rigorous this inspection should be.

3. Flotation ...Inflatable boats should have multiple air chambers and be test-inflated before launching.

4. Have strong, properly sized paddles or oars for controlling your craft. Carry sufficient spares for the length and difficulty of the trip.

5. Outfit your boat safely. The ability to exit your boat quickly is an essential component of safety in rapids. It is your responsibility to see that there is absolutely nothing to cause entrapment when coming free of an upset craft. This includes... loose ropes which cause entanglement. Beware of any length of loose line attached to a whitewater boat. All items must be tied tightly and excess line eliminated; painters, throw lines, and safety rope systems must be completely and effectively stored. Do not knot the end of a rope, as it can get caught in cracks between rocks.

6. Provide ropes which permit you to hold on to your craft so that it may be rescued.... Rafts and dories may have taut perimeter lines threaded through the loops provided. Footholds should be designed so that a paddler's feet cannot be forced through them, causing entrapment. Flip lines should be carefully and reliably stowed.

7. Know your craft's carrying capacity, and how added loads affect boat handling in whitewater. Most rafts have a minimum crew size which can be added to on day trips or in easy rapids....

8. Car top racks must be strong and attach positively to the vehicle. Lash your boat to each crossbar, then tie the ends of the boats directly to the bumpers for added security. This arrangement should survive all but the most violent vehicle accident.

III. GROUP PREPAREDNESS AND RESPONSIBILITY.

1. Organization. A river trip should be regarded as a common adventure by all participants, except on instructional or commercially guided trips as defined below. Participants share the responsibility for the conduct of the trip, and each participant is individually responsible for judging his or her own capabilities and for his or her own safety as the trip progresses. Participants are encouraged (but are not obligated) to offer advice and guidance for the independent consideration and judgement of others.

2. River Conditions. The group should have a reasonable knowledge of the difficulty of the run. Participants should evaluate this information and adjust their plans accordingly. If the run is exploratory or no one is familiar with the river, maps and guidebooks, if available, should be examined. The group should secure accurate flow information; the more difficult the run, the more important this will be. Be aware of possible changes in river level and how this will affect the difficulty of the run. If the trip involves tidal stretches, secure appropriate information on tides.

3. Group equipment should be suited to the difficulty of the river. The group should always have a throw line available, and one line per boat is recommended on difficult runs. The list may include carabiners, prussick loops, first aid kit, flashlight, folding saw, fire starter, guidebooks, maps, food, extra clothing, and any other rescue or survival items suggested by conditions. Each item is not required on every run, and this list is not meant to be a substitute for good judgement.

4. Keep the group compact, but maintain sufficient spacing to avoid collisions. If the group is large, consider dividing into smaller groups or using the "Buddy System" as an additional safeguard. Space yourselves closely enough to permit good communication, but not so close as to interfere with one another in rapids.

A. The lead paddler sets the pace. When in front, do not get in over your head. Never run drops when you cannot see a clear route to the bottom or, for advanced paddlers, a sure route to the next eddy. When in doubt, stop and scout.

B. Keep track of all group members. Each boat keeps the one behind it in sight, stopping if necessary. Know how many people are in your group and take head counts regularly. No one should paddle ahead or walk out without first informing the group. Weak paddlers should stay at the center of a group, and not allow themselves to lag behind. If the group is large and contains a wide range of abilities, a designated "Sweep Boat" should bring up the rear.

C. Courtesy. On heavily used rivers, do not cut in front of a boater running a drop. Always look upstream before leaving eddies to run or play. Never enter a crowded drop or eddy when no room for you exists. Passing other groups in a rapid may be hazardous; it's often safer to wait upstream until the group ahead has passed.

5. Float plan. If the trip is into a wilderness area or for an extended period, plans should be filed with a responsible person who will contact the authorities if you are overdue. It may be wise to establish checkpoints along the way where civilization could be contacted if necessary. Knowing the location of possible help and preplanning escape routes can speed rescue.

6. Drugs. The use of alcohol or mind altering drugs before or during river trips is not recommended. It dulls reflexes, reduces decision making ability, and may interfere with important survival reflexes.

7. Instructional or Commercially Guided Trips. In contrast to the common adventure trip format, in these trip formats, a boating instructor or commercial guide assumes some of the responsibilities normally exercised by the group as a whole, as appropriate under the circumstances. These formats recognize that instructional or commercially guided trips may involve participants who lack significant experience in whitewater. However, as a participant acquires experience in whitewater, he or she takes on increasing responsibility for his or her own safety, in accordance with what he or she knows or should know as a result of that increased experience. Also, as in all trip formats, every participant must realize and assume the risks associated with the serious hazards of whitewater rivers. It is advisable for instructors and commercial guides to acquire trip or personal liability insurance.

A. An "instructional trip" is characterized by a clear teacher/pupil relationship, where the primary purpose of the trip is to teach boating skills, and which is conducted for a fee.

B. A "commercially guided trip" is characterized by a licensed, professional guide conducting trips for a fee.

IV. GUIDELINES FOR RIVER RESCUE

1. Recover from an upset... (and get out of the way of the raft)... if there is imminent danger of being trapped against rocks, brush, or any other kind of strainer.

2. If you swim, hold on to your boat. It has much flotation and is easy for rescuers to spot. Get to the upstream end so that you cannot be crushed between a rock and your boat by the force of the current. Persons with good balance may be able to climb on top of a... flipped raft and paddle to shore.

3. Release your craft if it will improve your chances, especially if the water is cold or dangerous rapids lie ahead. Actively attempt self-rescue whenever possible by swimming for safety. Be prepared to assist others who may come to your aid.

A. When swimming in shallow or obstructed rapids, lie on your back with feet held high and pointed downstream. Do not attempt to stand in fast moving water; if your foot wedges on the bottom, fast water will push you under and keep you there. Get to slow or very shallow water before attempting to stand or walk. Look ahead! Avoid possible pinning situations including undercut rocks, strainers, downed trees, holes, and other dangers by swimming away from them.

B. If the rapids are deep and powerful, roll over onto your stomach and swim aggressively for shore. Watch for eddies and slackwater and use them to get out of the current. Strong swimmers can effect a powerful upstream ferry and get to shore fast. If the shores are obstructed with strainers or undercut rocks, however, it is safer to "ride the rapid out" until a safer escape can be found.

4. If others spill and swim, go after the boaters first. Rescue boats and equipment only if this can be done safely. While participants are encouraged (but not obligated) to assist one another to the best of their ability, they should do so only if they can, in their judgment, do so safely. The first duty of a rescuer is not to compound the problem by becoming another victim.

5. The use of rescue lines requires training; uninformed use may cause injury. Never tie yourself into either end of a line without a reliable quick-release system. Have a knife handy to deal with unexpected entanglement. Learn to place set lines effectively, to throw accurately, to belay effectively, and to properly handle a rope thrown to you.

6. When reviving a drowning victim be aware that cold water may greatly extend survival time underwater. Victims of hypothermia may have depressed vital signs so they look and feel dead. Don't give up; continue CPR for as long as possible without compromising safety.

WATER LEVEL INFORMATION

Bureau of Reclamation, Commissioner's Office, Department of the Interior, C Street, between 18th and 19th Streets, Washington, DC 20240; (202) 343-1100

Hydrological Information Unit, United States Geological Survey, 419 National Center, Reston, VA 22092; (703) 860-7531

National Weather Service, National Oceanic And Atmospheric Administration, Department of Commerce, 8060 13th Street, Silver Spring, MD, 20910; 301=427-7622

· United States Army Corp of Engineers, Public Affairs Office, 20 Massachusetts Ave., NW, Washington, DC 20314-1000; (202) 272-0010

UNITED STATES MAPS

BUREAU OF LAND MANAGEMENT: Office of Public Affairs, Bureau of Land Management, Department of the Interior, Washington, DC, 20240; (202) 343-9435

Denver Service Center, Bureau of Land Management, Denver Federal Center, Building 50, PO Box 25047, Denver, CO; 80225-0047; (303) 236-6452

NATIONAL CARTOGRAPHIC INFORMATION CENTER: National Cartographic Information Center, 507 National Center, 12201 Sunrise Valley Drive, Reston, VA 22092; (703) 860-6045

NATIONAL FOREST SERVICE: Region 1 (ID, MT): Regional Forester, Northern Region, Forest Service, Federal Building, PO Box 7669, Missoula, MT 59807; (406) 329-3011

Region 2 (CO, NB, SD, WY): Regional Forester, Rocky Mountain Region, Forest Service, 11177 West 8th Avenue, Lakewood, CO 80225; (303) 234-4185

Region 3 (AZ, NM): Regional Forester, Southwestern Region, Forest Service, 517 Gold Avenue SW, Albuquerque, NM 87102; (505) 766-2444

Region 4 (Southern ID, NV, UT, WY): Regional Forester, Intermountain Region, Forest Service, Federal Building, 324 25th Street, Ogden, UT 84401; (801) 625-5182

Region 5 (CA): Regional Forester, Pacific Southwest Region, Forest Service, 630 Sansome Street, San Francisco, CA 94111; (415) 556-0122

Region 6 (OR, WA): Regional Forester, Pacific Northwest Region, Forest Service, 319 SW Pine Street, Portland, OR 97208; (503) 221-2877

Region 8 (AL, AR, FL, GA, KY, LA, MS, NC, SC, TN, TX, VA): Forest Service Information Center, Southern Region, 1720 Peachtree Road NW, Room 850S, Atlanta, GA; (404) 347-2384

Region 9 (MO, PA, WV): Regional Forester, Eastern Region, 310 West Wisconsin Avenue, Room 500, Milwaukie, WI 53203; (414) 291-3693

NATIONAL PARK SERVICE: Pacific Northwest, 83 South King Street, Suite 212, Seattle, WA 98104; (206) 442-5366

Rocky Mountains, PO Box 25287, Denver, CO 80225; (303) 969-2000

Western, 450 Golden Gate Ave., PO Box 36063, San Francisco, CA 94102; (415) 556-8313

Southwest, PO Box 728, Sante Fe, NM 87504-0728; (505) 988-6886

Midwest, 1709 Jackson St, Omaha, NE 68102; (402) 221-3482

Mid-Atlantic, 143 South Third Street, Philadelphia, PA 19106; (215) 597-7386

Southeast, 75 Spring Street SW, Atlanta, GA 30303; (404) 331-5838

UNITED STATES GEOLOGICAL SURVEY: Mapping Distribution, US Geological Survey, Box 25286 Federal Center, Building 41, Denver, CO 80225; (303) 236-7477

CANADIAN MAPS

Map Distribution Office, 615 Booth Street, Ottawa, Ontario K1A 0E9

Canadian Heritage Rivers Board, c/o Canadian Parks Service, Environment Canada, Ottawa, Ontario K1A 0H3

REGIONAL GUIDEBOOKS (US)

Armstead, L.D. *Whitewater Rafting in Eastern America: A Guide to Rivers and Outfitters for Beginning and Advanced Whitewater Rafters.* The Globe Pequot: Chester, CT, 1974.

Armstead, L.D. *Whitewater Rafting in Western America: A Guide to Rivers and Professional Outfitters.* The Globe Pequot: Chester, CT, 1990.

Bennett, J. *Class Five Chronicles: Things Mother Never Told You 'Bout Whitewater.* Swiftwater Publishing Company: Portland, OR, 1992.

Cassady, J. and B. Cross and F. Calhoun. *Western Whitewater: From the Rockies to the Pacific.* North Fork Press: Berkeley, CA, 1993.

Hulick, K. and Wright, L. *Paddler's Atlas of U.S. Rivers West.* Stackpole Books: Harrisburg, PA, 1993.

Penny, R. *The Whitewater Sourcebook: A Directory of Information on American Whitewater Rivers.* Menasha Ridge Press: Birmingham, AL, 1989.

Shears, N. *Paddle America, A Guide to Trips and Outfitters in All 50 States.* Starfish Press: Washington D.C., 1992.

Wood, P. *Running the Rivers of North America: A Guide to Canoeing, Kayaking, and Rafting Down More than 50 US and Canadian Rivers—From Lazy Streams to White Water.* Barre Publishing, Barre, MA, 1978.

LOCAL GUIDEBOOKS (US)

FAR WEST (CA AND NV):

Cassady, J. and F. Calhoun. *California Whitewater: A Guide to the Rivers.* North Fork Press: Berkeley, CA, 1990.

Cassady, J. and F. Calhoun. *River Maps: Forks of the Kern, Upper Kern, Lower Kern, Tuolumne and South Fork American.* Cassady and Calhoun River Publications: Berkeley, CA, Miscellaneous Years.

Cassidy, J. *A Guide to Three Rivers: The Stanislaus, Tuolumne, and South Fork of the American.* Friends of the River Books: Stanford, CA, 1981.

Holbeck, L. and C. Stanley. *A Guide to the Best Whitewater in the State of California.* Friends of the River Books: Stanford, CA, 1984.

Margulis, R.K. *The Complete Guide to Whitewater Rafting Tours: California Edition 1986.* Aquatic Adventure Publications: Palo Alto, CA, 1986.

Quinn, J.M. and J.W. Quinn. *Handbook to the Klamath River Canyon.* Educational Adventures Inc.: Medford, OR, 1983.

Robinson, K. and F. Lehman. *South Fork of the American River: From Chili Bar Dam to Salmon Forks Road.* Lore Unlimited: Freemont, CA, 1982.

Robinson, K. and F. Lehman. *Stanislaus River: From Camp Nine to Parrots Ferry.* Lore Unlimited: Freemont, CA, 1982.

Robinson, K. and F. Lehman. *Tuolumne River: From Lumsden Bridge to Ward's Ferry.* Lore Unlimited: Freemont, CA, 1982.

PACIFIC NORTHWEST (AK, OR, and WA):

Bennett, Jeff. *A Guide To The Whitewater Rivers of Washington: A Comprehensive Handbook to Over 150 Runs in the Cascades and Beyond.* Swiftwater Publishing Company: Portland, OR, 1991.

Campbell, A. *John Day River: Drift and Historical Guide.* Frank Amato Pubs: Portland, OR, 1980.

Jettmar, K. *The Alaska River Guide: Canoeing, Kayaking, and Rafting in the Last Frontier.* Graphic Arts Center Publishing Center: Seattle, WA, 1993.

Furrer, W. *Water Trails of Washington.* Signpost: Edmonds, WA, 1979.

Garren, J. *Oregon River Tours.* Garren Publishing: Portland, OR. No date of publication.

Korb, G. *A Paddler's Guide to the Olympic Peninsula: A Comprehensive Guide to 69 River Runs on Washington's Beautiful Olympic Peninsula*. Self Published, 1992.

North, D. *Washington Whitewater*. Mountaineers: Seattle, WA, 1992.

Quinn and Quinn. *Handbook to the Klamath River Canyon*. (see California)

Quinn, J.M., J.W. Quinn, and J.G. King. *Handbook to the Illinois River Canyon*. Educational Adventures, Inc.: Medford, OR, 1979.

Quinn, J.M., J.W. Quinn, and J.G. King. *Handbook to the Rogue*. Educational Adventures, Inc.: Medford, OR, 1979.

Quinn, J.W., J.M. Quinn, and J.G. King. *Handbook to the Deschutes River Canyon*. Educational Adventures, Inc.: Medford, OR, 1979.

Wilderness Public Rights Fund. *Whitewater Primer: Including Selway and Illinois Rivers*. (see Idaho).

Willamette Kayak and Canoe Club. *Soggy Sneakers Guide to Oregon, 2nd Rev. Ed.* Willamette Kayak and Canoe Club: Corvallis, OR, 1986.

NORTHERN ROCKIES (ID, MT, AND WY):

Amaral, G. *Idaho: The Whitewater State*. Watershed Books: Boise, ID, 1990.

Conley, C. and J. Carrey. *The Middle Fork and Sheepeater War*. Backeddy Books: Cambridge, ID, 1977.

Conley, C. and J. Carrey. *River of No Return*. Backeddy Books: Cambridge, ID, 1978.

Conley, C. and J. Barton. *Snake River of Hell's Canyon*. Backeddy Books: Cambridge, ID, 1979.

Fischer, H. *The Floater's Guide to Montana, 2nd Ed.* Falcon Press: Helena, MT, 1986.

Garren, J. *Idaho River Tours*. Touchstone Press: Beaverton, OR, 1980.

Graeff, T. *River Runner's Guide to Idaho*. Idaho Department of Parks and Recreation: Boise, ID, 1986.

Huser, V. and Buzz Belknap. *Snake River Guide: Grand Teton National Park*. Westwater: Boulder City, NV, 1972.

Moore, G. and McClaren, D. *Idaho Whitewater: The Complete Guide For Canoeists, Rafters and Kayakers*. Class VI Whitewater: McCall, ID 1989.

Quinn, J.M., T.L. Quinn, J.W. Quinn and J.G. King. *Handbook to the Middle Fork of the Salmon*. Educational Adventures Inc.: Medford, OR, 1979.

Wilderness Public Rights Fund. *Whitewater Primer: Including Selway and Illinois Rivers*. Wilderness Public Rights Fund: Portland, OR.

Lewis, D. *Paddle and Portage: The Floater's Guide to Wyoming Rivers*. The Wyoming Naturalist: Casper, WY, 1991.

SOUTHWEST (UT, CO, AZ, NM, AND TX):

Aitchison, S. *A Naturalist's San Juan River Guide*. Pruett: Boulder, CO, 1983.

Anderson, F. and A. Hopkinson. *Rivers of the Southwest: A Boaters' Guide to the Rivers of Colorado, New Mexico, Utah and Arizona. 2nd. Ed.* Pruett: Boulder, CO, 1987.

Baars, D. and G. Stevenson. *San Juan Canyons: A River Runner's Guide*. Westwater: Boulder City, Nevada, 1986.

Belknap, Bill and Buzz Belknap. *Canyonlands River Guide*. Westwater: Boulder City, NV, 1974.

Belknap, Buzz. *Grand Canyon River Guide*. Westwater: Boulder City, Nevada, 1969.

Cassady, J. and Calhoun, F. *River Maps: Upper Arkansas, Lower Arkansas, and the Rio Grande*. Cassady-Calhoun River Publications: Berkeley, CA, Miscellaneous Years.

Crumbo, K. *History of the Grand Canyon: A River Runners's Guide*. Johnson: Boulder, CO, 1981.

Evans, L. and Buzz Belknap. *Desolation River Guide*. Westwater: Boulder City, NV, 1969.

Evans, L. and Buzz Belknap. *Dinosaur River Guide*. Westwater: Boulder City, NV, 1969.

Hamblin, W.K. and J.K. Rigby. *Guidebook to the Colorado River, Part I: Lee's Ferry to Phantom Ranch in Grand Canyon National Park. 2nd Ed.* Brigham Young University: Salt Lake City, UT, 1969.

Hamblin, W.K. and J.K. Rigby. *Guidebook to the Colorado River, Part II: Phantom Ranch in Grand Canyon National Park to Lake Mead, Arizona-Nevada*. Brigham Young University: Salt Lake City, UT, 1969.

Hayes, P.T. and G.C. Simmons. *River Runner's Guide to the Green and Colorado Rivers with Emphasis on Geologic Features, Vol. I: River Runner's Guide to Dinosaur National Monument and Vicinity, with Emphasis on Geologic Features*. Powell Society: Denver, CO, 1973.

Maurer, S. G. *A Guide to New Mexico's Popular Rivers and Lakes*. Heritage Associates Inc: Albuquerque, NM, 1983.

Humphrey, M. *Running the Rio Grande: A Floater's Guide to the Big Bend*. AAR/Tantalus: Austin, TX, 1981.

Kirkley, G. *A Guide to Texas Rivers and Streams*. Lone Star Books: Houston, TX, 1983.

Mutschler, F.E. *River Runner's Guide to the Green and Colorado Rivers with Emphasis on Geologic Features, Vol. II: Rivers Runner's Guide to Canyonlands National Park and Vicinity with Emphasis on Geologic Features*. Powell Society: Denver, CO, 1977.

Mutschler, F.E. *River Runner's Guide to the Green and Colorado Rivers with Emphasis on Geologic Features, Vol. IV: Rivers Runner's*

Guide to Desolation and Gray Canyons with Emphasis on Geologic Features. Powell Society: Denver, CO, 1972.

New Mexico State Park Division. *New Mexico Whitewater: A Guide to River Trips*. Santa Fe, NM, 1983.

Nichols, G.C. *River Runner's Guide to Utah and Adjacent Areas, 2nd Ed*. Univ. of Utah Press: Salt Lake City, UT, 1986.

Nolen, B.M. and R.E. Narramore. *Texas Rivers and Rapids, Vol. VI*. Ben Nolen Graphics: Bandera, TX, 1983.

Pearson, L.R. *River Guide to the Rio Grande: General Information*. Big Bend Natural History Assoc.: Big Bend National Park, TX, 1982.

Pearson, J.R. *River Guide to the Rio Grande, Vol, I: Colorado and Santa Elena Canyons*. Big Bend Natural History Assoc.: Big Bend National Park, TX, 1982.

Pearson, J.R. *River Guide to the Rio Grande, Vol. II: Mariscal and Boquillas Canyons*. Big Bend Natural History Assoc.: Big Bend National Park, TX, 1982.

Pearson, J.R. *River Guide to the Rio Grande, Vol. III: The Lower Canyons*. Big Bend Natural History Assoc.: Big Bend National Park, TX, 1982.

Rigby, J.K., W.H. Hamblin, R. Matheny, and S.L. Welsh. *Guidebook to the Colorado River, Part 3: Moab to Hite, Utah, Through Canyonlands National Park*. Brigham Young Univ. Press: Salt Lake City, UT, 1969.

Simmons, G.C. and D.L. Gaskill. *River Runner's Guide to the Green and Colorado Rivers with Emphasis on Geologic Features, Vol. III. River Runner's Guide: Marble Gorge and Grand Canyon*. Powell Society: Denver, CO, 1969.

Stevens, L. *The Colorado River in the Grand Canyon: A Comprehensive Guide to its Natural History*. Red Lake Books: Flagstaff, AZ, 1986.

Stohlquist, J.R. *Colorado Whitewater*. Colorado Kayak Supply: Buena Vista, CO, 1982.

Wheat, D. *The Floater's Guide to Colorado*. Falcon Press: Helena, MT, 1983.

SOUTHERN APPALACHIANS (AL, GA, KY, NC, SC, AND TN):

Benner, F. *Carolina Whitewater: A Canoeist's Guide to the Western Carolinas, 5th Ed*. Menasha Ridge Press: Hillsborough, NC, 1987.

Benner, F. and T. McCloud. *A Paddler's Guide to Eastern North Carolina*. Menasha Ridge Press: Hillsborough, NC, 1987.

Burmeister, W.F. *Appalachian Water, IV: Southeastern U.S. Rivers*. Appalachian Books: Oakton, VA, 1974.

Burmeister, W.F. *Appalachian Waters, V: The Upper Ohio and Its Tributaries*. Appalachian Books: Oakton, VA 1974.

Foshee, J. *Alabama Canoe Rides and Float Trips*. Strode Press: Huntsville, AL, 1975.

Nealy, W. *Whitewater Home Companion, Volume I, Southeastern Rivers*. Menasha Ridge Press: Birmingham, AL, 1981.

Nealy, W. *Whitewater Home Companion, Vol. II: Southeastern Rivers*. Menasha Ridge Press: Hillsborough, NC, 1984.

Sehlinger, B., D. Otey, B. Benner, W. Nealy, and B. Lantz. *Appalachian Whitewater, Volume I, The Southern Mountains*. Menasha Ridge Press: Birmingham, AL, 1986.

Sehlinger, B. *A Canoeing and Kayaking Guide to the Streams of Kentucky*. Menasha Ridge Press: Hillsborough, NC, 1978.

Sehlinger, B. and B. Lantz. *A Canoeing and Kayaking Guide to the Streams of Tennessee, Volume I*. Menasha Ridge Press: Hillsborough, NC, 1981.

Sehlinger, B. and B. Lantz. *A Canoeing and Kayaking Guide to the Streams of Tennessee, Vol. II*. Menasha Ridge Press: Hillsborough, NC, 1983.

Sehlinger, B. and D. Otey. *Northern Georgia Canoeing*. Menasha Ridge Press: Hillsborough, NC, 1980.

Sehlinger, B. and D. Otey. *Southern Georgia Canoeing*. Menasha Ridge Press: Hillsborough, NC, 1986.

Smith, M. *A Paddler's Guide to the Obed-Emory Watershed*. Menasha Ridge Press: Hillsborough, NC.

CENTRAL APPALACHIANS (DC, MD, OH, PA, VA, AND WV):

Burmeister, W.F. *Appalachian Waters, I: The Delaware River and Its Tributaries*. Appalachian Books: Oakton, VA, 1974.

Burmeister, W.F. *Appalachian Waters, III: The Susquehanna River and Its Tributaries*. Appalachian Books: Oakton, VA, 1974.

Burmeister. *Appalachian Water, IV.* (see Southern Appalachians)

Burmeister. *Appalachian Waters, V.* (see Southern Appalachians)

Matacia, L.J. and D. Cecil. *Blue Ridge Voyages, Vol IV: The Shenandoah River*. Matacia: Oakton, VA, 1974.

Combs, R. and S.E. Gillen. *A Canoeing and Kayaking Guide to the Streams of Ohio, Vol. I*. Menasha Ridge Press: Hillsborough, NC, 1983.

Combs, R. and S.E. Gillen. *A Canoeing and Kayaking Guide to the Streams of Ohio, Vol. II*. Menasha Ridge Press: Hillsborough, NC, 1983.

Corbett, H.R. *Virginia Whitewater*. Seneca Press: Springfield, VA, 1977.

Davidson, P. and W. Eister, with D. Davidson. *Wildwater West Virginia, Vol. I: The Northern Streams, 3rd Ed.* Menasha Ridge Press: Hillsborough, NC, 1985.

Davidson, P. and W. Eister, with D. Davidson. *Wildwater West*

Virginia, Vol. II: The Northern Streams, 3rd Ed. Menasha Ridge Press: Hillsborough, NC, 1985.

Falcomer, K. and R. Corbett. *The Delaware River.* Appalachian Books: Oakton, VA, 1981.

Grove, E., B. Kirby, C. Walbridge, W. Eister, P. Davidson, and D. Davidson. *Appalachian Whitewater. Vol. II. The Central Mountains: The Premier Canoeing and Kayaking Streams of Pennsylvania, West Virginia, Maryland, Delaware, and Virginia.* Menasha Ridge Press: Hillsborough, NC, 1987.

Matacia, L.J. and O.S. Cicil III. *An Illustrated Canoe Log of the Shenandoah River and its South Fork.* Matacia: Oakton, CA, 1974.

Matacia, L.J. and R. Corbett. *Blue Ridge Voyages, Vol. III: An Illustrated Guide to Ten Whitewater Canoe Trips.* Matacia: Oakton, VA, 1972.

Nealy. *Whitewater Home Companion, Vol. I.* (see Southern Appalachians)

Nealy. *Whitewater Home Companion, Vol. II.* (see Southern Appalachians)

NORTHERN APPALACHIANS (CT, MA, ME, NH, NY, AND VT):

AMC Appalachian River Guide Committee (R. Schweiker, Ed). *River Guide, Vol. I: Maine.* Appalachian Mountain Club: Boston, MA, 1986.

AMC Appalachian River Guide Committee (R. Schweiker, Ed). *River Guide, Vol. II: New Hampshire and Vermont.* Appalachian Mountain Club: Boston, MA, 1986.

AMC Appalachian River Guide Committee (R. Schweiker, Ed). *River Guide, Vol. III. Massachusetts, Connecticut and Rhode Island.* Appalachian Mountain Club: Boston, MA, 1985.

AMC (K. Yates, C. Phillips, Ed.) *River Guide, Maine.* Appalachian Mountain Club: New York, NY, 1991.

AMC (Steve Tuckerman, Ed.) *River Guide, Massachusetts, Connecticut, and Rhode Island.* Appalachian Mountain Club Books: Boston, MA, 1990.

Burmeister. *Appalachian Waters, I.* (see Central Appalachians)

Burmeister, W.F. *Appalachian Waters, II: The Hudson River and Its Tributaries.* Appalachian Books: Oakton, VA, 1974.

Burmeister. *Appalachian Waters, III.* (see Central Appalachians)

Burmeister. *Appalachian Waters, V.* (see Central Appalachians)

Connelly, J. and J. Porterfield. *Appalachian Whitewater, Vol. III. The Northern Mountains: The Premier Canoeing and Kayaking Streams of Connecticut, Massachusetts, Eastern New York State, Vermont, New Hampshire, and Maine.* Menasha Ridge Press: Hillsborough, NC, 1987.

Gabler, R. *New England Whitewater River Guide.* Appalachian

Mountain Club: Boston, MA, 1981.

OZARKS (AS AND MO):
Kennon, T. *Ozark Whitewater: A Paddler's Guide to the Mountain Streams of Arkansas and Missouri.* Menasha Ridge Press: AL.

NORTHWOODS (MI, MN, AND WI):
Breining, G. and L. Watson. *A Gathering of Waters: A Guide to Minnesota's Rivers.* Minnesota Dept. of Natural Resources: St. Paul, MN, 1977.

Palzer, F. and J. Palzer. *Whitewater/Quietwater: A Guide to the Rivers of Wisconsin, Upper Michigan and NE Minnesota, 5th Ed.* Evergreen Paddlers: Two Rivers, WI, 1983. (supplt. 1985)

LOCAL GUIDEBOOKS (CANADA)

Madsen, K. and Wilson, G. *Rivers of the Yukon: A Paddling Guide.* Primrose Publishing: Whitehorse, Yukon, 1989.

Pratt-Johnson, Betty. *Whitewater Trips and Hot Springs in the Kootenays of British Columbia: For Kayakers, Canoeists and Rafters.* Adventure Publishing: Seattle, WA, 1989.

Pratt-Johnson, Betty. *Whitewater Trips for Kayakers, Canoeists and Rafters in British Columbia: Greater Vancouver Through Whistler, Okanagan and Thompson River Regions.* Adventure Publishing: Seattle, WA, 1986.

Pratt-Johnson, Betty. *Whitewater Trips for Kayakers, Canoeists and Rafters on Vancouver Island.* Pacific Search Press: Seattle, WA, 1984.

VanDine, Doug and Fandrich, Bernard. *Rafting in British Columbia, Featuring the Lower Thompson River.* Hancock House: Surrey, BC, 1984.

INTERNATIONAL GUIDEBOOKS

Bangs, R. and C. Kallen. *Rivergods: Exploring the World's Wild Rivers.* Sierra Club Books: San Francisco, CA, 1985.

Bennett, Jeff. *Class Five Chronicles: Things Mother Never Told You 'Bout Whitewater.* Swiftwater Publishing Company: Portland, OR, 1992.

Gallo, R. and Mayfield, M. *The Rivers of Costa Rica, A Canoeing, Kayaking and Rafting Guide.* Menasha Ridge Press: Birmingham, AL, 1988.

Holbek, L. *The Rivers of Chile.* American Whitewater Association: Phoenicia, NY, 1992.

236

Walker, W. *Paddling the Frontier, Guide to Pakistan's Whitewater.* (Publishing information unknown)

ADDITIONAL CANADIAN INFORMATION

BRITISH COLUMBIA: Ministry of Tourism, Parliament Buildings, Victoria, B.C. V8V 1X4

Ministry of Environment and Parks, Conservation and Parks Division, 4000 Seymour Place, Victoria, B.C. V8V 1X5

Department of Lands, Forests and Resources, Parliament Buildings, Victoria, B.C. V8V 1X4

MANITOBA: Department of Tourism, 7-155 Carlton Street, Winnipeg, Manitoba R3C 3H8

NEW BRUNSWICK: Department of Tourism Information Service, Box 12345, Fredericton, New Brunswick E3B 5C3

NEWFOUNDLAND: Parks Division, Department of Culture, Recreation and Youth, PO Box 4750, St. John's, Newfoundland A1C 5T7

NORTHWEST TERRITORIES: TravelArctic, Government of the Northwest Territories, Yellowknife, NWT X1A 2L9

ONTARIO: Director, Park Management Branch, Ministry of Natural Resources, Public Information Centre, Room 1640, 99 Wellesly Street West, Toronto, Ontario M7A 1W3

QUEBEC: Parks and Recreation, Place de la Capitale, 150 East Street, Cyrille Blvd., Quebec City, Quebec G1R 2B2

SASKATCHEWAN: Saskatchewan Economic Development and Tourism, 1919 Saskatchewan Drive, Regina, Saskatchewan S4P 3V7

YUKON TERRITORY: Tourism Yukon, Box 2703, Whitehorse, Yukon Y1A 2C6

PERIODICALS

American Whitewater (The Journal of the American Whitewater Affiliation), PO Box 85, Phoenicia, NY 12464.

Canoe, 10526 NE 68th, Suite 3, Kirkland, WA 98033.

Currents, National Organization for River Sports, Box 6847, Colorado Springs, CO 80934.

Outside, Box 54729, Boulder, CO 80322-4729.

Paddle Sports, PO Box 3000, Denville, NJ 07834.

Paddler, PO Box 697, Fallbrook, CA 92028.

RAFTING EQUIPMENT/CATALOGS_____

Alpenglow Marine and Sport, Inc., I-70 and Colfax, 885 Lupine St. #B, Golden, CO 80401; (800) 274-0133

B and A Distributing, 201 SE Oak St., Portland, OR 97214; (503) 230-0482

Cascade Outfitters, PO Box 209, Springfield, OR 97477; (800) 223-RAFT (7238)

Clavey Equipment, PO Box 1149, Point Reyes Station, CA 94956; (415) 663-1921

Colorado Kayak Supply, PO Box 3059, Buena Vista, CO 81211; (800) 535-3565

Down River Equipment Company, 12100 W. 52nd Ave., Wheat Ridge, CO 80033; (303) 467-9489

Downstream Products, Inc., 12112 NE 195th, Bothell, WA, 98011; (206) 486-0220

Four Corners Rivers Sports, PO Box 379, Durango, CO 81302; (303) 259-0379

Long Beach Water Sports, 730 E. 4th Street, Long Beach, CA 90802; (310) 432-0187

Nantahala Outdoor Center, Outfitters Store, 41 Hwy 19 West, Bryson City, NC 28713-9114; (800) 367-3521

North American River Runners, US Route 60, PO Box 81, Hico, WV 25854; (800) 950-2585

Northwest River Supplies, 2009 S. Main, Moscow, ID; (800) 635-5202

Pacific River Supply, 3675 San Pablo Dam Rd., El Sobrante, CA 94803; (415) 223-3675

Predator, 1652 Duranleau, Granville Island, Vancouver, B.C. V6H 3S4; (604) 688-1928

Recreational Equipment Incorporated (REI), Department N2045, Sumner, WA 98352; (800) 426-4840

Sierra South, Box Y, Kernville, CA 93238; (619) 376-3745

Wildwater Designs, 230 Penllyn Pike, Penlynn, PA 19422; (215) 646-5034

Wyoming River Raiders, 601 SE Wyoming Blvd., Casper, WY 82609; (800) 247-6068

RAFT MANUFACTURERS_____

Achilles Inflatable Craft, 1407 80th St. S.W., Everett, WA 98203; (206) 353-7000

AIRE, Inc., PO Box 3412, Boise, ID 83703; (208) 344-7506

Avon Seagull Marine, 1851 McGaw Ave., Irvine, CA 92714; (714) 250-0880

B & A Distributing Co. (Riken and Momentum Rafts), 201 S.E. Oak St., Portland, OR 97214-1079; (503) 230-0482

Demaree Inflatable Boats, PO Box 307, Friendsville, MD 21531; (301) 746-5815

Hyside Inflatables, PO Box Z, Kernville, CA 93238; (619) 376-3723

Jack's Plastic Welding, 115 S. Main, Aztec, NM 87410; (505) 334-8748

Maravia Corporation, Box 404, Boise, ID 83701; (208) 322-4949

Northwest River Supplies, 2009 S. Main, Moscow, ID 83843; (800) 635-5202

Sevylor, 66511 E. 26th St., Los Angeles, CA 90040; (213) 727-6013

Whitewater Manufacturing, 1700 SW Nebraska Ave., Grants Pass, OR 97527; (503) 476-1344

Zodiac of North America, Inc. (Metzler), PO Box 400, Stevensville, MD 21668; (301) 643-4141

REUSABLE COMMODE COMPANIES

Canyon R.E.O., PO Box 3493, Flagstaff, AZ 86003; (602) 526-4663

Four Corners Marine, PO Box 3173, Durango, CO 81302; (303) 259-5380

Jack's Plastic Welding, 115 S. Main, Aztec, NM 87410; (505) 334-8748

Northwest Dories, 1127B Airway, Lewiston, ID 83501; (208) 743-4201

Partner Steel Co., 3187 Poleline Rd., Pocatello, ID 83201; (208) 233-2371

Professional River Outfitters, 1802 W. Kaibab Lane, Flagstaff, AZ 86001; (602) 779-1512

Thetford Corp., PO Box 1285, Ann Arbor, MI 48106; (313) 769-6000

Waterman Welding, Kanab, UT 84741; (801) 644-5729

OUTFITTERS ORGANIZATIONS (US)

America Outdoors, PO Box 1348, Knoxville, TN 37901; (615) 525-4765

National Organization of Canoe Liveries and Outfitters; R.R. 2, Box 249, Butler, KY 41006-9674; (606) 472-2205

North American Paddlesports Association, 12455 North Wauwatosa Rd., Mequon, WI 53092; (414) 242-5228

OUTFITTERS ORGANIZATIONS (CANADA)

Ministry of Tourism, Queen's Park, Toronto, Ontario M7A 2R9

The Quebec Outfitters Association, 2900, boul. Saint-Martin Quest, Laval, Quebec H7L 2J2

TravelArctic, Yellowknife, N.W.T. X1A 2L9

Yukon Outfitters Association, Bag Service 2762, Whitehorse, Yukon Y1A 5B9

PRIVATE BOATERS' ORGANIZATIONS

American Canoe Association (ACA), 7432 Alban Station Blvd., Suite B226, Springfield, VA 22150; (703) 451-0141

The American Whitewater Affiliation, PO Box 85, Phoenicia, NY 12464

The National Organization for River Sports, Box 6847, Colorado Springs, CO 80934

The North West Rafters Association, PO Box 19008, Portland, OR 97219

RAFTING SCHOOLS

Running Wild Whitewater School, PO Box 658, Ashland, OR 97520; (503) 482-WAVE (courses for both private boaters and professional guides)

To locate outfitters offering professional guiding schools contact one of the outfitters organizations.

SAFETY INSTRUCTION ORGANIZATIONS

Rescue 3 International, PO Box 519, Elk Grove, CA 95759; 1-(800)-45RESCU

Rescue 3 Northwest, 12112 N.E. 195th, Bothell, WA 98011; 1-(800)-234-4644

Rescue 3 Canada, 5075 Angus Drive, Vancouver, B.C., Canada, V6M 3M6; (604) 263-3580

For additional safety instruction programs, contact one of the rafting schools in your area.

CONSERVATION GROUPS

American Rivers, 800 Pennsylvania Avenue SE, Suite 303, Washington DC 20003; (202) 547-6900

Environmental Defense Fund, 2728 Durant, Berkeley, CA 94704

Friends of the Earth, 530 7th Street SE, Washington DC 20003; (202)543-4312

Friends of the River, Fort Mason Center, Building C, San Francisco, CA 94123; (415) 771-0400

National Audubon Society, 950 Third Avenue, New York, NY 10022

The Nature Conservancy, 1800 North Kent Street, Arlington, VA 22209; (703) 841-5300

The River Conservation Fund, 323 Pennsylvania Avenue NE, Washington DC 20003; (202) 547-6900

River Watch (see American Rivers, above)

The Sierra Club, 730 Polk Street, San Francisco, CA 94109

Wilderness Society, Suite S 176, 3900 Wisconsin Avenue NW, Washington DC 20016

SPECIALTY MAPS

The following specialty maps are available through Rivers and Mountains, 862 San Antonio Rd., Palo Alto, CA 94305; (415) 424-1213:

Riverguide and Trailguide Tee Shirts and Bandanas:
    California: American (South, Middle and North Forks), Kern, Stanislaus, Tuolumne
    Northwest: Deschutes, McKenzie, Rogue, Salmon, Snake, Wenatchee
    Rockies: Arkansas, Colorado, Snake
    Southwest: Colorado, Green Rio Grande, Yampa
    East Coast: Nantahala, New, Ocoee, Youghiogheny

Whitewater Maps, by Jim Cassady and Fryar Calhoun:
    South Fork American
    Tuolumne
    Upper Arkansas
    Lower Arkansas
    Rio Grande
    Lower Kern
    Upper Kern
    Forks of the Kern

CHECKLISTS

BASIC GEAR FOR DAY TRIPS

___ Raft	___ Paddle jacket or dry top
___ Frame	___ Spare oarlocks, pins & clips
___ Paddles	___ Rescue/safety gear (sep. list)
___ Oars and blades	___ First aid kit (separate list)
___ Pumps (manual and electric)	___ Repair kit (separate list)
___ Life jackets	___ Waterproof containers
___ Helmets	___ Water and food
___ Bow and stern lines	___ Other:
___ Bail buckets	
___ Straps	
___ Wet or dry suit	

REPAIR KIT

___ Patch materials (6" x 48")	___ Pliers
___ Glue and catalyst	___ Scissors
___ Solvent (mek or toluol)	___ Large needle and cord
___ Mixing cup	___ Wirecutters
___ Small paintbrush	___ Screwdrivers
___ Roller	___ Halkey-Roberts valve tool
___ Rag (cheesecloth)	___ Spare parts
___ Sandpaper or scuffing tool	___ Other:
___ Pen and hard eraser	
___ Nitrile gloves	

RESCUE/SAFETY GEAR

___ Carabiners (5)	___ 100' Static rope
___ River knife	___ Prussik Loops (3-4)
___ Throw bags (1 for each raft)	___ Z-Drag Crib Cards
___ Flip lines (2 for each raft)	___ Anchor Slings (3-4)
___ Whistle	___ Paddle Hook
___ 2" Pulleys (3-4)	___ Other:
___ Web Slings	

CAMPING AND COOKING GEAR

___ Dry bags/ammo cans	___ Forks, knives & spoons
___ Tent or tarp	___ Pots and pans
___ Sleeping bag	___ Cups, plates & bowls
___ Ground pad	___ Can opener
___ Lantern/fuel	___ Spatula
___ Pillow	___ Seasonings
___ Clothing	___ Scouring pads
___ Toiletries	___ Biodegradable soap
___ Camera gear	___ Trash bags
___ Firepan	___ Portable table
___ Presto log	___ Dutch oven
___ Portable toilet	___ Washing buckets
___ Stove/fuel	___ Food
___ Matches/lighters	___ Ice
___ Cooler	___ Water purifiers/filters
___ Water containers	___ Other:

FIRST AID KIT

___ First Aid Book	___ Oral Gluecose/Sugar/Candy
___ Bandaids	___ Powdered Sports Drink
___ Adhesive Tape	___ Penlight
___ Gauze (4" x 4")	___ Large Syringe/Rubber Bulb
___ Roll Gauze (2")	___ Moleskin
___ Compresses	___ Venom Extraction Kit
___ Ace Bandages	___ Space Blanket
___ Paramedic Shears	___ Tylenol or Ibuprofen
___ 10% Proridine-Iodine Solut'n	___ Lomotil
___ 19% Hydro-Cortisone Cream	___ Exlax
___ Neosporin Ointment	___ Dramamine
___ Small Tweezers	___ Robitussin DM
___ Knife	___ Prescription Medications
___ Needles	___ Triangular Bandages (opt'l)
___ Safety Pins	___ Sam Splint (optional)
___ CPR Face Shield	___ Total Sun Block
___ Hypothermia Thermometer	___ Waterproof Carry Case
___ Disposable Gloves	___ Other:
___ Alcohol Swabs	
___ Small Package Liquid Soap	

(NOTE: Consult a physician before taking any prescription medications. Many of the items included in this list require some expertise to use effectively. Obtain adequate first aid and CPR training through the Red Cross or other certified medical training programs.)

TRIP PLANNER

____ Assemble group of rafters
____ Choose river from guidebook or outfitter's brochure
____ Read guidebooks for best season, access points, rapids, etc.
____ Add to your knowledge from local boaters or outfitters
____ Call government to see if permits are required
____ Acquire any river and camping permits you may need
____ Check additional government regulations (i.e., toilets, gear, etc)
____ Arrange and plan shuttles
____ Plan menu
____ Check the equipment list (in appendix, above)
____ Check safety gear list (in appendix, above)
____ Check first aid kit list (in appendix, above)
____ Check kitchen and camping gear list (in appendix, above)
____ Buy or rent any missing items or rafting gear
____ Check river levels
____ Check weather forecast
____ Have fun!
____ Other:

(This is primarily designed to be used as a basic guideline for inexperienced rafters. There are many more steps that go into a pre-trip agenda. As your river experience grows, so will your ability to quickly assemble groups of rafters and plan river trips.)

HAND SIGNALS

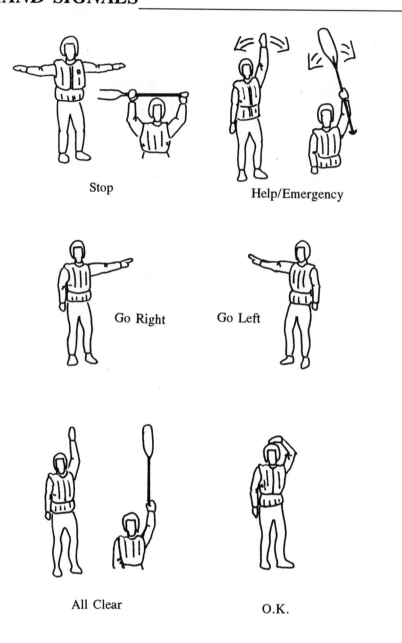

Stop

Help/Emergency

Go Right   Go Left

All Clear

O.K.

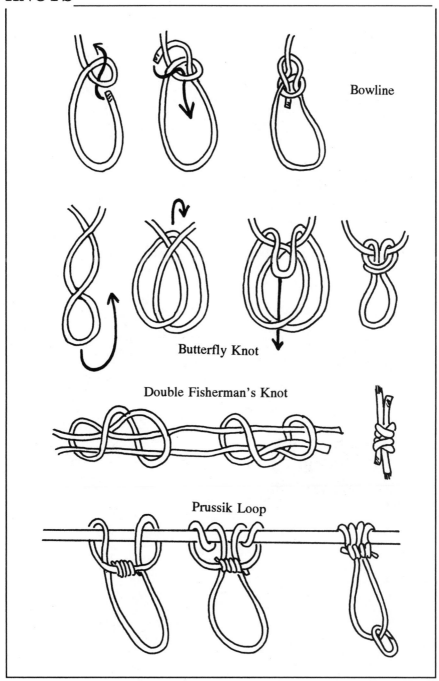

Bowline

Butterfly Knot

Double Fisherman's Knot

Prussik Loop

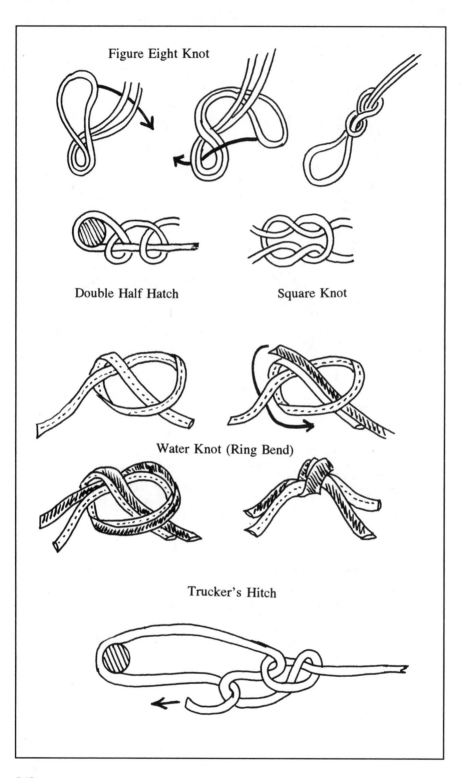

Figure Eight Knot

Double Half Hatch

Square Knot

Water Knot (Ring Bend)

Trucker's Hitch

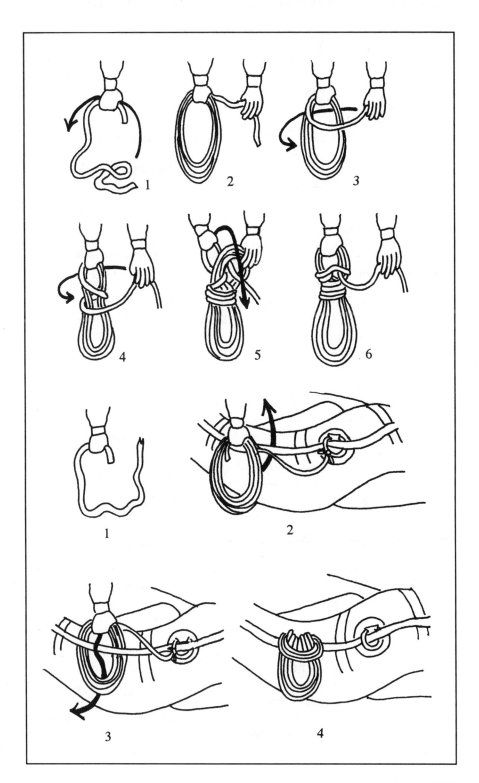

1

2

3

4

5

6

1

2

3

4

GLOSSARY

Baffle: a diaphragm which divides the interior of tubes into separate compartments

Bank: the river's shore

Bar: a shallow part of the river channel with sand, gravel or small rocks

Belay: A method of slowing or stopping a rope from sliding

Big Water: refers to rivers with large volume and powerful hydraulics

Blade: the wide, flat part of a paddle or oar

Boat: raft

Boater: rafter

Boils: ascending currents that rise above surface level unpredictably

Boulder Garden: a rapid densely strewn with boulders

Bow: the front or nose of a raft

Bowline: the rope tied to the front or nose of the raft (also a type of knot)

Brace: using the paddles to assist a paddler in staying in the raft or to prevent the raft from flipping over

Breaking Wave: a standing wave that falls upstream

Bulkhead: see baffle

CFS: cubic feet per second. Measures the current's velocity past a fixed point in the river (35.3 cfs equals one cubic meter per second)

CMS: cubic meters per second

Carabiner: a metal clip used to attach lines to rafts, secure gear, or to substitute for a pulley

Chamber: one interior compartment of a raft tube

Chute: a narrow, constricted portion of the river

Clean: a word used to describe a route free of obstructions

Classification: a system for rating the difficulty of whitewater rapids

Confluence: the point where two rivers or streams meet

Current: moving water

Cushion: see pillow

D-ring: a steel ring attached to the raft and used as a tie down point

Diaphragm: see baffle

Downstream: the part of the river to where the current flows (A.K.A. downriver)

Drawstroke: a stroke used to move the raft sideways by placing the paddle out to the side of the raft and pulling it back to the raft

Drop: a steep, sudden change in the level of the riverbottom. Drops taller than 6-7 feet are frequently called waterfalls

Dry Bag: a waterproof bag designed to keep its contents dry

Drysuit: a waterproof suit that encloses a paddler in impermeable layers of fabric. Designed to be worn over insulating layers of clothing

Eddy: a pocket of water downstream of an obstacle which flows upstream or back against the main current

Eddy Line: the interface between the eddy current and the main current (a high eddy line is called an *eddy fence*)

Entrapment: a situation where a raft or rafter gets pinned by the river's current against an obstacle

Falls: a drop where the river plummets steeply over boulders or broken riverbottom. Can refer to a waterfall, or to the upstream side of a hole.

Feather: to turn a paddle or oar blade horizontal to the water

Ferry: a maneuvering technique used to move a raft back and forth laterally across the river

Flipline: a short rope used to flip a raft back upright

Footcup: a loop, cone, cup or stirrup mounted on the raft's floor and used to brace the foot

Frame: a solid structure used to secure and provide a fulcrum for oars

Gradient: a term used to measure a river's descent in feet per mile or meters per kilometer.

Guide: the person in charge of the raft (also see *paddle captain*)

Handle: the handgrip of a paddle or oar

Haystack: A large, unstable standing wave

Helmet: rigid headgear designed to protect a rafter's head from impact

Highside: lean on the downstream side of the raft to prevent flips or wraps

Hole: a swirling vortex of water wherein the river pours over an obstacle and drops toward the riverbottom leaving a pocket behind the obstacle which is filled in by an upstream surface current

Hypothermia: a lowering of the body's core temperature

Keeper: a large hole or reversal that can keep and hold a raft or swimmer for a long period of time

Lifejacket: a personal flotation device designed to float a swimmer in water

Lining: a technique used to maneuver unmanned rafts around difficult rapids through the use of ropes

PSI: pounds per square inch. A way of measuring air pressure in a raft

Pillow: a cushion of water which forms on the upstream side of obstacles

Pivot: to turn the raft in place

Pool: a flat section of river with no rapids

Pool-drop: a type of river that has intermittent rapids followed by long, easy sections of calm water

Portage: to carry a raft around a rapid

Portegee: a pushstroke with oars

Power Face: the side of an oar or paddle blade that normally pulls against the current

Pry Stroke: a stroke used to turn or side-slip a raft away from the paddle

Put-in: the place where your raft trip begins

Rapid: a place where the river leaves its two-dimensional state and enters a three-dimensional state complete with faster currents, rocks, and various types of liquid surface features

Reversal: see hole

Riffle: shallow, gentle rapids caused by rocks or streambeds

River Left: the left side of the river looking downstream

River Right: the right side of the river looking downstream

Roller: a big curling wave that falls back upstream on itself

Roostertail: a fountain of water which explodes in a fan pattern off a submerged obstacle.

Scout: walk along a bank to inspect the river

Section: a portion of river between two points

Shaft: the long cylindrical tube between the blade and handle of a paddle or oar

Sneak Route: the easiest route through a rapid (A.K.A., *cheat route*)

Standing Wave: a stationary river wave

Stern: the back end of a raft

Stopper: a hole, reversal or breaking wave capable of stopping, holding, or flipping a raft or swimmer

Strainer: obstacles, such as trees, which let water flow freely through them, but which catch swimmers, rafts, and debris. (A.K.A. *sweeper, logjam, boulder sieve*)

Sweep Stroke: a turning stroke wherein the blade is swept in an arc pattern fore or aft

Tailwaves: standing waves that form at the base of a rapid

Take-out: the place where raft trips end and rafts depart from the river

Technical: a type of river that has many obstacles and therefore requires constant maneuvering

Throw bag: a bag which holds a long coiled rope, used as a rescue device to be tossed to swimmers

Thwart: the cross tubes of a raft

Tongue: a smooth V of fast moving water that frequently appears at the top of a rapid

Undercut: an overhanging rock or ledge with water flowing underneath it

Volume: the amount of water in a river

Waterfall: see drop

Wave: a hump in the river's flowing water

Wave Train: a series of standing waves

Whitewater: rapids. AKA, *fun!*

Wrap: a raft pinned flat by river currents against an obstacle

Z-drag: A pulley system used to rescue pinned or wrapped rafts

INDEX

ABOUT THE AUTHOR

Jeff Bennett started running rivers in flatwater canoes a few years before rafting Wyoming's Snake River in 1978. Since then he has spent more than a decade running the rivers of North America, Central America, and Norway as a professional river guide, whitewater instructor, and international racer. His captivating tales of whitewater travels have been captured in two guidebooks—*Class Five Chronicles* and *A Guide to the Whitewater Rivers of Washington*—and have landed him appearances in *Soggy Sneakers*, *The Inflatable Kayak Handbook*, *Western Whitewater*, and *Classic Images Calenders*. He even lurks buried beneath a wall of water on the video sleeve of *Blazing Paddles*. His writings, photography, and lectures have also emblazoned the pages of every major paddling magazine while delighting river runners far and wide.

ORDERING OTHER BOOKS

Class Five Chronicles: Things Mother Never Told You 'Bout Whitewater, ($13.95) edited by Jeff Bennett, is the ultimate guidebook to Class V rivers. Complete descriptions of 29 rivers, plus 34 hilarious tales of misadventure. "You'll have a ball with this book!"
— *David Bolling*, Former Director, *Friends of the River*

A Guide to the Whitewater Rivers of Washington: A Comprehensive Handbook to Over 150 Runs in the Cascades and Beyond, ($19.95) by Jeff Bennett. The most complete guide to Washington State's extraordinary rivers. "A public service to paddlers everywhere...."
— *Dave Harrison* , Editor-in-Chief, *Canoe Magazine*

Rafting! The Complete Guide to Whitewater Rafting Techniques and Equipment, ($15.95) by Jeff Bennett, is the most widely used "how to raft" manual available for guides and recreational river runners today. "The river will always be the truest teacher. This is the next best thing."
— *Eugene Buchanan*, Editorial Director, *Paddler Magazine*

Send checks or money orders to:
Swiftwater Publishing Company, P.O. Box 3031, Portland, OR 97208
(Include $2.00 S & H for first book, and $.50 for each book thereafter)